ON SYNCHRONICITY AND

THE PARANORMAL

ENCOUNTERING

JUNG

JUNG ON ALCHEMY

JUNG ON EVIL

JUNG ON ACTIVE IMAGINATION

JUNG ON MYTHOLOGY

JUNG ON SYNCHRONICITY
AND THE PARANORMAL

ENCOUNTERING

JUNG

ON SYNCHRONICITY
AND THE
PARANORMAL

SELECTED AND INTRODUCED BY RODERICK MAIN

PRINCETON UNIVERSITY PRESS · PRINCETON, NEW JERSEY

Published by Princeton University Press, 41 William Street, Princeton, New Jersey 08540
In the United Kingdom by Routledge, 11 New Fetter Lane, London EC4P 4EE

Typeset in Times by Ponting-Green Publishing Services, Chesham, Buckinghamshire

ISBN 0-691-05837-7

http.//pup.princeton.edu

Printed in the United States of America

10 9 8 7 6 5 4 3

Contents

Acknowledgements

I would like to thank the following for their help with the introduction: Adrian Cunningham for his sage and scholarly advice; Robert Segal for his meticulous stylistic suggestions as well as much general advice and encouragement; David Curtis for his numerous stimulating conversations and shared insights on synchronicity; and Clark Chilson for his thoughtful comments.

R. M.

ENDNOTES TO THE SELECTIONS

Except for some necessary minor changes, the notes at the end of each chapter of extracts are as they appear in Jung's works. Notes by the editors of those works are in square brackets. All other notes are Jung's. For fuller bibliographical details of works cited in the notes, see the volumes of Jung's works from which the extracts are taken.

Introduction

From practically the beginning of his life right through to its end C.G. Jung was involved with the kinds of phenomena which can broadly be classified as paranormal – that is, phenomena which defy explanation in normal rational terms.[1] This involvement was crucial for his personal and professional development. Almost all of his major theoretical formulations were influenced by, and in some cases may even have taken their origin from, his attempts to come to terms with his experiences, observations, and studies of paranormal phenomena (see Charet 1993).

The culmination of Jung's lifelong engagement with the paranormal is his theory of *synchronicity*, the view that the structure of reality includes a principle of acausal connection which manifests itself most conspicuously in the form of meaningful coincidences. Difficult, flawed, prone to misrepresentation, this theory none the less remains one of the most suggestive attempts yet made to bring the paranormal within the bounds of intelligibility. It has been found relevant by psychotherapists, parapsychologists, researchers of spiritual experience and a growing number of non-specialists. Indeed, Jung's writings in this area form an excellent general introduction to the whole field of the paranormal.

The selections in the present volume – drawn from Jung's letters, seminars, and autobiographical *Memories, Dreams, Reflections* (1963), as well as from his *Collected Works* – provide a thematic and roughly chronological overview of his experiences and ideas. Part I, 'Encountering the Paranormal', contains writings on mediumistic trance phenomena (Chapter 1), the reality of spirits and hauntings (Chapter 2), anomalous events involved in the development and practice of analytical psychology (Chapter 3) and the synchronistic basis of the divinatory techniques of astrology and the *I Ching* (Chapter 4). Part II, 'The Theory of Synchronicity', contains Jung's most lucid presentation of his theory of synchronicity (Chapter 5), then illustrates more fully his ideas, both earlier and later, on some of the central subjects involved in its elaboration, specifically parapsychology (Chapter 6), his astrological experiment (Chapter 7) and physics (Chapter 8). Part III, 'Outer Limits', illustrates those of Jung's experiences and speculations which touch most directly on questions of transcendence and spiritual reality: unitive and other bewildering visions (Chapter 9), intimations of life after death (Chapter 10), the UFO enigma (Chapter 11) and a variety of miscellaneous topics such as the subtle body, the underlying unity of reality, religious miracles and the role of synchronicity in the evolution of consciousness (Chapter 12).

The remainder of this introduction follows the same pattern as the selections. First, Jung's experiences and interpretations of the paranormal are discussed. Then the various other influences that contributed to his formulation of the theory of synchronicity are considered. Next, the central ideas of the theory of synchronicity itself are examined in detail and a number of possible criticisms noted. Finally, there is a review of some of the areas of paranormal experience which Jung addressed once he was equipped with the theory of synchronicity.

JUNG AND THE PARANORMAL

Jung's early life was spent in a milieu conducive to his developing an interest in paranormal phenomena. Living in the Swiss countryside, he continually heard stories of uncanny happenings (Jung 1963: 102) such as 'dreams which foresaw the death of a certain person, clocks which stopped at the moment of death, glasses which shattered at the critical moment' (Jung 1963: 104). The reality of these events, he says, was 'taken for granted in the world of my childhood' (Jung 1963: 104). More specifically, paranormal experiences were virtually commonplace in Jung's family. His maternal grandfather, Samuel Preiswerk, had believed himself to be continually surrounded by ghosts and would devote one day every week to conversing with the spirit of his deceased first wife, for whom he kept a special chair in his study (Jaffé 1984: 40). Jung's grandmother Augusta, Preiswerk's second wife, was believed to be clairvoyant (Jaffé 1984: 40). And the couple's daughter, Jung's mother, experienced 'strange occurrences' with sufficient regularity to write a diary exclusively dedicated to them (Jaffé 1971: 2).[2]

Jung's own experiences of the paranormal began at the age of seven or eight. During a period when his parents were sleeping apart and there was considerable tension in the house, he would sometimes see nocturnal apparitions: 'One night I saw coming from [my mother's] door a faintly luminous, indefinite figure whose head detached itself from the neck and floated along in front of it, in the air, like a little moon' (Jung 1963: 31).

Jung early came to consider his own, and his mother's, tendency towards these kinds of experiences to be related to the possession of a dual personality. In addition to what he called personality No. 1, the normal personality aiming at social integration, he believed he had a personality No. 2, which was ancient, deeply knowledgeable, and 'close to nature, . . . to the night, to dreams, and to whatever "God" worked directly in him' (Jung 1963: 45, 55). The tension between Jung's No. 2 acceptance of the fundamental reality of his paranormal experiences and his No. 1 need to articulate this reality in an intellectually and socially respectable form continued throughout his life.

When Jung was twenty-three and by that time a medical student, a couple of incidents happened which he says were 'destined to influence me profoundly' (Jung 1963: 108). On one occasion a round walnut table in his family home suddenly and inexplicably split with a loud bang. Two weeks later another loud explosion was heard, and it was discovered that a steel knife which was in perfect condition and had been used to cut bread just an hour before had miraculously shattered into four in a closed drawer (Jung 1963: 107–9). These experiences contributed to his decision to enter the then widely despised field of psychiatry (Jung 1963: 107, 110–11; also Baumann-Jung 1975: 46).

Jung's own account presents these incidents as connected prefiguratively with séances which he claims he heard about and started attending a few weeks later (Jung 1963: 109; Jung 1973: 181) but which in fact he had already been attending for several years and had even initiated (Hillman 1976: 125; Charet 1993: 155–6). His observations at these séances formed the basis for his doctoral dissertation, later published as 'On the Psychology and Pathology of So-Called Occult Phenomena' (1902). The desire to present his findings in an optimally objective light is undoubtedly why this as well as his various subsequent accounts (Jung 1925: 3–6, 9–10; Jung 1973: 181–2; Jung 1963: 109–10) all conceal to various degrees the full extent of his personal involvement. As F.X. Charet summarizes what is now known:

> the séances were conducted in Jung's own home, the medium was his cousin, and the participants, members of his own family. In addition, a number of the spirits with which the medium was allegedly in communication were none other than Jung's ancestors.
>
> (Charet 1993: 288)

This degree of engagement is consistent with other information about Jung's interests at the time. In particular, one of the lectures he delivered to his student fraternity, the Zofingia Society, consists largely of an impassioned and informed appeal for the serious scientific study of spiritualistic (i.e., paranormal) phenomena (Jung 1897; see also Oeri 1970: 187–8).

Jung describes his experiments with his medium cousin as 'the one great experience which wiped out all my earlier philosophy and made it possible for me to achieve a psychological point of view. I had discovered some objective facts about the human psyche' (Jung 1963: 110). The primarily descriptive account given in his dissertation prefigures several of the themes of his mature psychology. The medium's ability when in the trance state to manifest a variety of seemingly autonomous personalities provided evidence for the dissociability and unconscious functioning of the psyche – observations which would eventually lead to the formulation first of complexes and later of archetypes. While analysing his cousin's trances psychiatrically, Jung did not dismiss the psychic dissociation as simply pathological; the secondary personalities she was manifesting could also be therapeutic, representing 'attempts of the future character to break through' (Jung 1902: 79).[3] The emphasis here on the positive, prospective tendency of apparently pathological symptoms foreshadows Jung's later ideas of compensation, individuation and active imagination.[4]

Jung continued to attend séances for at least another thirty years (Charet 1993: 172–4, 197, 269). Already by 1905 he could report that he had investigated a total of eight mediums (Jung 1905: 301). His publicly expressed view at this time was that the results were 'of purely psychological interest. . . . Everything that may be considered a scientifically established fact belongs to the domain of the mental and cerebral processes and is fully explicable in terms of the laws already known to science' (Jung 1905: 301–2).

Even after the beginning of his association with Freud in 1907, Jung's preoccupation with the paranormal continued. Initially, Freud was highly sceptical and dismissive about the entire field – an attitude expressed most vividly in his exhortation to Jung to make the sexual theory 'a dogma, an unshakable bulwark' against 'the black tide of mud . . . of occultism' (Jung 1963: 147–8). It is true that this resistance eventually mellowed to the point where he was actually encouraging Jung's experiments and even attending séances himself (Charet 1993: 196–7).[5] 'In matters of occultism', he wrote to Jung on 15 June 1911, 'I have grown humble . . . my hubris has been shattered' (in Jung 1963: 335). However, he was still not willing to expose the full extent of his interest publicly, nor would he accede to Jung's demand that the theoretical basis of psychoanalysis be broadened to take account of spiritualistic phenomena that were inadequately explained in terms of sexuality.[6]

Once, in March 1909, this tension between Freud and Jung resulted in an argument that had both an interesting psychological context and an even more interesting parapsychological outcome. Earlier in the evening Freud had, as he afterwards wrote in a letter to Jung, 'formally adopted you as an eldest son, anointing you as my successor and crown prince' (in Jung 1963: 333). Later in the evening, however, in the course of an argument about paranormal phenomena, a seemingly unaccountable detonation went off in Freud's bookcase. When Freud dismissed Jung's parapsychological interpretation of this event, Jung predicted that the same thing would happen again and so, to Freud's consternation, it did (Jung 1963: 152). Freud's letter to Jung continues by remarking of this phenomenon, by which he admitted to having been impressed, that it 'then and there [i.e., immediately after his "anointing" of Jung] . . . divested me of my paternal dignity' (in Jung 1963: 333). Whether or not consciously realized at the time, this incident symbolized the inevitable divergence between the two psychologists. One of the main causes of this divergence was the significance each attached to paranormal phenomena.

In spite of Freud's unaccommodating attitude, Jung's understanding of paranormal phenomena undoubtedly benefited from their association. He was led by Freud to appreciate the important role that sexuality can indeed play in spiritualistic phenomena. As he recognized only after he had written his dissertation, the medium had fallen in love with him (Jung 1925: 5) and her inadmissible passion for her cousin – which may in fact have been reciprocal[7] – had contributed significantly to her experiences, many of which involved supposed romances of past members of their shared ancestry.

In effecting his break with Freud, Jung was greatly assisted by the influence of the psychologists Théodore Flournoy and William James (Shamdasani 1995: 126–7). Like Jung, both of them were deeply interested in psychical research and had made close observations of mediums; moreover, they were willing, as Freud was not, to consider the phenomena that emerged in these contexts in a nonpathological light. While James's influence on Jung was mainly through his writings (Jung 1976: 452), Flournoy's was more personal. In an appendix contained in the Swiss but omitted in the English edition of *Memories, Dreams, Reflections*, Jung recounts that during the period of his disaffection with Freud he would regularly see Flournoy, who both helped him formulate his understanding of Freud's limitations and encouraged him in his own researches on somnambulism, parapsychology and the psychology of religion (summarized in Charet 1993: 235). It was also through Flournoy that Jung became interested in the creative imagination and specifically in the 'Miller Fantasies', which were to form the basis for his *Symbols of Transformation* (1911–12/1952)[8] – the work in which Jung first expressed openly his divergence from Freud (Jung 1963: 158; Charet 1993: 235).

Validating the creative or, as he came to call it, the 'active' imagination was also important to Jung personally. He himself had a facility for imaginative thinking, and what he learned about this faculty from the Miller material enhanced his ability to cope with the deluge of dreams, visions and paranormal experiences that were released in him in the years following his rupture with Freud (Jung 1963: 165–91).

Prominant among these experiences were Jung's inner encounters with a variety of seemingly autonomous fantasy figures with whom he conversed as though they were spirits (Jung 1963: 174–8). The most important such figure was 'Philemon', whom Jung described as his 'ghostly guru', his 'psychagogue', a representation of 'superior insight' who 'conveyed to me many an illuminating idea', above all 'the insight that there are things in the psyche which I do not produce, but which produce themselves and have their own life' (Jung 1963: 176–7). One of the earliest experiences Jung mentions specifically of a meaningful coincidence concerns this figure: Philemon had appeared in his dreams with kingfisher's wings, and Jung, in order to understand the image better, did a painting of it. While engaged on this, he happened to find in his garden, for the first and only time, a dead kingfisher (Jung 1963: 175–6).

Later, in 1916, Jung relates that he felt 'compelled from within, as it were, to formulate and express what might have been said by Philemon' (Jung 1963: 182). The composition of the resulting *Septem Sermones ad Mortuos*, a series of texts addressed to the spirits of the dead, was immediately preceded by a remarkable haunting of Jung's house, involving an 'ominous atmosphere' and various apparitional and poltergeist phenomena experienced not just by himself but by his children and other members of the household (Jung 1963: 182–3). As several writers have noted, the *Septem Sermones* – whose relation to spiritualistic communications is obvious, if also rather eccentric (see Segal 1992: 37–8) – express in germinal form almost all of Jung's developed ideas: the nature of the unconscious, individuation, the problem of opposites, the archetypes, and the self (see, for example, Charet 1993: 265–7).

In 1919, while in England, Jung delivered to the Society for Psychical Research a lecture on 'The Psychological Foundations of Belief in Spirits' (1920/1948). In this lecture he explained experiences of one's own soul in terms of complexes of the personal unconscious, while seemingly autonomous spirits were explained in terms of complexes of the collective unconscious, that is, archetypes (Jung 1920/1948: 309–12). Towards the end of the lecture he admitted to having 'repeatedly observed the telepathic effects of un-conscious complexes, and also a number of parapsychic phenomena' (Jung 1920/1948: 318). But on the question of the objective existence of spirits he took a cautious position, in spite of his own experience of three years earlier. While acknowledging that, from the point of view of feeling, it might well be legitimate to believe in spirits, he considered that, from the point of view of thinking, there are no grounds for holding that they can be known to exist other than as 'the exteriorized effects of unconscious complexes': 'I see no proof whatever', he remarked, 'of the existence of real spirits, and until such proof is forthcoming I must regard this whole territory as an appendix of psychology' (Jung 1920/1948: 318).

But Jung was in fact less sceptical than he says here. For example, in a footnote added at this point to the 1948 revision of the lecture, he admits:

> After collecting psychological experiences from many people and many countries for over fifty years, I no longer feel as certain as I did in 1919, when I wrote this sentence. To put it bluntly, I doubt whether an exclusively psychological approach can do justice to the phenomena in question.
>
> (Jung 1920/1948: 318)

In the year following his SPR lecture he was again in England and had some very disturbing experiences while staying over a series of weekends in a house which he learned afterwards was reputed to be haunted: he heard loud thumping and dripping noises, smelled foul odours, and on one occasion saw a figure with part of its face missing lying in the bed beside him – all of which phenomena simply disappeared at the first light of dawn (Jung 1950b: 320–4). For at least one of these phenomena, the loud dripping noise, he could find no adequate physical or psychological explanation (Jung 1950b: 325).

Jung was also influenced by his continued witnessing of spiritualistic trance phenomena. We are told, for instance, of his attendance at séances with Rudi Schneider in 1925 at which 'telekinetic phenomena and the materialization of human limbs were observed' (Charet 1993: 282–3,

n. 230).[9] At a séance with Oscar Schlag in 1931 'a sample of ectoplasm was secured', and on another occasion Jung 'embraced Schlag when suddenly Schlag's Jacket dematerialized' (Charet 1993: 283, nn. 230–1).[10] On the 'question of materialization' Jung wrote in 1945: 'I have seen enough of this phenomenon to convince me entirely of its existence' (Jung 1973: 390). He recalled in 1946 his discussions many years earlier with the American psychologist and psychical researcher James Hyslop:

> He [Hyslop] admitted that, all things considered, all these metapsychic phenomena could be explained better by the hypothesis of spirits than by the qualities and peculiarities of the unconscious. And here, on the basis of my own experience, I am bound to concede he is right. In each individual case I must of necessity be sceptical, but in the long run I have to admit that the spirit hypothesis yields better results in practice than any other.
>
> (Jung 1973: 431)

Of Jung's experiences in this period after 1919 one more deserves mention for the significant bearing it had on the development of his concept of the self as the centre of psychic totality (Jung 1963: 188). He relates that after he had worked this concept out in isolation, he experienced a powerful confirmatory coincidence in which a painting he had done, based on a dream, was paralleled by the core idea of a Taoist–alchemical treatise, *The Secret of the Golden Flower*, sent to him by Richard Wilhelm (Jung 1963: 188–9). The timely receipt of this treatise was, he says, 'the first event which broke through my isolation. I became aware of an affinity; I could establish ties with something and someone' (Jung 1963: 189).

Finally, Jung's thinking was also furthered by the experiences accompanying his heart attack in 1944. A series of altered states of consciousness, including a near-death experience, attendant coincidence and some profound states of mystical union, gave him the insight, and ultimately the courage, to express himself much more forthrightly on a number of controversial topics, including that of synchronicity itself (Jung 1963: 270–7).

Jung's paranormal experiences and the resulting need adequately to understand them were probably the greatest influences on the development of his theory of synchronicity. Such intimate personal engagement both gave him an inside view of the kind of psychological dynamics that can be involved in paranormal experiences and, even more importantly, impressed on him the extent to which the experiences can be meaningful. Thus, Jung's own experiences seemed to occur at critical junctures in his life: paranormal events accompanied his decision to make a career of psychiatry, his conflict and eventual breach with Freud, his relationship with his 'ghostly guru' Philemon, the writing of the *Septem Sermones ad Mortuos* in which he adumbrated much of his later psychology, his formulation of the concept of the self as the centre of psychic totality, and his heart attack and transformative near-death experience of 1944.

TOWARDS SYNCHRONICITY

In addition to his personal experiences and observations of paranormal phenomena, a number of further influences also played a significant part in Jung's eventual formulation of the theory of synchronicity. On the level of spontaneous events, there were the meaningful coincidences which he noticed occurring to individual analysands during therapeutic sessions as well as to others during seminars that were being held in analytical psychology. Other sources of insight were Jung's practical engagement with the mantic procedures of astrology and the *I Ching*,[11] and his cultural researches into alchemy and other esoteric traditions. No less important again was his awareness of recent developments in science, above all in the new discipline of parapsychology and the then radically transformed field of physics. It is worth looking at each of these influences in turn, since their contributions to his developing theory are varied and at times complex.

The therapeutic context

Jung's specific interest in meaningful coincidence dates from the mid-1920s,[12] when, as he says,

> I was investigating the phenomena of the collective unconscious and kept coming across connections which I could not explain as chance groupings or 'runs.' What I found were 'coincidences' which were connected so meaningfully that their 'chance' concurrence would represent a degree of improbability that would have to be expressed by an astronomical figure.
>
> (Jung 1952: 437)

In his analytic practice, Jung was impressed both by the frequency with which coincidence phenomena occurred and by their meaningfulness to those who experienced them:

> As a psychiatrist and psychotherapist I have often come up against the phenomena in question and could convince myself how much these inner experiences meant to my patients. In most cases they were things which people do not talk about for fear of exposing themselves to thoughtless ridicule. I was amazed to see how many people have had experiences of this kind and how carefully the secret was guarded.
>
> (Jung 1952: 420)

For example, a patient, whose problem lay in her excessive and seemingly intractable rationalism, was telling Jung about an impressive dream in which she had been given a costly jewel in the form of a scarab beetle. Just at that moment an insect began tapping against the consulting room window. Jung let it in, caught it in his hands and, realizing it was a form of scarabaeid beetle, presented it to his patient with the words, 'Here is your scarab'. The irrationality yet obvious meaningfulness of this paralleling between real life and her dream was so striking that it broke through the patient's resistances and enabled her treatment to proceed (Jung 1951b: 525–6; 1952: 438–9).

The special value of events such as this for the development of the theory of synchronicity lay in the fact that they occurred in a psychotherapeutic context, so that their accompanying psychological dynamics could be observed particularly closely. Jung noted, for instance, that the meaning which coincidences have for their subject, including their attendant emotional charge or numinosity, seems to stem from the underlying presence of an archetype, activated usually in response to the person having reached some kind of psychological impasse. Thus, in the above case, Jung believed the archetype of rebirth had been activated by the patient's inability to see beyond her rationalism, by her need for 'psychic renewal' (1952: 439). As Robert Aziz has shown (Aziz 1990: 66–90), implicit in Jung's analysis of this and other cases is his understanding of synchronicity as an expression of the process of individuation furthered through compensation. Thus, only after the excessive rationalism of the patient's conscious attitude had been compensated from the unconscious by the powerful irrational event of the synchronicity, could her 'process of transformation [i.e., her individuation] . . . at last begin to move' (Jung 1952: 439).[13] Cases such as this also enabled Jung to observe that coincidences can be symbolic in their meaning. His reason for supposing the archetype of rebirth to have been active in the woman's experience was his knowledge that 'The scarab is a classic example of a rebirth symbol' (Jung 1952: 439).

The seminar context

From 1925 to 1939 Jung held a series of English language seminars at the Psychological Club in Zurich,[14] during which meaningful coincidences sometimes occurred. Indeed, during the course of the 1928–30 seminars on dream analysis, one can actually monitor Jung moving towards a first formulation of the concept of synchronicity.

On 14 November 1928 the seminar group was discussing the meaning of certain forms of ritual sport, since one of the dreams being examined (the important 'initial dream' of the analysis) contained an image of a square amphitheatre, which made the dreamer think of the game of *jeu de paume*, an early form of tennis. Amplifying on the idea that this game could be viewed as a form of symbolic ceremonial, Jung associated the game with the sport of bull-fighting, which he in turn connected with the ancient cult of Mithras, the bull god (Jung 1928–30: 24–5). This turned out to be the first coincidence, for it happened that, unknown to Jung, one of the participants at the seminar had dreamed the night before that she had been present at a bull-fight in Spain (Jung 1928–30: 35).

When this dream was mentioned at the next meeting a week later on 21 November, it was followed by a discussion of its meaning and the meaning of the bull symbol generally, during which Jung reported that 'not long ago

I had a letter from a patient [in Mexico], a lady who had just been to a bull-fight . . .' (Jung 1928–30: 36). Then, at the meeting following this, on 28 November, Jung began by announcing that the discussion of the bull dream and the meaning of the bull-fight had 'brought interesting coincidences to light' (Jung 1928–30: 43). For he had just received another letter from the woman in Mexico in which she commented on the bull-fight she had been to in terms very similar to those used by Jung when he had initially spoken about the bull-fight symbol. Allowing time for postage, Jung calculated that the letter must have been written 'just about the day when we first spoke of the bull in the seminar' (Jung 1928–30: 44). He remarks: 'My friend is a quite independent observer, but she got the gist of [the symbolic significance of the bull-fight] and in that moment found it necessary to convey it to me' (Jung 1928–30: 44).

Equally strikingly, Jung reported that the person whose dreams were being analyzed in the seminar (a patient, not a participant at the seminar) had spent from the 20th to the 24th November 'making a picture which he could not understand' (Jung 1928–30: 43). It was of a bull's head holding the disc of the sun between its horns, as in representations of sacred bull gods. Thus he drew just what was being discussed by the seminar group and over the very period when they were discussing it. 'I told him', Jung reported, 'that we were talking of the bull in connection with his dream, and that his drawing *synchronizes* with that' (Jung 1928–30: 43; emphasis added).

Coincidences such as these, Jung told the seminar group, have a sort of 'irrational regularity' (Jung 1928– 30: 43), which is why we notice them. 'The East bases much of its science on this irregularity', he continued, 'and considers coincidences as the reliable basis of the world rather than causality. *Synchronism* is the prejudice of the East; causality is the modern prejudice of the West' (Jung 1928–30: 44–5; emphasis added).

In November 1928 Jung is recorded as having used the words 'synchronize' and 'synchronism'. A year later, on 4 December 1929, another incident occurred. The five-year-old child of one of the participants at the seminar made two drawings incorporating symbols (principally the cross and the crescent) that were being talked about, yet the child had not actually been exposed to any information about the seminars. Jung remarks:

> Since I have seen many other examples of the same kind in which people not concerned were affected, I have invented the word *synchronicity* as a term to cover these phenomena, that is, things happening at the same time moment as an expression of the same time content.
>
> (Jung 1928–30: 417)

From this series of incidents two important points can be noted about the way Jung was initially conceiving of synchronicity. First, he was understanding it to be a phenomenon which could have its impact on the widest collective level. Thus, the whole nexus of bull coincidences manifested via four different people: Jung himself, who first mentioned the cult of the bull god Mithras; the seminar participant who dreamed of a bull-fight the night before Jung mentioned the bull god; the person whose dreams were being analyzed and who felt moved to draw a bull's head; and the correspondent who wrote to Jung with her symbolic interpretation of the bull-fight she had recently attended. The last two of these people were not even present at the seminars, and one of them was many thousands of miles away in Mexico. Again, of the bull-fight dream Jung remarked that 'any one of us might have dreamt it' (Jung 1928–30: 36).

The second point is that Jung was stressing the idea of the quality of particular moments of time. 'In 1929', he remarked at the end of one seminar (27 November 1929), 'everything has the cast and brand of this year. And the children born in this year will be recognisable as part of a great process and marked by a particular condition' (Jung 1928–30: 412). This idea also played a central role in the way Jung generally articulated his understanding of astrology and the *I Ching*.

Astrology

Jung's interest in astrology dates from around 1911. In a letter to Freud of 12 June of that year he reports:

> My evenings are taken up very largely with astrology. I make horoscopic calculations in order to find a clue to the core of psychological truth. Some remarkable things have turned up. . . I dare say that one day we shall find in astrology a good deal of knowledge that has been intuitively projected into the heavens. For instance, it appears that the signs of the zodiac are character pictures, in other words libido symbols which depict the typical qualities of the libido at a given moment.
>
> (Jung 1973: 24)

This interest continued to the end of Jung's life. For example, in a letter to B.V. Raman dated 6 September 1947, he reaffirmed the practical importance of astrology for the psychologist:

> In cases of difficult psychological diagnosis I usually get a horoscope in order to have a further point of view from an entirely different angle. I must say that I very often found that the astrological data elucidated certain points which I otherwise would have been unable to understand.
>
> (Jung 1973: 475)

This practical involvement provided Jung with data which seemed to support the idea of moments of time having particular qualities. Thus, in a letter to B. Baur (29 January 1934), after discussing the precession of the equinoxes, he remarks:

The fact that astrology nevertheless yields valid results proves that it is not the apparent positions of the stars which work, but rather the times which are measured or determined by arbitrarily named stellar positions. Time thus proves to be a stream of energy filled with qualities and not, as our philosophy would have it, an abstract concept or precondition of knowledge.

(Jung 1973: 138–9)

Initially, Jung seems to have hoped that astrology might be able to demonstrate objectively a relationship of synchronicity between temporal determinants and individual character (Jung 1976: 476; Jung 1952: 454–5). Later, however, his attitude became more complex and ambivalent. This change stemmed partly from his own astrological experiment, which revealed the extent of the astrologer's psychic participation in the handling of astrological material (Jung 1952: 459–84; see also Hyde 1992: 121–39), and partly from recent discoveries concerning the possible influence of planetary positions on solar proton radiation. Those discoveries suggested that there might be some causal basis for the apparent efficacy of astrology (Jung 1951b: 527–8; Jung 1976: 23–4) – or even that astrology might be partly causal and partly synchronistic (Jung 1976: 177, 421, 428–30). Finally, for all his early enthusiasm for the idea of qualitative time, which was articulated even more fulsomely in relation to the *I Ching*, Jung did eventually (in a letter of 1954) express dissatisfaction with this notion, rejecting it as tautological and, rather than using it as the basis for an explanation of synchronicity, claiming to have 'replaced it with the idea of synchronicity' (Jung 1976: 176).

The I Ching

Around 1920, Jung began experimenting with the ancient Chinese oracle system of the *I Ching*, or *Book of Changes*, and was deeply impressed by its effectiveness in yielding pertinent answers to his questions. He relates how, one summer, he

resolved to make an all out attack on the riddle of this book. . . . I would sit for hours on the ground beneath the hundred-year-old pear tree, the *I Ching* beside me, practising the technique by referring the resultant oracles to one another in an interplay of questions and answers. All sorts of undeniably remarkable results emerged – meaningful connections with my own thought processes which I could not explain to myself. . . . Time and again I encountered amazing coincidences which seemed to suggest the idea of an acausal parallelism (a synchronicity as I later called it).

(Jung 1963: 342)

Jung's appreciation of the *I Ching* deepened considerably a couple of years later when he became friends with the German Sinologist Richard Wilhelm, who had just produced a new German translation of the book. Jung refers to his friendship with Wilhelm as 'one of the most significant events of my life' (Jung 1930: 53). He appears to have been particularly impressed by Wilhelm's own mastery of the *I Ching*:

At his first lecture at the Psychological Club in Zurich [in 1923], Wilhelm, at my request, demonstrated the use of the *I Ching* and at the same time made a prognosis which, in less than two years, was fulfilled to the letter and with the utmost clarity.

(Jung 1930: 57)

It was with reference to the *I Ching*, at a memorial address for Wilhelm in 1930, that Jung made his second recorded use of his new concept: 'The science of the *I Ching*', he asserted, 'is based not on the causality principle but on one which – hitherto unnamed because not familiar to us – I have tentatively called the *synchronistic* principle' (Jung 1930: 56). He referred to 'psychic parallelisms which simply cannot be related to each other causally, but must be connected by another kind of principle altogether' (Jung 1930: 56). The essence of this other principle he considered to consist 'in the relative simultaneity of the events', for time, as he still understood it,

far from being an abstraction, is a concrete continuum which possesses qualities or basic conditions capable of manifesting themselves simultaneously in different places by means of an acausal parallelism, such as we find, for instance, in the simultaneous occurrence of identical thoughts, symbols, or psychic states.

(Jung 1930: 56).

Referring also to the data and claims of astrology, he asserted that 'whatever is born or done at this particular moment of time has the quality of this moment of time', adding confidently that 'Here we have the basic formula for the use of the *I Ching*' (Jung 1930: 56–7).

A fuller exposition of the principle, again preceding the publication of his main essays on synchronicity, was also made with reference to the *I Ching* in Jung's 'Foreword' to the English rendering of Wilhelm's German translation (Jung 1950a: 590–3). Here, as late as 1949, Jung was still emphasizing the factor of the quality of moments of time. He writes that 'synchronicity takes the coincidence of events in space and time as meaning something more than mere chance, namely, a peculiar interdependence of objective events among themselves as well as with the subjective (psychic) states of the observer or observers' (Jung 1950a: 592). The specific style of thinking implied in this is then explicated as follows:

How does it happen that A', B', C', D', etc., appear all at the same moment and in the same place? It happens in the first place because the physical events A' and B' are of the same quality as the psychic events C' and D', and further because all are the exponents of one and the same momentary situation. The situation is assumed to represent a legible or understandable picture.

(Jung 1950a: 593)

Apart from consolidating his understanding of qualitative time, the *I Ching* provided Jung with a means of generating experiences of meaningful coincidence with some measure of regularity. At times he practically recommended it to others for such experimental purposes (Jung 1976: 491). Again, largely because of this amenability to experimental investigation, the system offered a context for looking at some of the dynamics of synchronicity. The *I Ching* hexagrams, for example, seemed to Jung to be a kind of readable representation of archetypes (Jung 1963: 294; Jung 1976: 584). This connection between hexagrams and archetypes, combined with the fact that the method of consulting the oracle is essentially based on number, led Jung to speculate on the archetypes of natural numbers and on the possibility of their having a special relationship to synchronicity (Jung 1952: 456–8). Finally, the simple fact that the *I Ching* was such a prominent cultural force throughout Chinese history encouraged Jung's efforts to present his ideas on synchronicity by providing him with a major precedent for the recognition of an acausal principle of connection between events.

Alchemy and other esoteric research

No less significant for the development of the concept of synchronicity was Jung's extensive research into the esoteric traditions of the West. The ancient Greek conception of 'the sympathy of all things', the medieval and Renaissance theory of correspondences, and above all the alchemical understanding of the *unus mundus* (one world) and of the relationship between microcosm and macrocosm also provided acausal connections between events (see Jung 1952: 485–98). At times, Jung presents his theory of synchronicity as simply an up-dating of these esoteric views: 'Synchronicity', he writes at the end of his 1951 Eranos lecture, 'is a modern differentiation of the obsolete concept of correspondence, sympathy, and harmony' (Jung 1951b: 531). At other times he recognizes that his theory differs from these earlier views – for example, in his rejection of the notion of 'magical causality', the view that coincidences and paranormal phenomena, rather than being acausal, are 'somehow due to magical influence' (Jung 1952: 501). What the early theories suggest to him instead is that there may be a dimension of meaning that does not depend on human subjectivity or projection but is 'transcendental' or 'self-subsistent' – 'a meaning which is *a priori* in relation to human consciousness and apparently exists outside man' (Jung 1952: 501–2).

Not only did these esoteric worldviews themselves present a challenge to causality, but Jung believed that in the course of his researches into them he had actually uncovered some extraordinary objective synchronicities: 'my researches into the history of symbols', he writes in the 'Foreword' to his

1952 essay, 'and of the fish symbol in particular, brought the problem [of synchronicity] ever closer to me' (Jung 1952: 419). The reference here is to the coincidence, mapped out in detail in *Aion* (Jung 1951a), 'between the life of Christ and the objective astronomical event, the entrance of the spring equinox into the sign of Pisces'; his discovery of this was another of the factors which 'led to the problem of synchronicity' (Jung 1963: 210).

Parapsychology

While Jung was actively interested in psychical research throughout his life, few bodies of work within this field made such a deep impression on him as the parapsychological experiments carried out by J.B. Rhine in the first parapsychology laboratory, established at Duke University in 1932.[15] These experiments appeared to give statistical, that is to say, scientifically respectable, confirmation of the reality of both extrasensory perception (ESP) and psychokinesis (PK). More importantly, the positive results of Rhine's experiments did not diminish if the subjects attempting the ESP or PK tasks were separated from the target objects by even great distances in space or time (Jung 1952: 435). Jung concluded that 'in relation to the psyche space and time are, so to speak, "elastic" and can apparently be reduced almost to vanishing point' (Jung 1952: 435). Another of the ways in which Jung came to characterize synchronicity was therefore as 'a psychically conditioned relativity of time and space' (Jung 1952: 435). In fact, Jung suggests that spatio–temporal relativity of this kind is the basic condition within the unconscious psyche, as though space and time 'did not exist in themselves but were only "postulated" by the conscious mind' (Jung 1952: 435). Knowledge of events at a distance or in the future is possible because, within the unconscious psyche, all events co-exist timelessly and spacelessly:

> For the unconscious psyche space and time seem to be relative; that is to say, knowledge finds itself in a space–time continuum in which space is no longer space, nor time time. If, therefore, the unconscious should develop or maintain a potential in the direction of consciousness, it is then possible for parallel events to be perceived or 'known'.
>
> (Jung 1952: 481)

This space–time relativity is different from the notion of qualitative time. In qualitative time the idea of a 'moment', and hence of relative simultaneity, is of paramount importance. In space–time relativity any natural understanding of 'moments', and certainly of simultaneity, becomes irrelevant, as the experience of foreknowledge clearly indicates.

Apart from experimental confirmation of this crucial insight concerning space–time relativity, Rhine's work also appeared to support Jung's observation that paranormal experiences are usually attended by heightened emotionality. For Rhine's work identified the so-called 'decline effect', the fact that the most significant results were generally obtained towards the beginning of the experimental session when the subject's interest (emotional engagement) can be supposed to have been at its greatest (Jung 1952: 434, 436–7).

On Rhine's initiative, a correspondence between him and Jung developed, which continued intermittently from 1934 to 1954. Rhine repeatedly pressed Jung to write down accounts of his paranormal experiences and observations as well as his theoretical reflections concerning them (see Jung 1973: 180–2, 378–9). Though somewhat reluctant, because fearing incomprehension on the part of the public (Jung 1973: 190), Jung did comply to a certain extent, and in a letter of November 1945 he gave in response to a series of direct questions submitted by Rhine a tentative preliminary formulation of the theory of synchronicity as he would eventually present it in terms of the psychic relativization of space and time (Jung 1973: 493–5).

Physics

Jung's language in discussing the implications of Rhine's experiments – his references to 'relativity' and a 'space–time continuum' – is clearly reminiscent of Einstein's theories of relativity in physics, and in fact the influence of Einstein on Jung is a real and substantial one. When the physicist was working in Zurich in 1909 and 1912, he was Jung's dinner guest on several occasions, and, as Jung recalls, 'tried to instil into us the elements of [his first theory of relativity], more or less successfully' (Jung 1976: 109; see also Jung 1935: 67–8). Jung continues:

> It was Einstein who first started me off thinking about a possible relativity of time as well as space, and their psychic conditionality. More than thirty years later this stimulus led to my relation with the physicist Professor W. Pauli and to my thesis of psychic synchronicity.
>
> (Jung 1976: 109; see also Progoff 1989: 151–2)

Perhaps even more significant influences on Jung were certain developments within the other great physics theory that arose in the early part of the twentieth century: quantum mechanics. Jung was impressed by both the principle of complementarity formulated by Niels Bohr and the ability to predict subatomic events only probabilistically. It was to the legitimacy of mere probabilistic prediction that Jung most often appealed in support of his concept of acausality. With reference to one such subatomic event, radioactive decay, he quotes Sir James Jeans: 'Radioactive break-up appeared to be an effect without a cause, and suggested that the ultimate laws of nature were not even causal' (in Jung 1952: 512).

The principle of complementarity was utilized by Jung in his presentation of the status of synchronicity. Bohr considered that one of the central paradoxes of quantum physics – the fact that subatomic entities behave in contradictory ways, either as particle or as wave, depending on the method by which they are observed – cannot be resolved by considering one of the forms of manifestation more essential than the other. Both, in his view, are fundamental: the two forms of manifestation complement each other and together give as complete a picture of the actual subatomic entity as is possible given the intrinsic limitations of human cognition (see, e.g., Honner 1987). Jung saw causality and acausality as standing in a similar relationship. As the title of his principal essay indicates, synchronicity is for him 'an acausal connecting principle'. As such, it is 'a hypothetical factor equal in rank to causality as a principle of explanation' (Jung 1952: 435). It is 'equal in rank' precisely in the sense of being complementary to the principle of causality: causality accounts for one kind of connection between events – 'constant connection through effect', as Jung epitomizes it (Jung 1952: 514) – and synchronicity accounts for the complementary kind of connection – 'in-constant connection through contingency, equivalence, or "meaning"' (Jung 1952: 514). Together, the two principles give, in Jung's view, a complete account of the kinds of connections that can exist between events. Jung also draws attention to the complementarities between consciousness and the unconscious and between physics and psychology (Jung 1947/1954: 231–2).

The implications of these points from physics were explored by Jung largely through his friendship with the physicist Wolfgang Pauli, which lasted from 1932 until Pauli's death in 1958. The full extent of Pauli's and Jung's influence on each other has only recently begun to be evaluated (see, e.g., Erkelens 1991; Meier 1992; Zabriskie 1995; Lindorff 1995a and 1995b). One can note in particular that Jung's principal essay on synchronicity was originally published in the same volume as a companion essay by Pauli on 'The Influence of Archetypal Ideas on the Scientific Theories of Kepler' (Jung and Pauli 1955). In his own essay Jung credits Pauli with having helped him formulate the *quaternio* diagram in which the complementary relationships between causality and synchronicity and between indestructible energy and the space–time continuum were set out (Jung 1952: 514). Indeed, Pauli himself appears to have been particularly prone to experiencing synchron-icities, especially of the psychokinetic variety, and discussed them in detail in his letters to Jung (Hinshaw 1995: 129–30). Furthermore, in a letter to the physicist M. Fierz (22 June 1949) Jung actually refers to a draft of one of his essays on synchronicity as a 'manuscript which Pauli has prompted me to write' (Jung 1973: 530).

THE THEORY OF SYNCHRONICITY

Jung's various thoughts on synchronicity converged from these diverse sources and were integrated in two essays: 'On Synchronicity', originally delivered as a lecture at the 1951 Eranos Conference, and 'Synchronicity: An Acausal Connecting Principle', a vastly expanded version of the 1951 paper, originally published in 1952 alongside an essay by Pauli in *The Interpretation of Nature and the Psyche* (English translation 1955). The 1951 essay, contained in the present volume, is probably Jung's clearest piece of writing on this subject, but because of its brevity it inevitably skips over many difficulties and implications. The 1952 essay, by contrast, is replete with so many difficulties and nuances that it ends up seeming rather confused and so risks doing poor justice to the important ideas it contains. Although this essay is not included in the present volume,[16] its central ideas do figure in one form or another in the ensuing selections. It may therefore be useful, before addressing the key issues of the theory, to give a summary of the core argument of this essay.

'Synchronicity: An Acausal Connecting Principle'

In his 'Foreword' (Jung 1952: 419–20) Jung states that he is aiming 'to give a consistent account of everything I have to say on this subject'. In the first chapter, 'Exposition' (Jung 1952: 421–58), he notes that modern physics has shown natural laws to be statistical truths and the principle of causality to be only relatively valid, so that at the microphysical[17] (i.e., subatomic) level there can occur events which are acausal. He then addresses the question of whether acausal events can also be demonstrated at the macrophysical level of everyday experience. The most decisive evidence in support of this possibility he considers to have been provided by Rhine's experiments. These experiments have revealed statistically significant correlations between events in spite of the fact that the possibility of any known kind of energy transmission and hence of causal relationship between the events was completely ruled out. Jung thereby concludes that under certain psychic conditions time and space can both become relative and can even appear to be transcended altogether. The fact that Rhine's positive results fell off once his subjects began to lose interest suggests to Jung that the necessary psychic condition has to do with affectivity. Affectivity in turn suggests the presence of an activated archetype, and in fact this archetypal background is especially evident in the kind of spontaneous acausal events Jung encountered in his therapeutic work. In these spontaneous cases, however, a certain amount of symbolic interpretation is often needed in order to detect the operation of the archetype. Jung is now in a position to define synchronicity, which he does in a variety of ways (see below, pp. 20–4). He also suggests a possible psychological dynamic to explain how an activated archetype might result in synchronicities: the presence of the active archetype is accompanied by numinous effects, and this numinosity or affectivity results in a lowering of the mental level, a relaxing of the focus of consciousness. As the energy of consciousness is lowered, the energy of the unconscious is correspondingly heightened, so that a gradient from the unconscious to the conscious is established and unconscious contents flow into consciousness more readily than usual. Included among these unconscious contents are items of what Jung calls 'absolute knowledge', knowledge that transcends the space–time limitations of consciousness in the manner demonstrated by Rhine's experiments. If there is then the recognition of a parallel between any of this 'absolute knowledge' and co-occurring outer physical events, the result will be the experience of synchronicity. Finally in this chapter, Jung discusses a number of mantic procedures and concludes that astrology is the one most suitable for his purposes, which are to yield measurable results demonstrating the existence of synchronicity and to provide insight into the psychic background of synchronicity.

The second chapter, 'An Astrological Experiment' (Jung 1952: 459–84), describes Jung's attempt to carry out these aims. He collected and analyzed 483 pairs of marriage horoscopes (obtained from friendly donors) in three batches of 180, 220 and 83, looking for conjunctions and oppositions of sun, moon, ascendant, descendant, Mars and Venus. He found that the maximal figure for each of the three batches was one of the traditional aspects for marriage (moon conjunct sun, moon conjunct moon, or moon conjunct ascendant). Although the figures do not exceed the kind of dispersions that might be expected due to chance, Jung considers it psychologically interesting that they appear to confirm astrological expectation; moreover, if the probabilities of the three individual sets of results are combined, the overall result does become statistically significant. In Jung's view, his results fortuitously imitate astrological expectation and therefore constitute a synchronistic phenomenon. The archetypal background to this synchronicity he finds indicated by the lively interest taken in the experiment by himself and his co-worker. Rejecting as primitive and regressive the hypothesis of magical causality, he concludes that if the connecting principle between astrological expectation and the results obtained is not causal, it must consist in meaning.

This conclusion is supported in the third chapter, 'Forerunners of the Idea of Synchronicity' (Jung 1952: 485–504). Jung surveys a range of traditional views – Oriental and Western; primitive, classical, medieval and Renaissance – which express the possibility of there being a realm of transcendental, objective, or 'self-subsistent' meaning. In particular, he looks at the notions of Tao, microcosm and macrocosm, sympathy, correspondence and pre-established harmony. He also notes that the idea of self-subsistent meaning is sometimes suggested in dreams.

In the fourth and final chapter, 'Conclusion' (Jung 1952: 505–19), Jung acknowledges that his views concerning synchronicity have not been proved, but he nevertheless suggests tentatively, on the basis of observations of out-of-the-body and near-death experiences, that the relationship between mind and body may yet prove to be one of synchronicity. He then elaborates on the theoretical status of synchronicity as a fourth explanatory principle, one in addition to time, space and causality (or in addition to indestructible energy, the space–time continuum, and causality). According to Jung, synchronicity 'makes possible a whole judgment' (Jung 1952: 512) by introducing the 'psychoid factor' (Jung 1952: 513) of meaning into one's description of nature. It thereby also helps bring about a rapprochement between psychology and physics. More specifically, the psychoid factor at the basis of synchronicity is the archetype – a factor which Jung proceeds to characterize.

Archetypes provide the shared meaning by virtue of which two events are considered to be in a relationship of synchronicity. They cannot be determined with precision and are capable of expressing themselves in physical as well as psychic processes. They manifest their meaning through whatever psychic and physical content is available, but might equally well have manifested the same meaning through other content. They represent psychic probability, making it likely that certain types of events will occur but not enabling one actually to predict the occurrence of any particular event. At this point Jung introduces the broader category of general acausal orderedness, of which meaningful coincidence experiences are considered to be one particular instance. He states in conclusion that general acausal orderedness (which includes such phenomena as the properties of natural numbers and the discontinuities of modern physics) is a universal factor existing from all eternity, whereas meaningful coincidences are individual acts of creation in time. Both, however, are synchronistic phenomena occurring within the field of the contingent.

As can be seen from this summary, the essential concepts running through the argument of the 1952 essay are time, acausality, meaning and probability, with the final chapter also highlighting the mind–body relationship, the notion of general acausal orderedness, and the question of the epistemological status of the principle of synchronicity. Clarifying Jung's thinking on each of these key topics should make it possible to move through his various writings on synchronicity much more confidently and profitably.

Time

Jung's definitions of synchronicity confront one with an immediate puzzle. Almost invariably, they highlight the factor of simultaneity, and yet one important category of events which Jung wants to call synchronistic – namely, precognitive experiences – by definition cannot be simultaneous. Jung himself was certainly aware of this apparent contradiction and made an interesting, if ultimately unsuccessful, attempt to resolve it.

In his 1951 Eranos lecture he offers a definition which recognizes three categories of events to which the term synchronicity can be applied. The first category includes such happenings as the scarab incident where a psychic event (the patient's recalling her dream of a scarab) and a physical event (the actual appearance of a scarabaeid beetle) occur at the same time and in the same place (during the analytic session in Jung's consulting room). Here there is indeed simultaneity between the psychic and physical events (Jung 1951b: 526).

The second category includes happenings where a psychic event occurs and a corresponding physical event takes place more or less simultaneously but at a distance, so that the approximate simultaneity can only be established afterwards (Jung 1951b: 526). Jung cites as an illustration Emanuel Swedenborg's well-attested vision of the great fire in Stockholm in 1759. Swedenborg was at a party in Gottenburg about 200 miles from Stockholm when the vision occurred. He told his companions at six o'clock in the evening that the fire had started, then described its course over the next two hours, exclaiming in relief at eight o'clock that it had at last been extinguished, just three doors from his own house. All these details were confirmed when messengers arrived in Gottenburg from Stockholm over the next few days (Jung 1952: 481, 483).[18]

The third category includes happenings where a psychic event occurs and a corresponding physical event takes place in the future. Here there is not even approximate simultaneity (Jung 1951b: 526). An example mentioned by Jung is of a student friend of his whose father had promised him a trip to Spain if he passed his final examinations satisfactorily. The friend then had a dream of seeing various things in a Spanish city: a particular square, a Gothic Cathedral and, around a certain corner, a carriage drawn by two cream-coloured horses. Shortly afterwards, having successfully passed his examinations, he actually visited Spain for the first time and encountered all the details from his dream in reality (Jung 1951b: 522).

Jung's emphasis is generally on the first of these categories. He presents the scarab incident as a paradigm case (Jung 1951b: 526) and tries to assimilate the second and third categories to its basic pattern by writing that 'In groups 2 and 3 the coinciding events are not yet present in the observer's field of perception, but have been anticipated in time' (Jung 1951b: 526) – in other words, they are present to consciousness as though actually being perceived (see also Jaffé 1967: 270–1).

When Jung elaborates his thoughts in the 1952 essay, he introduces an important additional factor: a second psychic state (Jung 1952: 441–5). After first speaking, as in the 1951 essay, of the simultaneity of psychic and physical events (Jung 1952: 441), he later shifts to speaking of 'the simultaneous occurrence of two different psychic states' (Jung 1952: 444). He explains that 'One of them is the normal, probable state (i.e., the one that is causally explicable), and the other, the critical experience, is the one that cannot be causally derived from the first' (Jung 1952: 444–5). If one wonders what has happened here to the physical event, it is understood as the 'objective existence' (Jung 1952: 445) of the 'critical' psychic event. Jung is now claiming that the synchronicity actually consists of the coincidence not between the critical psychic event and its objective correlate but between the two psychic events: 'An unexpected content which is directly or indirectly connected with some objective external event coincides with the ordinary psychic state: this is what I call synchronicity' (Jung 1952: 445). For instance, in the apparently precognitive experience of Jung's student friend, the 'unexpected content' is the dream of the Spanish city with its square, its cathedral and its carriage drawn by cream-coloured horses, while the 'objective external event' with which the content is 'directly or indirectly connected' is the fact of seeing these things in reality. The 'ordinary psychic state' – the new presence in the definition – we must suppose to be the ongoing state of mind of the student at the time of his dream. It is this ordinary state which is simultaneous with the unexpected content of the dream and which Jung, rather surprisingly, says 'coincides' with it.

This thinking receives unambiguous expression in the definition of synchronicity that occurs in the 'Résumé' added to the 1955 English translation of the principal essay. With the specific aim of clearing up misunderstandings that had arisen, Jung writes:

> By synchronicity I mean the occurrence of a *meaningful coincidence in time*. It can take three forms:
>
> a The coincidence of a certain psychic content with a corresponding objective process which is perceived to take place simultaneously.
> b The coincidence of a subjective psychic state with a phantasm (dream or vision) which later turns out to be a more or less faithful reflection of a 'synchronistic', objective event that took place more or less simultaneously, but at a distance.
> c The same, except that the event perceived takes place in the future and is represented in the present only by a phantasm that corresponds to it.
>
> Whereas in the first case an objective event coincides with a subjective content, the synchronicity in the other two cases can only be verified subsequently, though the synchronistic event as such is formed by the coincidence of a neutral psychic state with a phantasm (dream or vision).
>
> (Jung 1955: 144–5)

This definition is clearly similar to the three-pronged 1951 definition summarized earlier. Now, however, instead of the coincidence in the second and third cases being between a psychic state and an objective external event which has been 'anticipated in time', it is between one psychic state and another psychic state (a 'phantasm') which is 'a more or less faithful reflection' of an objective external event.

For Jung's purposes, the advantage of introducing the normal psychic state is that it allows him to retain the notion of simultaneity in the case of each of his three categories of synchronicity, for in each case there is both a normal psychic state and an unexpected psychic content occurring simultaneously with it. The simultaneity of these two psychic states is not compromised no matter how great a separation there is either in space or in time between the unexpected psychic content and its corresponding objective external event. Referring to the occurrence of the unexpected contents which mark the actual synchronicities – of whatever kind – Jung maintains that 'we are dealing with exactly the same category of events whether their objectivity appears separated from my consciousness in space or in time' (Jung 1952: 445).

However, for all its advantage in terms of preserving simultaneity, this definition is itself fraught with problems. First, it means that there are now actually two acausal relationships involved in the synchronicity: that between the two psychic events (Jung 1952: 444–5), and that between the second psychic event and the physical event with which it corresponds (Jung 1952: 447). Though Jung says of the two critical events – the second psychic event and the physical event – that 'The one is as puzzling as the other' (Jung 1952: 447), he nowhere shows explicit awareness of the fact that he is claiming they are both, in different respects, acausal.

Second, any acausal relationship that may exist between the two psychic events will be virtually impossible to demonstrate. Since both events are intrapsychic, the possibility of there being some associative causal connection between them can scarcely be even improbable, let alone, as Jung requires, 'unthinkable' (Jung 1952: 518). At any rate, it is not acausality of this kind, but of the kind between a psychic and a physical event, that Jung considered to have been so impressively demonstrated by Rhine's experiments.

A third problem is that of identifying the neutral psychic state at all. For example, we are able only to guess about the normal psychic state simultaneously with which the student's dream of the Spanish city took place. In the light of Aziz's work, one might identify this normal psychic state with the conscious orientation of the experiencer (Aziz 1990: 66) – in the student's case, a state of anxiety concerning his impending examinations. The unexpected content which arises simultaneously with this conscious orientation would, according to Aziz, be an unconscious compensation serving the purposes of individuation (Aziz 1990: 66–7); the student's dream, for example, might have compensated his anxiety by impressing on him that he would indeed earn the trip to Spain by passing his examinations. This compensatory relationship between the two psychic events is indeed acausal in that the conscious orientation does not cause the compensation but only provides the conditions in which it might occur. Again, inasmuch as the compensatory relationship is involved ultimately in the furthering of individuation, it is also meaningful. However, even if this understanding proves workable up to a point, it also involves at least one notable discrepancy from Jung's explicit statements elsewhere: two psychic states in a compensatory relationship may be meaningfully related in terms of individuation, but they do not in any obvious sense have, as Jung specifies, 'the same or a similar meaning' (Jung 1952: 441). If they did, the one would hardly be compensated by the other.

As noted above, Jung's first theorizing about synchronicity was done with reference to astrology and the *I Ching* and focused on the fact that things arising in a particular moment of time all share the characteristics of that moment. It appears to have been this understanding of the role of time, an understanding in which simultaneity does indeed play an essential part, which led Jung to coin the term 'synchronicity', with its emphasis on the element of time (Gk. *syn* = together, *chronos* = time). Later, Jung came to question the notion of qualitative time (Jung 1976: 176) and, under the influence of parapsychology and physics, began to emphasize instead the idea of the psychic relativization of space and time. That he none the less went to such lengths to uphold the component of simultaneity in the concept of synchronicity may have been because he wished to preserve enough of the original meaning of the concept to justify its continued use.

In any case, it is clear that Jung would have done better to drop the notion of simultaneity altogether in relation to synchronistic experiences, and instead to have operated consistently with the more flexible notion of space–time relativization.[19] He could in fact have done this and still highlighted the defining factor of time by giving more prominence to his characterization of synchronicities as 'acts of creation in time' (Jung 1952: 517), emphasizing their nature as spontaneous momentary states in contrast to constant or reproducible ones (see below on 'General acausal orderedness').

Acausality

Jung's personal paranormal experiences confronted him with events which seemed inexplicable in terms of normal physical and psychological causes. There was, for example, no apparent cause of the walnut table splitting or the bread knife shattering in a closed drawer. The impression Jung gained from events such as these – that normal causality was insufficient as a comprehensive principle of explanation – was later reinforced by the results of Rhine's experiments:

> since experience [i.e., Rhine's experimental work] has shown that under certain conditions space and time can be reduced almost to zero, causality disappears along with them, because causality is bound up with the existence of space and time and physical changes, and consists essentially in the succession of cause and effect. For this reason synchronistic phenomena cannot in principle be associated with any conceptions of causality. Hence the interconnection of meaningfully coincident factors must necessarily be thought of as acausal.
>
> (Jung 1952: 445–6)

Supporting these conclusions from another angle was Jung's cultural research into such pre-modern concepts as the 'sympathy of all things' and 'correspondences', and especially into the workings of the *I Ching*. This research made him aware of the fact that other kinds of connection than causality not only exist but have in fact received wide traditional recognition and been put to orderly cultural use.

Usually, however, when Jung attempts to explain what he means by calling synchronicity an 'acausal connecting principle', his first recourse is to the following argument based on quantum physics. 'The discoveries of modern physics', he informs us, 'have shattered the absolute validity of natural law and made it relative' (Jung 1952: 421). Since 'very small quantities [i.e., subatomic particles] no longer behave in accordance with natural laws', it follows that 'natural laws are *statistical* truths' (Jung 1952: 421). Further:

> The philosophical principle that underlies our conception of natural law is *causality*. But if the connection between cause and effect turns out to be

only statistically valid and only relatively true, then the causal principle is only of relative use for explaining natural processes and therefore pre-supposes the existence of one or more other factors which would be necessary for an explanation.

(Jung 1952: 421)

This 'other factor' is Jung's 'acausal connecting principle'. He believes the above argument to have proved the existence of the principle in 'the realm of very small quantities' (Jung 1952: 421). Regarding its existence in the realm of normal sensory experience, he says:

We shall naturally look round in vain in the macrophysical world for acausal events, for the simple reason that we cannot imagine events that are connected non-causally and are capable of a non-causal explanation. But that does not mean that such events do not exist. Their existence – or at least their possibility – follows logically from the premise of statistical truth.

(Jung 1952: 421–2)

Presumably Jung emphasized this argument from physics because it promised to give his concept of acausality the greatest degree of scientific respectability and the most fundamental level of epistemological grounding. However, it brings with it several problems of its own. For instance, the fact that Jung's understanding of causality and acausality is so closely tied to physics threatens to make it too restrictive. He himself clearly intended the notion of acausality to apply to psychological as well as to physical causes: synchronistic events are not caused by psychological states. Yet it is at least questionable whether physical terms alone are adequate to account for the dynamics of psychological causes. As John Beloff points out, 'the concept of cause was not invented by physicists, physics is merely one of the domains for its application, the concept as such is a very basic logical notion of wide generality' (Beloff 1977: 577). In response to Jung's claim that Rhine's parapsychological data have furnished 'decisive evidence for the existence of acausal combinations of events' (Jung 1952: 432), Beloff writes that it is

nonsensical to say . . . that there are events that are related experimentally that are not related causally. For the crux of the experimental method is precisely carrying out certain procedures that we may call A so as to find out whether or not they are necessary in order to obtain a result B.

(Beloff 1977: 577)

If Rhine's experiments are indeed statistically significant and there is no way to account for them in normal causal terms, what they demonstrate, according to Beloff, is the existence not of absolute acausality but of some form of paranormal causality.

Even if one rejects Beloff's understanding of causality, it remains the case that many broader conceptions than Jung's are both possible and have in fact been regularly invoked not only in the ancient world (e.g., Aristotle's material, efficient, formal and final causes [Ross 1928]) but also in the modern period (e.g., Sheldrake's hypothesis of formative causation [1981]), and not only in the West but also in the East (e.g., in Buddhist philosophy [see Kalupahana 1975]). Whether one evaluates Jung's concept of acausality favourably or critically, it is important to bear in mind the restricted understanding of causality on which it is based.

Jung's actual argument for acausality involves two stages. First, he argues that the inability of modern science to predict the behaviour of subatomic particles proves that the relationship between the particles is not simply causal but must also involve some element of acausality. Second, he argues that because this acausality exists in the microphysical world of subatomic particles, it ought also to exist in the macrophysical world of normal sensory experience. Both stages of the argument can be challenged.

Jung makes at least three illegitimate jumps, two in the first stage of his argument and one in the second stage. The first jump is from asserting that subatomic events are merely probabilistic to asserting that they are acausal. In fact, the acausal cannot simply be inferred from the merely probabilistic: if event A is followed by event B only 75 per cent of the time, this does not entail that B is not caused by A. In fact, since B, when it does occur, would not have done so but for A, it is reasonable to think that it has been caused by A.

Jung's second jump is from present knowledge to future knowledge. He assumes that because in his day the behaviour of individual subatomic particles could not be predicted other than probabilistically, this would always be the case. However, although it has not yet been done, it is quite possible that scientists in the future may prove the behaviour of subatomic particles not to be irreducibly probabilistic but the result of deterministic factors which just happen to be too complex and subtle to discern at present. In this respect chaos theory should make one cautious. Since the emergence of this theory in the 1980s, it has become increasingly clear that apparently random or chaotic behaviour can be just as much the product of regular causal factors as is conspicuously ordered behaviour. As the mathematician Ian Stewart has remarked, some scientists now appreciate 'the ability of even simple equations to generate motion so complex, so sensitive to measurement, that it appears random' (Stewart 1990: 16), so that they 'are beginning to view order and chaos as two distinct manifestations of an underlying determinism' (Stewart 1990: 22).

Even without invoking chaos theory, a number of eminent physicists have been dissatisfied with the view which sees certain subatomic events as inescapably random and unpredictable. Einstein, for example, famously resisted the view of a universe in which 'God plays dice', that is, allows things to happen by pure chance. He initiated a search for 'hidden variables' – as yet unknown factors which could account causally for the seemingly random behaviour of subatomic particles. More recently this approach has been favoured by Roger Penrose (Penrose 1989: 383–6) and was also pursued by David Bohm, who stressed that his was a 'causal interpretation' of quantum phenomena (Bohm 1990: 276–81). Even a contemporary physicist who personally considers that there are indeed quantum phenomena for which 'both theory and experiment converge in making the prospect of a causal explanation . . . exceedingly unlikely' (Mansfield 1995: 32) none the less cautions that 'the key issues [in the acausality debate] are not yet fully resolved' (Mansfield 1995: 80).

Let us suppose, however, that certain events at the subatomic level are genuinely acausal. Even so, the next stage of Jung's argument – that there must also be acausal events in the macrophysical world – does not follow, as he puts it, 'logically from the premise of statistical truth' (Jung 1952: 422). This is his third illegitimate jump. There is no reason to expect that a property existing on the subatomic level will also exist in the realm of normal sensory experience. Perhaps what Jung had in mind was that the subatomic indeterminacy which he thought implied acausality could in some way be expected to be scaled up to the level of normal experience. If so, the very way in which probability operates in fact suggests the contrary: the indeterminacy attaching to an individual event on one scale will progressively diminish as one views ever larger aggregates of such events on a higher scale. Acausality on the subatomic level cannot prove or even make probable its existence on other levels. The most it can do is to make its possible existence on those higher levels less intellectually outrageous (cf., Mansfield 1995: 50).

Problematic though the concept of acausality is, it is certainly not an incoherent or absurd notion. There is strong, if not conclusive, evidence that acausality does indeed exist on the subatomic level, and there are no *a priori* reasons that it should not also exist on the level of normal sensory experience. On the normal sensory level it may not be possible actually to prove either its existence as understood by Jung or the inappropriateness of explaining it in terms of broader conceptions of causality than Jung's. Granted this limitation, a case remains for speaking of acausality in a relative and provisional sense, as applying to the relationship between events within a certain domain of consideration or level of current understanding (see Main 1996: 40–3, 154–5). As the paranormal events experienced and observed by Jung indicate, acausality appears to be an accurate enough term phenomenologically. As his definitions of synchronicity also emphasize, it is an extremely useful concept psychologically inasmuch as it shifts attention away from the causes of events and onto their possible meaning.

Meaning

Rather surprisingly, Jung nowhere sets out systematically his thoughts concerning what actually makes synchronicities meaningful. He does, however, provide a substantial clue to his implicit understanding when he states that 'by far the greatest number of synchronistic phenomena that I have had occasion to observe and analyse can easily be shown to have a direct connection with the archetype' (Jung 1952: 481). Though he appears to recognize not one but several kinds of meaning that can adhere to synchronicities, all of these can ultimately be related back to the single factor of the archetype. Aziz, for example, has identified four levels of meaning referred to by Jung at different times. These are: (1) simply the fact of two or more events paralleling one another (the paralleling is by virtue of a shared content or meaning); (2) the emotional charge or 'numinosity' attending the synchronicity (a source of non-rational meaning); (3) the significance of the synchronicity interpreted subjectively, from the point of view of the experiencer's personal needs and goals; and (4) the significance of the synchronicity objectively, as the expression of archetypal meaning which is transcendental to human consciousness (Aziz 1990: 64–6, 75–84; see also Main 1996: 155–79).

Aziz calls this fourth level of meaning the 'archetypal level' (Aziz 1990: 66). It is based on the fact that the archetype represents in itself a form of meaning which is '*a priori* in relation to human consciousness and apparently exists outside man' (Jung 1952: 501–2). Thus in synchronicities 'one and the same (transcendental) meaning might manifest itself simultaneously in the human psyche and in the arrangement of an external and independent event' (Jung 1952: 482). In fact, each of the other three levels of meaning also depends on the presence of the archetype. The shared meaning by virtue of which two or more events are taken to be in a synchronistic relationship derives from an archetype (e.g., underlying the scarab symbol in both its psychic and its physical appearances is the archetype of rebirth). Again, the numinous charge of synchronicities derives from the presence of an activated archetype – the association with such numinosity being precisely one of the characteristics of archetypes as presented by Jung (Jung 1952: 436). Third, the subjective level of meaning, insofar as this is evaluated with reference to the process of individuation, will also be based on archetypes, since it is the archetypes – shadow, animus/anima, self, etc. – which essentially govern individuation for Jung.

The appreciation of this archetypal foundation of synchronicities helps resolve a pervasive ambiguity in Jung's use of the phrase 'meaningful coincidence'. On the one hand, the 'meaning' referred to in this phrase is clearly the significance the coincidence has for the experiencer – ultimately, its bearing on the experiencer's individuation. On the other hand, Jung also often uses the word 'meaning' to refer to the content that the coinciding events have in common: they have 'the same or similar meaning' or 'appear as meaningful parallels' (Jung 1952: 441). Here what the coincidence might signify for an experiencer is not germane; one can, in fact, replace 'meaning' with 'content'. It is true that the two senses of 'meaning' do not exclude each other – the meaning/content can be meaningful/significant to an experiencer or observer – but it is equally true that they do not entail each other. That Jung none the less moves ambiguously between the two different senses probably stems from the fact that for him the content of synchronicities is generally understood to be archetypal and therefore is bound also to be meaningful in the sense of significant.

The tension between the two understandings of 'meaning' is clearest in the case of parapsychological experiments such as those of Rhine. In these experiments what is important is primarily the paralleling of content between the image constituting the subject's guess and the target object. It is this paralleling of content that leads Jung to assert that 'Rhine's results confront us with the fact that there are events which are related to one another experimentally, and in this case *meaningfully*, without there being any possibility of proving that this relation is a causal one' (Jung 1952: 435). Whether the coincidence represented by the improbable number of successful guesses is also meaningful in the sense of being significant for the individuation or other personal needs or goals of the experimental subject is a question about which Jung appears to have remained uncertain. On the one hand, he acknowledges that Rhine's experiments 'contain no direct evidence of any constellation of the archetype' (Jung 1952: 440; see also Jung 1976: 399). On the other hand, he suggests that such a constellation may none the less be present inasmuch as 'the experimental set-up is influenced by the expectation of a *miracle*' and 'A miracle is an archetypal situation' (Jung 1976: 537; see also Progoff 1987: 105–6). Furthermore, the important emotional factor in the experiments, indicated by the decline effect, may also suggest the presence of an archetypal situation inasmuch as archetypal situations are typically 'accompanied by a corresponding emotion' (Jung 1976: 537).

Jung's astrological experiment

The section of Jung's 1952 essay on synchronicity which was most widely misunderstood when it first appeared was his astrological experiment. Indeed, many writers on synchronicity still tend to side-step this aspect of his work, dismissing it as, for example, 'peripheral' (Aziz 1990: 2) or 'fruitless' (Mansfield 1995: 33). Others, however, have found Jung's experiment to constitute one of the most interesting and original features of his work and to have suggestive implications for the understanding both of statistics (Fordham 1957) and of astrology (Hyde 1992).

It may be that Jung himself was unclear initially as to what his experiment could be expected to demonstrate. Michael Fordham writes that 'At one time [Jung] really thought that if his [astrological] material proved statistically significant it would prove his [synchronicity] thesis' (Fordham 1993: 105) – a suggestion reinforced by Jung's remark in a letter to B.V. Raman (6 September 1947) that 'What I miss in astrological literature is chiefly the statistical method by which fundamental facts could be scientifically established' (Jung 1973: 476; see also Hyde 1992: 129–30). Later, however, Jung was adamant that his experiment, as carried out, was never intended to prove anything about astrology or, through astrology, about synchronicity (Jung 1958a: 494, 497, 498). He had come to appreciate, Fordham suggests, that if the astrological material did prove statistically significant, 'it would make a cause for the data more likely' (Fordham 1993: 105), thereby undermining the synchronicity thesis. Rather, what Jung hoped was that his experiment would 'on the one hand demonstrate the existence of synchronicity [i.e., allow for its occurrence and make it visible in the form of measurable results] and, on the other hand, disclose psychic contents which would at least give us a clue to the nature of the psychic factor involved' (Jung 1952: 450). Arguably, he succeeded in both aims.

The key to an appreciation of the experiment is an understanding of Jung's use of statistics – a use which, as Fordham has remarked, is 'highly original and peculiarly his own' (Fordham 1957: 36). As they are usually employed, Fordham explains,

> Statistics distinguish between two sets of phenomena: those which are sufficiently ordered to indicate causal connections and to which the notion of prediction can be applied with considerable success, and those whose action is random and which as such obey the laws of chance where the notion of prediction is of little use.

> (Fordham 1957: 36)

With synchronicities, however, Jung introduces a third set of phenomena, since 'Considered statistically they will appear as chance, but they will not be due to chance; i.e. he cuts right across the duality chance–cause axiom on which statistics are based' (Fordham 1957: 36). Statistically, events are considered to be 'significant' (i.e., not chance) if their improbability rises above a certain level (technically, the 'Null hypothesis'). When they rise above this level of improbability, events are usually expected and found to have a cause. Since none of Jung's astrological results rose to such a level, they were unlikely to have been caused but were indeed chance happenings – which is what, as acausal events, he needed them to be. Thus, Jung's use of statistics 'had an aim exactly the reverse to the usual one. He used them to define the region in which synchronistic phenomena are most likely' (Fordham 1957: 37).

Rather than dismiss his results altogether because they did not rise to the level of statistical significance, Jung took the novel step of using the statistical distribution they presented as a monitor through which to investigate their possible psychological significance. As he remarks: 'it is just as important to consider the exceptions to the rule as the averages. . . . Inasmuch as chance maxima and minima occur, they are *facts* whose nature I set out to explore' (Jung 1952: 463).

Thus analysis of the three batches of 180, 220 and 83 pairs of marriage horoscopes showed the maximum frequencies to fall on the aspects respectively of moon conjunct sun, moon conjunct moon and moon conjunct Ascendant. These are precisely the three aspects that astrological tradition would expect to turn up most frequently in marriage horoscopes, as Jung and his co-worker well knew (Jung 1952: 454–5). Here, however, they have turned up in a way which is entirely random. The horoscopes 'were piled up in chronological order just as the post brought them in' (Jung 1952: 459), and Jung decided when to begin analyzing the first batch for no better reason than that he was unable to restrain his curiosity any longer (Jung 1958a: 495). As his subsequent analyses demonstrated, if the horoscopes had arrived in a different order or if he had waited until they had all come in and had analyzed them together, the three traditional marriage aspects would not have shown up with the same remarkable salience (Jung 1952: 479–80, 471–2). He concludes that, since the resulting figures

> actually fall within the limits of chance expectation, they do not support the astrological claim, they merely *imitate* accidentally the ideal answer to astrological expectation. It is nothing but a chance result from the statistical point of view, yet it is *meaningful* on account of the fact that it looks as if it validated this expectation. It is just what I call a synchronistic phenomenon.
>
> (Jung 1952: 477)

The fact that the result corresponded to the expectations of his co-worker and himself suggested to Jung that their psychic state might in some way have been involved in 'arranging' it, that there may have existed, in their case as with practitioners in the past, 'a secret, mutual connivance . . . between the material and the psychic state of the astrologer' (Jung 1952: 478). This conclusion was further suggested by his realization that in working on the statistics 'use had been made of unconscious deception', that he had been 'put off the trail by a number of errors' (Jung 1952: 478). The curious thing about these errors was that they '*all tend[ed] to exaggerate the results in a way favourable to astrology*, and add[ed] most suspiciously to the impression of an artificial or fraudulent arrangement of the facts' (Jung 1952: 479). Jung remarks:

> I know, however, from long experience of these things that spontaneous synchronistic phenomena draw the observer, by hook or by crook, into what is happening and occasionally make him an accessory to the deed. That is the danger inherent in all parapsychological experiments.
>
> (Jung 1952: 479)

Fortunately, the errors in the astrological experiment were eventually discovered and corrected (Jung 1952: 478). However, in the light both of these errors and of the remarkable correspondence between his expectation and the results he obtained, Jung conducted a further experiment to test for indications of possible psychic participation. He got three people 'whose psychological status was accurately known' (Jung 1952: 473) to draw by lot twenty pairs of marriage horoscopes from a random assortment of 200. In each case, he found that the person's random selection of twenty horoscopes produced maximal figures which, while not statistically significant, corresponded surprisingly well with the known psychic state of the subject (Jung 1952: 473–5). For example, one woman 'who, at the time of the experiment, found herself in a state of intense emotional excitement' drew horoscopes in which there was 'a predominance of the Mars aspects' (Jung 1952: 474). Inasmuch as 'The classical significance of Mars lies in his emotionality', this result 'fully agrees with the psychic state of the subject' (Jung 1952: 474). This informal experiment appeared to confirm what had happened under more rigorously controlled circumstances in the main experiment. Without exceeding the levels of dispersion that would be expected due to chance, the data none the less patterned themselves in ways which corresponded to a known psychic disposition. If, however, the astrologer's psychic condition can indeed participate in the arrangement of the material being considered, this means that astrology may be more a form of divination and less a form of science than many of its practitioners would like to believe. This conclusion has in fact been drawn by some astrologers and has led to a serious reassessment of their practice (see Hyde 1992).

The mind–body relationship

The relationship between mind and body is a source of unending perplexity for physicians, psychologists, and philosophers alike. Jung states a version of the problem as follows:

> The assumption of a causal relation between psyche and physis leads . . . to conclusions which it is difficult to square with experience: either there are physical processes which cause psychic happenings, or there is a pre-existent psyche which organizes matter. In the first case it is hard to see how chemical processes can ever produce psychic processes, and in the second case one wonders how an immaterial psyche could ever set matter in motion.
>
> (Jung 1952: 505–6)

He then suggests, ambitiously, that 'The synchronicity principle possesses properties that may help to clear up the body–soul problem' (Jung 1952: 506). The properties in question are the fact that the psyche can be meaningfully correlated with physical processes without any causal interaction – suggesting that the psyche may not need to be connected with the brain (Jung 1952: 505); and the hypothesis of 'absolute knowledge . . . a knowledge not mediated by the sense organs' which provides the means by which this acausal co-ordination of mental and bodily processes can be possible (Jung 1952: 506).

In the light of this suggestion Jung examines a number of cases of out-of-the-body and near-death experiences (Jung 1952: 506–9) which, he concludes, 'seem to show that in swoon states, where by all human standards there is every guarantee that conscious activity and sense perception are suspended, consciousness, reproducible ideas, acts of judgment, and perceptions can still continue to exist' (Jung 1952: 509). He considers this to 'indicate a shift in the localization of consciousness, a sort of separation from the body, or from the cerebral cortex or cerebrum which is conjectured to be the seat of conscious phenomena' (Jung 1952: 509). There now seem to be two possibilities: either 'there is some other nervous substrate in us, apart from the cerebrum, that can think and perceive' or else 'the psychic processes that go on in us during loss of consciousness are synchronistic phenomena, i.e., events which have no causal connection with organic processes' (Jung 1952: 509). Since there is evidence to support both possibilities (Jung 1952: 510–11), Jung remains uncommitted, concluding that 'psychophysical parallelism', by which he here seems to mean the mind–body relationship, is something 'which we cannot at present pretend to understand' (Jung 1952: 511; cf., Jung 1973: 76–7).

In the same period in which Jung was articulating his theory of synchronicity he was also giving serious thought to the possibility of there being a 'subtle body' that somehow mediates between the psyche and the physical body as we normally experience them (see, e.g., Jung 1973: 522–3; Jung 1976: 43–5). Quite what the implications of this are for the theory of synchronicity is unclear. Jung's colleague C.A. Meier, for instance, considered psychosomatic phenomena to be synchronistic and as such actually to presuppose the existence of the subtle body (Meier 1963: 116). Another colleague, however, Marie-Louise von Franz, argued that psychosomatic phenomena and other suggestions of the existence of a subtle body indicate rather a causal relationship between mind and body (Franz 1992: 249–51). In support of her view she refers to Jung's intriguing suggestion – which he admitted was 'highly speculative, in fact unwarrantably adventurous' (Jung 1976: 45) – that the psyche and the body should be viewed as different manifestations of a single energy and their relationship be understood in terms of the transformation of this energy into greater or lesser states of 'intensification' (Jung 1976: 45).

General acausal orderedness

Synchronicities such as Jung's scarab case – presented by him as paradigmatic – typically manifest themselves as random one-off events. However, certain kinds of acausal phenomena display a greater regularity than this. The results of Rhine's parapsychological experiments were sufficiently reproducible to achieve a high level of statistical significance (see Jung 1952: 516). Also, with mantic methods such as astrology and the *I Ching* Jung writes that 'Synchronistic phenomena are found to occur – experimentally – with some degree of regularity and frequency' (Jung 1952: 511). Again, if the mind–body relationship were found to be synchronistic – and Jung is at least open to this possibility – then this too would imply that acausality is not just 'a relatively rare phenomenon' (Jung 1952: 500, n. 70). Above all, however, the conception of synchronicity as having to do solely with irregular one-off events was called into question for Jung by such factors as the properties of natural numbers and certain quantum phenomena such as 'the orderedness of energy quanta, of radium decay, etc.' (Jung 1952: 517).[20] These are properties of the world which appear to have no deeper cause but are 'Just-So', i.e., acausal (Jung 1952: 516). In the light especially of this last factor, Jung was forced to consider 'whether our definition of synchronicity with reference to the equivalence of psychic and physical processes is capable of expansion, or rather, requires expansion' (Jung 1952: 516). He concluded that the definition was indeed too narrow and needed to be supplemented with the broader category of 'general acausal orderedness':

> I incline in fact to the view that synchronicity in the narrow sense is only a particular instance of general acausal orderedness – that, namely, of the equivalence of psychic and physical processes where the observer is in the fortunate position of being able to recognize the *tertium comparationis* [i.e., the meaning by which the psychic and physical processes are related].
>
> (Jung 1952: 516)

More specifically, synchronicity in the narrow sense is distinguished from general acausal orderedness in that phenomena belonging to the latter category 'have existed from eternity and occur regularly, whereas the forms of psychic orderedness [i.e., synchronicities] are *acts of creation in time*' (Jung 1952: 517). He then adds: 'That, incidentally, is precisely why I have stressed the element of time as being characteristic of these phenomena and called them *synchronistic*' (Jung 1952: 517). This represents a significant shift of emphasis – if not a different view altogether, and possibly a more coherent view – from his earlier explanation in terms of simultaneity (Jung 1952: 441).

Jung's statements about general acausal orderedness are few but have attracted interest. For example, Jung several times expresses the view that natural numbers may prove particularly important for an understanding of synchronicity: 'I feel that the root of the enigma', he writes, 'is to be found in the properties of whole numbers' (Jung 1976: 289; see also Jung 1976: 352, 400). This hint has been taken up by von Franz in a number of publications (Franz 1974, 1980, 1992).

Epistemological status of the principle of synchronicity

'Synchronicity', Jung insists, 'is not a philosophical view but an empirical concept which postulates an intellectually necessary principle' (Jung 1952: 512); 'It is based not on philosophical assumptions but on empirical experience and experimentation' (Jung 1951b: 531); from the material before him he claims that he 'can derive no other hypothesis that would adequately explain the facts (including the ESP experiments)' (Jung 1952: 505). Notwithstanding this last statement, it is 'only a makeshift model' and 'does not rule out the possibility of other hypotheses' (Jung 1976: 437).

Other writers, however, have found aspects of the theory of synchronicity to be less free from metaphysical presupposition than these statements imply. Explicitly or implicitly, Jung's claims to an empirical status for his work are invariably based on an appeal to Kant's epistemological distinction between phenomena (things as they appear to human consciousness) and noumena (things as they are in themselves) – Jung's professed concern being solely with phenomena (see, e.g., Voogd 1984). However, Wolfgang Giegerich has argued that many of the core concepts of Jung's psychology, including the concept of synchronicity, overstep the limits prescribed by Kantian epistemology: 'As long as Jung clings to his label "empiricist first and last," Kant would show him that he has no right to posit, for example, a psychoid archetypal level in which the subject-object dichotomy would be overcome' (Giegerich 1987: 111).

This issue, as Giegerich implies, goes to the heart of Jung's psychology as a whole. Jung himself does appear to have been aware that his thinking on at least synchronicity sometimes shifts into metaphysics. In a letter to Fordham (3 January 1957) he congratulates Fordham on his essay 'Reflections on the Archetypes and Synchronicity' (Fordham 1957) and remarks:

> I well understand that you prefer to emphasize the archetypal implication in synchronicity. This aspect is certainly most important from the psychological angle, but I must say that I am equally interested, at times even more so, in the metaphysical aspect of the phenomena, and in the question: how does it come that even inanimate objects are capable of behaving as if they were acquainted with my thoughts?
>
> (Jung 1976: 344)

Again, in a letter to K. Schmid (11 June 1958) Jung first asserts his empiricist position by stating that synchronicity 'is not a name that characterizes an "organizing principle"' but 'characterizes a modality' and therefore 'is not meant as anything substantive' (Jung 1976: 448). However, he then admits that it can sometimes be legitimate to conceptualize beyond the bounds of what is empirically knowable so long as this conceptualization does not come 'from my biased speculation but rather from the unfathomable law of nature herself . . . from the total man, i.e., from the co-participation of the unconscious [in the form of dreams etc.]' (Jung 1976: 448). 'This far-reaching speculation', he believes, 'is a psychic need which is part of our mental hygiene', adding, however, that 'in the realm of scientific verification it must be counted sheer mythology' (Jung 1976: 449). Thus, he is able to excuse some of his own more incautious statements regarding synchronicity: 'if', he concedes, 'I occasionally speak of an "organizer," this is sheer mythology since at present I have no means of going beyond the bare fact that synchronistic phenomena are "just so"' (Jung 1976: 449). Again, after quoting a paragraph from his 1952 essay affirming the transcendental nature of the '"absolute knowledge" which is characteristic of synchronistic phenomena' (Jung 1952: 506), he admits that 'This statement, too, is mythology, like all transcendental postulates' (Jung 1976: 449).[21]

AFTER SYNCHRONICITY

Once formulated, the theory of synchronicity provided Jung with insights into a variety of subjects and areas of experience – some of them, not surprisingly, the very ones which had challenged him to develop the theory in the first place.

At the most fundamental level, synchronicity led Jung to speculate about the nature of reality. The fact, for instance, that in synchronistic events the same archetypal pattern of meaning seems capable of expressing itself independently in both psychic and physical contexts suggested to him that 'all reality [may be] grounded on an as yet unknown substrate possessing material and at the same time psychic qualities' (Jung 1958b: 411). The synchronistic principle 'suggests that there is an inter-connection or unity of causally unrelated events, and thus postulates a unitary aspect of being which can very well be described as the *unus mundus*' (Jung 1954–5: 464–5). This postulated unitary background to existence, in which the concepts of psyche and matter and space and time merge into a psychophysical space–time continuum, was where Jung considered the archetypes themselves, as opposed to their phenomenal manifestations, ultimately to be located. To express this ambivalent nature – at once psychic and physical yet neither because beyond both – he was led to coin the term 'psychoid'. The ability of the archetype to manifest synchronistically in independent psychic and physical contexts is itself an indicator of its fundamentally psychoid nature.

Regarding the phenomenal world rather than its hypothetical substrate, synchronicity, as a connecting principle complementary to causality, directs attention to a whole dimension of experienceable relationships between events which would be disregarded or marginalized by any exclusively causalistic view. On a general level, this helps create conceptual space for the acknowledgment of radically anomalous or paranormal events which might otherwise be denied.

More specifically, in the field of psychical research, the concept of acausal connection offers a fresh way of looking at the kinds of phenomena usually designated as telepathy, clairvoyance, psychokinesis, precognition, and so on. Each of these terms, Jung felt, perpetuates the expectation of finding some kind of energic and hence causal relationship between the events involved, whereas the concept of synchronicity focuses attention on the main relationship actually present in experience, namely, the meaningful coincidence of the events (Jung 1955–56: 464; Jung 1976: 538). This implies a shift of emphasis away from seeking to discover some mechanism or means of transmission at work in the events and towards a potentially more illuminating exploration of their psychological background and meaning.

Even easier to overlook from the causal perspective are the kinds of meaningful acausal connections which constitute the correspondences upon which divinatory and similar forms of esoteric thinking are based. As Jung's astrological experiment demonstrated, these connections, unlike the more radical anomalies, often do not even achieve the salience of statistical significance, and so would in many cases not be noticed at all if one were not sensitized to their possibility by one's awareness of the principle of synchronicity.

There are also many important implications for the practice of psychotherapy. For example, Jung recognized that states of mind, such as bad conscience, can sometimes express themselves synchronistically in the thoughts and feelings of another person (Jung 1963: 60–1; Jung 1958d: 450–1) or even through the arrangement of events in the environment (Jung 1963: 123–4). In this light, it is not surprising that the occurrence of synchronicities can play various kinds of role in the transference/countertransference relationship – sometimes providing crucial insight to either the analyst or the patient (Gordon 1983: 138–44), at other times marking a critical or even fatal moment within the relationship (Jung 1963: 136–7). Again, Jung points out the possibility, on the part of certain patients, of interpreting genuine synchronistic events as delusions (i.e., the delusion of believing that quite ordinary events have special reference to them). Therapists capable of understanding synchronicity 'not as a psychotic but as a normal phenomenon' will be able to avoid the therapeutically negative consequences of the patients' – and, if they are not sensitive to synchronicity, their own – 'morbidly narrow' interpretation (Jung 1976: 409–10).

Spiritual experience is another area to which Jung's theory of synchronicity has been applied, both by himself directly and by others elaborating on the implications of the theory. Thus, the crucial role of synchronicity within Jung's overall psychology of religion has been clearly demonstrated by Aziz (1990). In particular, Aziz argues that synchronistic experiences enable one to view Jung's core religious process – individuation – not just intrapsychically but as involving the world beyond the psyche. Synchronicity therefore provides the key to freeing Jung from the criticism of psychological reductionism often levelled at him by theologians (Aziz 1990: 179–84).[22]

On the personal level, Jung's own visionary experiences of union, which attended his near-fatal illness in 1944, can also be understood in the light of synchronicity. Although he does not himself directly apply the concept of synchronicity to these experiences, his characterization of them in terms of 'a quality of absolute objectivity' and of 'a non-temporal state in which present, past, and future are one' (Jung 1963: 275) clearly reflects the 'absolute knowledge' and 'space–time relativity' involved in synchronicities. In fact, his sense of his visions as representing a kind of mystic marriage between self and world (the *hierosgamos* or *mysterium coniunctionis* (Jung 1963: 274–5)) suggests that they may actually constitute an experiential realization of the unitary dimension of existence (the *unus mundus*) towards which he considered the more familiar forms of synchronicity to be pointing.

Jung is more explicit concerning the implications of synchronicity for the question of possible life after death. For epistemological reasons, he does not think one can actually prove that there is survival of death, but he considers it significant that the unconscious psyches of people approaching death generally present dreams and other spontaneous imagery which imply an expected continuity (Jung 1934: 410–11; Jung 1963: 278–80). The hint provided by this is supported by two different aspects of synchronicity. On a general level, he argues that the space–time relativization involved in synchronicity implies that the psyche 'exists in a continuum outside time and space' (Jung 1976: 561; see also Jung 1934: 412–15; Jung 1963: 282–3). Although we do not know in detail what 'existence outside time' is like, we can at least infer that it is 'outside change' and 'possesses relative eternity' (Jung 1976: 561) – grounds for supposing that it may not end with the death of the body. More concretely, he considers that certain synchronistic phenomena that occur in relation to death – veridical dreams and apparitions, for instance – can express the idea of survival also in terms of their content (Jung 1963: 289–92).[23]

Jung sometimes refers to synchronistic events as miracles, though it is clear that he does so only in a loose way and certainly without any expectation of having to provide theological backing for his usage (e.g., Jung 1976: 537, 540).[24] Occasionally, however, he does address the issue of traditionally designated religious miracles and on these occasions sometimes refers to synchronicity. Thus, speaking of the identity of Christ the 'empirical man' with 'the traditional Son of Man type', he says: 'Wherever such identities occur, characteristic archetypal effects appear, that is *numinosity* and *synchronistic phenomena*, hence tales of miracles are inseparable from the Christ figure' (Jung 1976: 21). At other times he suggests that explanations for apparent miracles, such as the case of Brother Klaus living for twenty years without material sustenance, should be sought more specifically in the realm of parapsychology and mediumistic phenomena (Jung 1950/1951: 660). Even here, however, the implication is that the sustained paranormal phenomena constituting the miracle are synchronistic archetypal 'effects' rendered possible by the maintaining of a numinous religious attitude (cf., Jung 1976: 576).

Finally, Jung also had recourse to the concept of synchronicity when attempting to account for the baffling reports of UFOs. He had kept a close eye on this phenomenon since its emergence in the mid 1940s and recognized that it seemed to have both a physical aspect (the fact that UFOs are not only seen but are sometimes simultaneously picked up on radar) and a psychic aspect (the fact that they 'provoked, like nothing else, conscious and unconscious fantasies' [Jung 1958b: 313]). He was unable to decide, however, which was primary – whether there were indeed physical events followed by the fantasies, or whether the fantasies and visions were arising independently from an activated archetype (Jung 1958b: 313). In this perplexity he invokes synchronicity as a third possibility, suggesting that there may indeed be an anomalous physical phenomenon involved but that this meaningfully coincides with, rather than causes, the accompanying fantasizing or myth-making, which has its own independent reasons for surfacing at this time (Jung 1958b: 313, 416–17).[25]

These examples should suffice to indicate how Jung's theory of synchronicity can provide, if not conclusive explanations, at least some stimulating new perspectives on a wide range of anomalous phenomena. The theory of synchronicity brings more fully into awareness the experiential reality, the complexity, and above all the potential meaningfulness of paranormal events. In doing so, it perhaps furthers what Jung once described as the 'uncomprehended purpose' of 'any nocturnal, numinous experience': 'to make us feel the overpowering presence of a mystery ... shaking our certitudes and lending wings to the imagination' (Jung 1958c: 328–9).

NOTES

1 Jung himself more usually speaks of spiritualistic, parapsychological, or synchronistic phenomena. He does, however, use the term 'paranormal' on at least a couple of occasions (see Jung 1973: 389–90; Jung 1976: 538, 540). I have preferred 'paranormal' to any other term because it seemed to me the most current, comprehensive and theoretically and methodologically neutral. Recently Victor Mansfield has attempted to dissociate synchronicity from the paranormal (Mansfield 1995: 27–34). His attempt depends, however, on understanding both synchronicity and the paranormal (and its equivalents) in a narrower way than Jung.

2 A broader context for Jung's early interest in the paranormal is the widespread popular and psychiatric interest during the nineteenth century in the movements of mesmerism, hypnotism and Spiritualism. See Charet (1993), 27–58.

3 In this approach, as in the format of his dissertation generally, Jung was following the model of the seminal study of a medium by Théodore Flournoy, *From India to the Planet Mars* (1900).

4 James Hillman, however, cautions against too linear a view of the relationship between Jung's early observations and later theory: 'if we read about the early years of Jung's personal life in order to understand the later years of his theoretical life, we have the cart before the horse, and are working reductively, personalistically. To understand early Jung, we must read late Jung. To understand events of 1896, we must turn to his writing of 1946' (Hillman 1976: 133).

5 In this Freud was also greatly influenced by the Hungarian psychoanalyst Sandor Ferenczi (Charet 1993: 196–7).

6 For a full account of the conflict between Freud and Jung over spiritualistic phenomena, see Charet (1993), 171–227. For a collection of the writings which Freud eventually published on telepathy and occultism, as well as other psychoanalytic writings on these subjects up to the year 1951, see Devereux (1974).

7 This appears to be the view of Stefanie Zumstein-Preiswerk, a blood relation of both Jung and his medium (Zumstein-Preiswerk 1975: 110). Hillman, however, thinks the relationship should be understood more in terms of transference and participation mystique (Hillman 1976: 131–3).

8 Originally titled *Wandlungen und Symbole der Libido* (literally, *Transformations*

and Symbols of the Libido), translated into English in 1916 as *The Psychology of the Unconscious*.

9 Rudi Schneider's mediumship is, as John Beloff remarks, 'rightly considered among the best authenticated in the literature' (Beloff 1993: 107).

10 For an interesting account of Schlag, and the fate of his 'sample of ectoplasm', see Mulacz (1995).

11 He also mentions experimenting with geomancy (Jung 1952: 453; Jung 1976: 463, 538), but I can find no indication that he gained anything from this over and above what he gained from astrology and the *I Ching*.

12 One wonders whether Jung actually began to encounter more meaningful coincidences in the 1920s than he had done previously, perhaps because of having reached some significant point in his personal development and research, or whether he had simply become more cognisant of them as a category of experiences in their own right, perhaps as a result of his experiments with the *I Ching*.

13 The central points of Aziz's analysis of synchronicity in terms of compensation and individuation have been taken up by Kelly (1993) and Mansfield (1995).

14 The topics were analytical psychology (1925), dream analysis (1928–30), interpretations of visions (1930–4), Kundalini yoga (1932), and Nietzsche's *Thus Spoke Zarathustra* (1934–9).

15 For a lucid overview of Rhine's work, see Beloff (1993), 125–51. Though Rhine's work is no longer considered as unimpeachable as when it first appeared, equally challenging parapsychological results, meeting the more rigorous experimental standards that modern critics demand, have recently been produced by other researchers (see, e.g., Jahn and Dunne 1988).

16 This omission is for reasons of space and because the 1952 essay is in any case readily available as an individual volume (Jung 1955).

17 Where Jung uses 'microphysical' and 'macrophysical' it is now more common to find 'microscopic' and 'macroscopic'.

18 For Kant's relation of this incident, which appears to be Jung's source for it, see Jung (1905), 297–8.

19 Aziz attempts to refer Jung's use of the notion of 'simultaneity' to the situation in the unconscious psyche where 'in the space–time continuum everything exists en bloc' and therefore 'with a kind of simultaneity' (Aziz 1990: 71). For a discussion of this approach to the problem, see Main (1996), 138–41.

20 Mansfield has pointed out that the particular quantum phenomena singled out by Jung and, following him, von Franz are mostly inappropriate (Mansfield 1995: 30). Nevertheless, he considers that 'Jung and von Franz are quite right to appeal to quantum mechanics', since 'Innumerable quantum phenomena are acausal in the strict sense' (Mansfield 1995: 32). With appropriate examples substituted for the inappropriate ones, Jung's argument can be followed as it stands.

21 Interestingly, a number of attempts have been made to elucidate the nature of synchronicity by viewing it from the perspective of mythology, in particular by imagining it as the expression of one or another of the gods of the Greek pantheon: Hermes the trickster and transgressor of boundaries (Combs and Holland 1994); Pan the god of spontaneity (Hillman 1972); or Dionysus bestower of the experience of mystical fusion and timelessness (Burniston 1994).

22 For a broader exploration of the relationship between synchronicity and spiritual experience, see Main (1996).

23 For more on Jung's view of life after death, see Franz (1987).

24 For an explication of how, in theological terms, synchronicities might be accounted miracles, see Main (1996), 205–11.

25 The phenomenon of alien abduction, which represents one of the main topics of contemporary UFO investigation (see Mack 1994), had not emerged with any

salience in Jung's lifetime.

REFERENCES

Aziz, R. (1990) *C. G. Jung's Psychology of Religion and Synchronicity*, Albany: State University of New York Press.

Baumann-Jung, G. (1975) 'Some Reflections on the Horoscope of C. G. Jung', *Spring* 36: 35–55.

Beloff, J. (1977) 'Psi Phenomena: Causal versus Acausal Interpretation', *Journal of the Society for Psychical Research* 49: 573–82.

—— (1993) *Parapsychology: A Concise History*, London: The Athlone Press.

Bohm, D. (1990) 'A New Theory of the Relationship of Mind and Matter', *Philosophical Psychology* 3: 271–86.

Burniston, A. F. (1994) 'Synchronicity: A Dionysian Perspective', *Harvest* 40: 118–27.

Charet, F.X. (1993) *Spiritualism and the Foundations of C. G. Jung's Psychology*, Albany: State University of New York Press.

Combs, A. and Holland, M. (1994) *Synchronicity: Science, Myth and the Trickster*, Edinburgh: Floris Books.

Devereux, G. (ed.) (1974) *Psychoanalysis and the Occult*, London: Souvenir Press.

Erkelens, H. van (1991) 'Wolfgang Pauli's Dialogue with the Spirit of Matter', *Psychological Perspectives* 24: 34–53.

Flournoy, T. (1900) *From India to the Planet Mars: A Case of Multiple Personality with Imaginary Languages*, ed. Sonu Shamdasani, Princeton, NJ: Princeton University Press, 1996.

Fordham, M. (1957) 'Reflections on Archetypes and Synchronicity', in *New Developments in Analytical Psychology*, London: Routledge and Kegan Paul, 35–50.

—— (1993) *The Making of an Analyst: A Memoir*, London: Free Association Books.

Franz, M.-L. von (1974) *Number and Time: Reflections Leading Towards a Unification of Psychology and Physics*, trans. Andrea Dykes, London: Rider and Company.

—— (1980) *On Divination and Synchronicity: The Psychology of Meaningful Chance*, Toronto: Inner City Books.

—— (1987) *On Dreams and Death: A Jungian Interpretation*, trans. Emmanuel Xipolitas Kennedy and Vernon Brooks, Boston and London: Shambhala.

—— (1992) *Psyche and Matter*, Boston and London: Shambhala.

Giegerich, W. (1987) 'The Rescue of the World: Jung, Hegel, and the Subjective Universe', *Spring* 48: 107-14.

Gordon, R. (1983) 'Reflections on Jung's Concept of Synchronicity', in Molly Tuby (ed.), *In the Wake of Jung: A Selection from 'Harvest'*, London: Coventure, 129–46.

Hillman, J. (1972) 'An Essay on Pan', in W.H. Roscher and J. Hillman (eds), *Pan and the Nightmare*, Zurich: Spring Publications.

—— (1976) 'Some Early Background to Jung's Ideas: Notes on *C. G. Jung's Medium* by Stephanie Zumstein-Preiswerk', *Spring*: 123–36.

Hinshaw, R. (1995) 'Review' of C.A. Meier (ed.), *Wolfgang Pauli und C. G. Jung: Ein Briefweschel*, in *Psychological Perspectives* 31: 125–30.

Honner, J. (1987) *The Description of Nature: Niels Bohr and the Philosophy of Quantum Physics*, Oxford: Clarendon Press.

Hyde, M. (1992) *Jung and Astrology*, London: Aquarian Press.

Jaffé, A. (1967) 'C. G. Jung and Parapsychology', in J.R. Smythies (ed.), *Science and ESP*, London: Routledge and Kegan Paul, 263–80.

—— (1971) *From the Life and Work of C. G. Jung*, London: Hodder and Stoughton.

—— (1984) 'Details about C. G. Jung's Family', *Spring* 45: 35–43.

Jahn, R.G. and Dunne, B.J. (1988) *Margins of Reality: The Role of Consciousness in the Physical World*, San Diego, CA: Harcourt Brace Jovanovich.

Jung, C.G. (1897) 'Some Thoughts on Psychology', in *The Collected Works of C. G. Jung*, 21 vols, ed. Sir Herbert Read, Michael Fordham and Gerhard Adler, executive editor William McGuire, trans. R.F.C. Hull [hereafter *Collected Works*], Supplementary Volume A, *The Zofingia Lectures*, trans. Jan Van Heurck, with an Introduction by Marie-Louise von Franz, London: Routledge and Kegan Paul, 1983.

—— (1902) 'On the Psychology and Pathology of So-Called Occult Phenomena', in *Collected Works*, vol. 1, *Psychiatric Studies*, 2nd edn, London: Routledge and Kegan Paul, 1970.

—— (1905) 'On Spiritualistic Phenomena', in *Collected Works*, vol. 18, *The Symbolic Life*, London: Routledge and Kegan Paul, 1977.

—— (1911–12/1952) *Collected Works*, vol. 5, *Symbols of Transformation*, 2nd edn, London: Routledge and Kegan Paul, 1967.

—— (1920/1948) 'The Psychological Foundations of Belief in Spirits', in *Collected Works*, vol. 8, *The Structure and Dynamics of the Psyche*, 2nd edn, London: Routledge and Kegan Paul, 1969.

—— (1925) *Analytical Psychology: Notes of the Seminar Given in 1925*, ed. William McGuire, London and New York: Routledge, 1990.

—— (1928–30) *Dream Analysis: Notes of the Seminar Given in 1928–1930*, ed. William McGuire, London: Routledge and Kegan Paul, 1984.

—— (1930) 'Richard Wilhelm: In Memoriam', in *Collected Works*, vol. 15, *The Spirit in Man, Art and Literature*, London: Routledge and Kegan Paul, 1966.

—— (1934) 'The Soul and Death', in *Collected Works*, vol. 8, *The Structure and Dynamics of the Psyche*, 2nd edn, London: Routledge and Kegan Paul, 1969.

—— (1935) 'The Tavistock Lectures', in *Collected Works*, vol. 18, *The Symbolic Life*, London: Routledge and Kegan Paul, 1977.

—— (1938/1954) 'Psychological Aspects of the Mother Archetype', in *Collected Works*, vol. 9i, *The Archetypes and the Collective Unconscious*, 2nd edn, London: Routledge and Kegan Paul, 1968.

—— (1947/1954) 'On the Nature of the Psyche', in *Collected Works*, vol. 8, *The Structure and Dynamics of the Psyche*, 2nd edn, London: Routledge and Kegan Paul, 1969.

—— (1950a) 'Foreword to the "I Ching"', in *Collected Works*, vol. 11, *Psychology and Religion: West and East*, 2nd edn, London: Routledge and Kegan Paul, 1969.

—— (1950b) 'Foreword to Moser: "Spuk: Irrglaube oder Wahrglaube?"', in *Collected Works*, vol. 18, *The Symbolic Life*, London: Routledge and Kegan Paul, 1977.

—— (1950/1951) 'The Miraculous Fast of Brother Klaus', in *Collected Works*, vol. 18, *The Symbolic Life*, London: Routledge and Kegan Paul, 1977.

—— (1950–55) 'Letters on Synchronicity', in *Collected Works*, vol. 18, *The Symbolic Life*, London: Routledge and Kegan Paul, 1977.

—— (1951a) *Collected Works*, vol. 9ii, *Aion*, 2nd edn, London: Routledge and Kegan Paul, 1968.

—— (1951b) 'On Synchronicity', in *Collected Works*, vol. 8, *The Structure and Dynamics of the Psyche*, 2nd edn, London: Routledge and Kegan Paul, 1969.

—— (1952) 'Synchronicity: An Acausal Connecting Principle', in *Collected Works*, vol. 8, *The Structure and Dynamics of the Psyche*, 2nd edn, London: Routledge and Kegan Paul, 1969.

—— (1955) *Synchronicity: An Acausal Connecting Principle*, London: Ark Paperbacks, 1987.

—— (1955–6) *Collected Works*, vol. 14, *Mysterium Coniunctionis*, London: Routledge and Kegan Paul, 1963.

—— (1958a) 'An Astrological Experiment', in *Collected Works*, vol. 18, *The Symbolic Life*, London: Routledge and Kegan Paul, 1977.

—— (1958b) 'Flying Saucers: A Modern Myth of Things Seen in the Skies', in *Collected Works*, vol. 10, *Civilization in Transition*, 2nd edn, London: Routledge and Kegan Paul, 1970.

—— (1958c) 'Foreword to Jaffé: "Apparitions and Precognition"', in *Collected Works*, vol. 18, *The Symbolic Life*, London: Routledge and Kegan Paul, 1977.

—— (1958d) 'A Psychological View of Conscience', in *Collected Works*, vol. 10, *Civilization in Transition*, 2nd edn, London: Routledge and Kegan Paul, 1970.

—— (1963) *Memories, Dreams, Reflections*, recorded and edited by Aniela Jaffé, trans. Richard and Clara Winston, London: Collins and Routledge and Kegan Paul.

—— (1973) *Letters 1: 1906–1950*, selected and edited by Gerhard Adler in collaboration with Aniela Jaffé, trans. R.F.C. Hull, London: Routledge and Kegan Paul.

—— (1976) *Letters 2: 1951–1961*, selected and edited by Gerhard Adler in collaboration with Aniela Jaffé, trans. R.F.C. Hull, London: Routledge and Kegan Paul.

—— and Pauli, W. (1955) *The Interpretation of Nature and the Psyche*, trans. R.F.C. Hull, London: Routledge and Kegan Paul.

Kalupahana, D. (1975), *Causality: The Central Philosophy of Buddhism*, Honolulu: University of Hawaii Press.

Kelly, S. (1993) 'A Trip through Lower Town: Reflections on a case of double synchronicity', *Journal of Analytical Psychology* 38: 191–8.

Lindorff, D. (1995a) 'One Thousand Dreams: The spiritual awakening of Wolfgang Pauli', *Journal of Analytical Psychology* 40: 555–69.

—— (1995b) 'Psyche, Matter and Synchronicity: A collaboration between C. G. Jung and Wolfgang Pauli', *Journal of Analytical Psychology* 40: 571–86.

Mack, J.E. (1994) *Abduction: Human Encounters with Aliens*, London: Simon and Schuster.

Main, R. (1996) 'Synchronicity as a Form of Spiritual Experience', unpublished Ph.D. dissertation, Lancaster University.

Mansfield, V. (1995) *Synchronicity, Science, and Soul-Making: Understanding Jungian Synchronicity through Physics, Buddhism, and Philosophy*, Chicago and La Salle, ILL: Open Court.

Meier, C.A. (1963) 'Psychosomatic Medicine from the Jungian Point of View', *Journal of Analytical Psychology* 8: 103–21.

Meier, C.A. (ed.) (1992) *Wolfgang Pauli und C. G. Jung – Ein Brief Wechsel (1932–1958)*, Heidelberg: Springer.

Mulacz, W.P. (1995) 'Oscar R. Schlag', *Journal of the Society for Psychical Research* 60: 263–7.

Oeri, A. (1970) 'Some Youthful Memories of C. G. Jung', *Spring*: 182–9.

Penrose, R. (1989) *The Emperor's New Mind: Concerning Computers, Minds, and The Laws of Physics*, London: Vintage.

Progoff, I. (1987) *Jung, Synchronicity, and Human Destiny*, New York: Julian Press.

Ross, W.D. (ed.) (1928) *The Works of Aristotle*, vol. 8, 2nd edn, Oxford: The Clarendon Press.

Segal, R.A. (ed.) (1992) *The Gnostic Jung*, Princeton, NJ: Princeton University Press; London and New York: Routledge.

Shamdasani, S. (1995) 'Memories, Dreams, Omissions', *Spring* 57: 115–37.

Sheldrake, R. (1981) *A New Science of Life: The Hypothesis of Formative Causation*, London: Blond and Briggs.

Stewart, I. (1990) *Does God Play Dice? The New Mathematics of Chaos*, London: Penguin.

Voogd, S. de (1984) 'Fantasy versus Fiction: Jung's Kantianism Appraised', in R.K. Papadopoulos and G.S. Saayman (eds), *Jung in Modern Perspective*, Hounslow: Wildwood House.

Zabriskie, B. (1995) 'Jung and Pauli: A subtle asymmetry', *Journal of Analytical Psychology* 40: 531–53.

Zumstein-Preiswerk, S. (1975) *C. G. Jungs Medium: Die Geschichte der Helly Preiswerk*, Munich: Kindler.

Part I

Encountering the paranormal

1 Spiritualism

From: *Memories, Dreams, Reflections* (1963),
pp. 102–3, 107–10

At the end of my second semester, however, I made another discovery, which was to have great consequences. In the library of a classmate's father I came upon a small book on spiritualistic phenomena, dating from the seventies. It was an account of the beginnings of spiritualism, and was written by a theologian. My initial doubts were quickly dissipated, for I could not help seeing that the phenomena described in the book were in principle much the same as the stories I had heard again and again in the country since my earliest childhood. The material, without a doubt, was authentic. But the great question of whether these stories were physically true was not answered to my satisfaction. Nevertheless, it could be established that at all times and all over the world the same stories had been reported again and again. There must be some reason for this, and it could not possibly have been the predominance of the same religious conceptions everywhere, for that was obviously not the case. Rather it must be connected with the objective behaviour of the human psyche. But with regard to this cardinal question – the objective nature of the psyche – I could find out absolutely nothing, except what the philosophers said.

The observations of the spiritualists, weird and questionable as they seemed to me, were the first accounts I had seen of objective psychic phenomena. Names like Zoellner and Crookes impressed themselves on me, and I read virtually the whole of the literature available to me at the time. Naturally I also spoke of these matters to my comrades, who to my great astonishment reacted with derision and disbelief or with anxious defensiveness. I wondered at the sureness with which they could assert that things like ghosts and table-turning were impossible and therefore fraudulent, and on the other hand at the evidently anxious nature of their defensiveness. I, too, was not certain of the absolute reliability of the reports, but why, after all, should there not be ghosts? How did we know that something was "impossible"? And, above all, what did the anxiety signify? For myself I found such possibilities extremely interesting and attractive. They added another dimension to my life; the world gained depth and background. Could, for example, dreams have anything to do with ghosts? Kant's *Dreams of a Spirit Seer* came just at the right moment, and soon I also discovered Karl Duprel, who had evaluated these ideas philosophically and psychologically. I dug up Eschenmayer, Passavant, Justinus Kerner, and Görres, and read seven volumes of Swedenborg.

During the summer holidays, however, something happened that was destined to influence me profoundly. One day I was sitting in my room, studying my textbooks. In the adjoining room, the door to which stood ajar, my mother was knitting. That was our dining-room, where the round walnut dining-table stood. The table had come from the dowry of my paternal grandmother, and was at this time about seventy years old. My mother was sitting by the window, about a yard away from the table. My sister was at school and our maid in the kitchen. Suddenly there sounded a report like a pistol shot. I jumped up and rushed into the room from which the noise of the explosion had come. My mother was sitting flabbergasted in her arm-chair, the knitting fallen from her hands. She stammered out, 'W-w-what's happened? It was right beside me!' and stared at the table. Following her eyes, I saw what had happened. The table top had split from the rim to beyond the centre, and not along any joint; the split ran right through the solid wood. I was thunderstruck. How could such a thing happen? A table of solid walnut that had dried out for seventy years – how could it split on a summer day in the relatively high degree of humidity characteristic of our climate? If it had stood next to a heated stove on a cold, dry winter day, then it might have been conceivable. What in the world could have caused such an explosion? 'There certainly are curious accidents', I thought. My mother nodded darkly. 'Yes, yes', she said in her No. 2 voice, 'that means something.' Against my will I was impressed and annoyed with myself for not finding anything to say.

Some two weeks later I came home at six o'clock in the evening and found the household – my mother, my fourteen-year-old sister, and the maid – in a great state of agitation. About an hour earlier there had been another deafening report. This time it was not the already damaged table; the noise had come from the direction of the sideboard, a heavy piece of furniture dating from the early nineteenth century. They had already looked all over it, but had found no trace of a split. I immediately began examining the sideboard and the entire surrounding area, but just as fruitlessly. Then I began on the interior of the sideboard. In the cupboard containing the bread basket I found a loaf of bread, and, beside it, the bread knife. The greater part of the blade had snapped off in several pieces. The handle lay in one corner of the rectangular basket, and in each of the other corners lay a piece of the blade. The knife had been used shortly before, at four-o'clock tea, and afterwards put away. Since then no one had gone to the sideboard.

The next day I took the shattered knife to one of the best cutlers in the town. He examined the fractures with a magnifying glass, and shook his head. 'This knife is perfectly sound', he said. 'There is no fault in the steel. Someone must have deliberately broken it piece by piece. It could be done, for instance, by sticking the blade into the crack of the drawer and breaking off a piece at a time. Or else it might have been dropped on stone from a great height. But good steel can't explode. Someone has been pulling your leg.' I have carefully kept the pieces of the knife to this day.

My mother and my sister had been in the room when the sudden report made them jump. My mother's No. 2 looked at me meaningfully, but I could find nothing to say. I was completely at a loss and could offer no explanation of what had happened, and this was all the more annoying as I had to admit that I was profoundly impressed. Why and how had the table split and the knife shattered? The hypothesis that it was just a coincidence went much too far. It seemed highly improbable to me that the Rhine would flow backwards just once, by mere chance – and all other possible explanations were automatically ruled out. So what was it?

A few weeks later I heard of certain relatives who had been engaged for some time in table-turning, and also had a medium, a young girl of fifteen and a half. The group had been thinking of having me meet the medium, who produced somnambulistic states and spiritualistic phenomena. When I heard this, I immediately thought of the strange manifestations in our house, and I conjectured that they might be somehow connected with this medium. I therefore began attending the regular séances which my relatives held every Saturday evening. We had results in the form of communications and tapping noises from the walls and the table. Movements of the table independently of the medium were questionable, and I soon found out that limiting conditions imposed on the experiment generally had an obstructive effect. I therefore accepted the obvious autonomy of the tapping noises and turned my attention to the content of the communications. I set forth the results of these observations in my doctoral thesis. After about two years of experimentation we all became rather weary of it. I caught the medium trying to produce phenomena by trickery, and this made me break off the experiment – very much to my regret, for I had learned from this example how a No. 2 personality is formed, how it enters into a child's consciousness and finally integrates it into itself. She was one of these precociously matured personalities, and she died of tuberculosis at the age of twenty-six. I saw her once again, when she was twenty-four, and received a lasting impression of the independence and maturity of her personality. After her death I learned from her family that during the last months of her life her character disintegrated bit by bit, and that ultimately she returned to the state of a two-year-old child, in which condition she fell into her last sleep.

All in all, this was the one great experience which wiped out all my earlier philosophy and made it possible for me to achieve a psychological point of view. I had discovered some objective facts about the human psyche. Yet the nature of the experience was such that once again I was unable to speak of it. I knew no one to whom I could have told the whole story. Once more I had to lay aside an unfinished problem. It was not until two years later that my dissertation appeared.[1]

From: 'On the Psychology and Pathology of so-called Occult Phenomena' (1902) (*CW* 1)

36 The following case was under my observation during the years 1899 and 1900. As I was not in medical attendance upon Miss S.W., unfortunately no physical examination for hysterical stigmata could be made. I kept a detailed diary of the séances, which I wrote down after each sitting. The report that follows is a condensed account from these notes. Out of regard for Miss S.W. and her family, a few unimportant data have been altered and various details omitted from her 'romances', which for the most part are composed of very intimate material.

39 At home and from friends she heard about table-turning and began to take an interest in it. She asked to be allowed to take part in such experiments, and her desire was soon gratified. In July 1899, she did some table-turning several times in the family circle with friends, but as a joke. It was then discovered that she was an excellent medium. Communications of a serious nature arrived and were received amid general astonishment. Their pastoral tone was surprising. The spirit gave himself out to be the grandfather of the medium. As I was acquainted with the family, I was able to take part in these experiments. At the beginning of August 1899, I witnessed the first attacks of somnambulism. Their course was usually as follows: S.W. grew very pale, slowly sank to the ground or into a chair, closed her eyes, became cataleptic, drew several deep breaths, and began to speak. At this stage she was generally quite relaxed, the eyelid reflexes remained normal and so did tactile sensibility. She was sensitive to unexpected touches and easily frightened, especially in the initial stage.

40   She did not react when called by name. In her somnambulistic dialogues she copied in a remarkably clever way her dead relatives and acquaintances, with all their foibles, so that she made a lasting impression even on persons not easily influenced. She could also hit off people whom she knew only from hearsay, doing it so well that none of the spectators could deny her at least considerable talent as an actress. Gradually gestures began to accompany the words, and these finally led up to 'attitudes passionnelles' and whole dramatic scenes. She flung herself into postures of prayer and rapture, with staring eyes, and spoke with impassioned and glowing rhetoric. On these occasions she made exclusive use of literary German, which she spoke with perfect ease and assurance, in complete contrast to her usual uncertain and embarrassed manner in the waking state. Her movements were free and of a noble grace, mirroring most beautifully her changing emotions. At this stage her behaviour during the attacks was irregular and extraordinarily varied. Now she would lie for ten minutes to two hours on the sofa or the floor, motionless, with closed eyes; now she assumed a half-sitting posture and spoke with altered voice and diction;

now she was in constant movement, going through every possible panto-mimic gesture. The content of her speeches was equally variable and irregular. Sometimes she spoke in the first person, but never for long, and then only to prophesy her next attack; sometimes – and this was the most unusual – she spoke of herself in the third person. She then acted some other person, either a dead acquaintance or somebody she had invented, whose part she carried out consistently according to the characteristics she herself conceived. The ecstasy was generally followed by a cataleptic stage with *flexibilitas cerea*, which gradually passed over into the waking state. An almost constant feature was the sudden pallor which gave her face a waxen anaemic hue that was positively frightening. This sometimes occurred right at the beginning of the attack, but often in the second half only. Her pulse was then low but regular and of normal frequency; the breathing gentle, shallow, often barely perceptible. As we have already remarked, S.W. frequently predicted her attacks beforehand; just before the attacks she had strange sensations, became excited, rather anxious, and occasionally expressed thoughts of death, saying that she would probably die in one of these attacks, that her soul only hung on to her body by a very thin thread, so that her body could scarcely go on living. On one occasion after the cataleptic stage, tachypnoea was observed, lasting for two minutes with a respiration of 100 per minute. At first the attacks occurred spontaneously, but later S.W. could induce them by sitting in a dark corner and covering her face with her hands. But often the experiment did not succeed, as she had what she called 'good' and 'bad' days.

41   The question of amnesia after the attacks is unfortunately very unclear. This much is certain, that after each attack she was perfectly oriented about the specific experiences she had undergone in the 'rapture'. It is, however, uncertain how much she remembered of the conversations for which she served as a medium, and of changes in her surroundings during the attack. It often looked as if she did have a vague recollection, for often she would ask immediately on waking: 'Who was there? Wasn't X or Y there? What did he say?' She also showed that she was superficially aware of the content of the conversations. She often remarked that the spirits told her before waking what they had said. But frequently this was not the case at all. If at her request someone repeated the trance speeches to her, she was very often indignant about them and would be sad and depressed for hours on end, especially if any unpleasant indiscretions had occurred. She would rail against the spirits and assert that next time she would ask her guide to keep such spirits away from her. Her indignation was not faked, for in the waking state she could barely control herself and her affects, so that any change of mood was immediately reflected in her face. At times she seemed barely, if at all, aware of what went on around her during the attack. She seldom noticed when anyone left the room or came into it. Once she forbade me to enter the room when she was expecting special communications which she wished to keep secret from me. I went in,

nevertheless, sat down with the three other sitters, and listened to everything. S.W. had her eyes open and spoke to the others without noticing me. She only noticed me when I began to speak, which gave rise to a veritable storm of indignation. She remembered better, but still only vaguely, the remarks of participants which referred to the trance speeches or directly to herself. I could never discover any definite rapport in this connection.

42   Besides these 'big' attacks, which seemed to follow a certain law, S.W. also exhibited a large number of other automatisms. Premonitions, forebodings, unaccountable moods and rapidly changing fancies were all in the day's work. I never observed simple states of sleep. On the other hand, I soon noticed that in the middle of a lively conversation she would become all confused and go on talking senselessly in a peculiar monotonous way, looking in front of her dreamily with half-closed eyes. These lapses usually lasted only a few minutes. Then she would suddenly go on: 'Yes, what did you say?' At first she would not give any information about these lapses, saying evasively that she felt a bit giddy, had a headache, etc. Later she simply said: 'They were there again', meaning her spirits. She succumbed to these lapses very much against her will; often she struggled against them: 'I don't want to, not now, let them come another time, they seem to think I'm there only for them'. The lapses came over her in the street, in shops, in fact anywhere. If they happened in the street, she would lean against a house and wait till the attack was over. During these attacks, whose intensity varied considerably, she had visions; very often, and especially during attacks when she turned extremely pale, she 'wandered', or, as she put it, lost her body and was wafted to distant places where the spirits led her. Distant journeys during ecstasy tired her exceedingly; she was often completely exhausted for hours afterwards, and many times complained that the spirits had again drained the strength from her, such exertions were too much, the spirits must get another medium, etc. Once she went hysterically blind for half an hour after the ecstasy. Her gait was unsteady, groping; she had to be led, did not see the light that stood on the table, though the pupils reacted.

43   Visions also came in large numbers even without proper lapses (if we use this word only for higher-grade disturbances of attention). At first they were confined to the onset of sleep. A little while after she had gone to bed the room would suddenly light up, and shining white figures detached themselves from the foggy brightness. They were all wrapped in white veil-like robes, the women had things resembling turbans on their heads and wore girdles. Later (according to her own statement) 'the spirits were already there' when she went to bed. Finally she saw the figures in broad daylight, though only blurred and fleetingly if there was no real lapse (then the figures became solid enough to touch). But she always preferred the darkness. According to her account, the visions were generally of a pleasant nature. Gazing at the beautiful figures gave her a feeling of

delicious bliss. Terrifying visions of a daemonic character were much rarer. These were entirely confined to night-time or dark rooms. Occasionally she saw black figures in the street at night or in her room; once in the dark hallway she saw a terrible copper-red face which suddenly glared at her from very near and terrified her. I could not find out anything satisfactory about the first occurrence of the visions. She stated that in her fifth or sixth year she once saw her 'guide' at night – her grandfather (whom she had never known in life). I could not obtain any objective clues about this early vision from her relatives. Nothing more of the kind is said to have happened until the first séance. Except for the hypnagogic brightness and 'seeing sparks' there were never any rudimentary hallucinations; from the beginning the hallucinations were of a systematic nature involving all the sense organs equally. So far as the intellectual reaction to these phenomena is concerned, what is remarkable is the amazing matter-of-factness with which she regarded them. Her whole development into a somnambulist, her innumerable weird experiences, seemed to her entirely natural. She saw her whole past only in this light. Every in any way striking event from her earlier years stood in a clear and necessary relationship to her present situation. She was happy in the consciousness of having found her true vocation. Naturally she was unshakably convinced of the reality of her visions. I often tried to give her some critical explanation, but she would have none of it, since in her normal state she could not grasp a rational explanation anyway, and in her semi-somnambulistic state she regarded it as senseless in view of the facts staring her in the face. She once said: 'I do not know if what the spirits say and teach me is true, nor do I know if they really are the people they call themselves; but that my spirits exist is beyond question. I see them before me, I can touch them. I speak to them about everything I wish as naturally as I'm talking to you. They must be real'. She absolutely would not listen to the idea that the manifestations were a kind of illness. Doubts about her health or about the reality of her dream-world distressed her deeply; she felt so hurt by my remarks that she closed up in my presence and for a long time refused to experiment if I was there; hence I took care not to express my doubts and misgivings aloud.

From: 'On Spiritualistic Phenomena' (1905) (*CW* 18)

724 This psychological interest of mine has prompted me to keep track of persons who are gifted as mediums. My profession as a psychiatrist gave me ample opportunities for this, particularly in a city like Zurich. So many remarkable elements converging in so small a space can perhaps be found nowhere else in Europe. In the last few years I have investigated eight mediums, six of them women and two of them men. The total impression made by these investigations can be summed up by saying that one must

approach a medium with a minimum of expectations if one does not want to be disappointed. The results are of purely psychological interest, and no physical or physiological novelties came to light. Everything that may be considered a scientifically established fact belongs to the domain of the mental and cerebral processes and is fully explicable in terms of the laws already known to science.

725   All phenomena which the spiritualists claim as evidence of the activity of spirits are connected with the presence of certain persons, the mediums themselves. I was never able to observe happenings alleged to be 'spiritual' in places or on occasions when no medium was present. Mediums are as a rule slightly abnormal mentally. Frau Rothe, for example, although she could not be declared *non compos mentis* by forensic psychiatrists, nevertheless exhibited a number of hysterical symptoms. Seven of my mediums showed slight symptoms of hysteria (which, incidentally, are extraordinarily common in other walks of life too). One medium was an American swindler whose abnormality consisted chiefly of his impudence. The other seven acted in good faith. Only one of them, a woman of middle age, was born with her gifts; she had suffered since earliest childhood from alterations of consciousness (frequent and slightly hysterical twilight states). She made a virtue of necessity, induced the change of consciousness herself by auto-suggestion, and in this state of auto-hypnosis was able to prophesy. The other mediums discovered their gift only through social contacts and then cultivated it at spiritualistic séances, which is not particularly difficult. One can, with a few skilful suggestions, teach a remarkably high percentage of people, especially women, the simple spiritualistic manipulations, table-turning for instance, and, less commonly, automatic writing.

NOTES

1 *Zur Psychologie und Pathologie sogenannter occulter Phänomene: eine psychiatrische Studie* (1902); English trans.: 'On the Psychology and Pathology of So-called Occult Phenomena: A Psychiatric Study', in *Psychiatric Studies* (CW 1).

2   Spirits and hauntings

From: 'The Psychological Foundations of Belief in Spirits' (1920/1948) (*CW* 8)

585   Spirits, therefore, viewed from the psychological angle, are unconscious autonomous complexes which appear as projections because they have no direct association with the ego.[1]

586   I said earlier on that belief in souls is a necessary correlate of belief in spirits. Whilst spirits are felt to be strange and as not belonging to the ego, this is not true of the soul or souls. The primitive feels the proximity or the influence of a spirit as something uncanny or dangerous, and is greatly relieved when the spirit is banished. Conversely, he feels the loss of a soul as if it were a sickness; indeed, he often attributes serious physical diseases to loss of soul. There are innumerable rites for calling the 'soul-bird' back into the sick person. Children may not be struck because their souls might feel insulted and depart. Thus, for the primitive, the soul is something that seems normally to belong to him, but spirits seem to be something that normally should not be near him. He avoids places haunted by spirits, or visits them only with fear, for religious or magical purposes.

587   The plurality of souls indicates a plurality of relatively autonomous complexes that can behave like spirits. The soul-complexes seem to belong to the ego and the loss of them appears pathological. The opposite is true of spirit-complexes: their association with the ego causes illness, and their dissociation from it brings recovery. Accordingly, primitive pathology recognizes two causes of illness: loss of soul, and possession by a spirit. The two theories keep one another more or less balanced. We therefore have to postulate the existence of unconscious complexes that normally belong to the ego, and of those that normally should not become associated with it. The former are the soul-complexes, the latter the spirit-complexes.

588   This distinction, common to most primitive beliefs, corresponds exactly to my conception of the unconscious. According to my view, the unconscious falls into two parts which should be sharply distinguished from one another. One of them is the personal unconscious; it includes all those psychic contents which have been forgotten during the course of the individual's life. Traces of them are still preserved in the unconscious, even if all conscious memory of them has been lost. In addition, it contains all subliminal impressions or perceptions which have too little energy to

reach consciousness. To these we must add unconscious combinations of ideas that are still too feeble and too indistinct to cross over the threshold. Finally, the personal unconscious contains all psychic contents that are incompatible with the conscious attitude. This comprises a whole group of contents, chiefly those which appear morally, aesthetically, or intellectually inadmissible and are repressed on account of their incompatibility. A man cannot always think and feel the good, the true, and the beautiful, and in trying to keep up an ideal attitude everything that does not fit in with it is automatically repressed. If, as is nearly always the case in a differentiated person, one function, for instance thinking, is especially developed and dominates consciousness, then feeling is thrust into the background and largely falls into the unconscious.

589   The other part of the unconscious is what I call the impersonal or collective unconscious. As the name indicates, its contents are not personal but collective; that is, they do not belong to one individual alone but to a whole group of individuals, and generally to a whole nation, or even to the whole of mankind. These contents are not acquired during the individual's lifetime but are products of innate forms and instincts. Although the child possesses no inborn ideas, it nevertheless has a highly developed brain which functions in a quite definite way. This brain is inherited from its ancestors; it is the deposit of the psychic functioning of the whole human race. The child therefore brings with it an organ ready to function in the same way as it has functioned throughout human history. In the brain the instincts are preformed, and so are the primordial images which have always been the basis of man's thinking – the whole treasure-house of mythological motifs.[2] It is, of course, not easy to prove the existence of the collective unconscious in a normal person, but occasionally mythological ideas are represented in his dreams. These contents can be seen most clearly in cases of mental derangement, especially in schizophrenia, where mythological images often pour out in astonishing variety. Insane people frequently produce combinations of ideas and symbols that could never be accounted for by experiences in their individual lives, but only by the history of the human mind. It is an instance of primitive, mythological thinking, which reproduces its own primordial images, and is not a reproduction of conscious experiences.[3]

590   The personal unconscious, then, contains complexes that belong to the individual and form an intrinsic part of his psychic life. When any complex which ought to be associated with the ego becomes unconscious, either by being repressed or by sinking below the threshold, the individual experiences a sense of loss. Conversely, when a lost complex is made conscious again, for instance, through psychotherapeutic treatment, he experiences an increase of power.[4] Many neuroses are cured in this way. But when, on the other hand, a complex of the collective unconscious becomes associated with the ego, that is, becomes conscious, it is felt as strange, uncanny, and at the same time fascinating. At all events the

conscious mind falls under its spell, either feeling it as something pathological, or else being alienated by it from normal life. The association of a collective content with the ego always produces a state of alienation, because something is added to the individual's consciousness which ought really to remain unconscious, that is, separated from the ego. If the content can be removed from consciousness again, the patient will feel relieved and more normal. The irruption of these alien contents is a characteristic symptom marking the onset of many mental illnesses. The patients are seized by weird and monstrous thoughts, the whole world seems changed, people have horrible, distorted faces, and so on.[5]

591   While the contents of the personal unconscious are felt as belonging to one's own psyche, the contents of the collective unconscious seem alien, as if they came from outside. The reintegration of a personal complex has the effect of release and often of healing, whereas the invasion of a complex from the collective unconscious is a very disagreeable and even dangerous phenomenon. The parallel with the primitive belief in souls and spirits is obvious: souls correspond to the autonomous complexes of the personal unconscious, and spirits to those of the collective unconscious. We, from the scientific standpoint, prosaically call the awful beings that dwell in the shadows of the primeval forests 'psychic complexes'. Yet if we consider the extraordinary role played by the belief in souls and spirits in the history of mankind, we cannot be content with merely establishing the existence of such complexes, but most go rather more deeply into their nature.

597 Spirits are complexes of the collective unconscious which appear when the individual loses his adaptation to reality, or which seek to replace the inadequate attitude of a whole people by a new one. They are therefore either pathological fantasies or new but as yet unknown ideas.

598   The psychogenesis of the spirits of the dead seems to me to be more or less as follows. When a person dies, the feelings and emotions that bound his relatives to him lose their application to reality and sink into the unconscious, where they activate a collective content that has a deleterious effect on consciousness. The Bataks and many other primitives therefore say that when a man dies his character deteriorates, so that he is always trying to harm the living in some way. This view is obviously based on the experience that a persistent attachment to the dead makes life seem less worth living, and may even be the cause of psychic illnesses. The harmful effect shows itself in the form of loss of libido, depression and physical debility. There are also universal reports of these post-mortem phenomena in the form of ghosts and hauntings. They are based in the main on psychic facts which cannot be dismissed out of hand. Very often the fear of superstition – which, strangely enough, is the concomitant of universal enlightenment – is responsible for the hasty suppression of extremely interesting factual reports which are thus lost to science. I have

not only found many reports of this kind among my patients, but have also observed a few things myself. But my material is too slender for me to base any verifiable hypothesis on it. Nevertheless, I myself am convinced that ghosts and suchlike have to do with psychic facts of which our academic wisdom refuses to take cognizance, although they appear clearly enough in our dreams.

599   In this essay I have sketched out a psychological interpretation of the problem of spirits from the standpoint of our present knowledge of unconscious processes. I have confined myself wholly to the psychological side of the problem, and purposely avoided the question of whether spirits exist in themselves and can give evidence of their existence through material effects. I avoid this question not because I regard it as futile from the start, but because I am not in a position to adduce experiences that would prove it one way or the other. I think the reader will be as conscious as I am that it is extraordinarily difficult to find reliable evidence for the independent existence of spirits, since the usual spiritualistic communications are as a rule nothing but very ordinary products of the personal unconscious.[6] There are, nevertheless, a few exceptions worth mentioning. I would like to call attention to a remarkable case Stewart E. White has described in a number of books. Here the communications have a much profounder content than usual. For instance, a great many archetypal ideas were produced, among them the archetype of the self, so that one might almost think there had been borrowings from my writings. If we discount the possibility of conscious plagiarism, I should say that cryptomnesic reproduction is very unlikely. It appears to be a case of genuine, spontaneous production of a collective archetype. This is not in itself anything extraordinary, since the archetype of the self is met with everywhere in mythology as well as in the products of individual fantasy. The spontaneous irruption of collective contents whose existence in the unconscious has long been known to psychology is part of the general tendency of mediumistic communications to filter the contents of the unconscious through to consciousness. I have studied a wide range of spiritualistic literature precisely for these tendencies and have come to the conclusion that in spiritualism we have a spontaneous attempt of the unconscious to become conscious in a collective form. The psychotherapeutic endeavours of the so-called spirits are aimed at the living either directly, or indirectly through the deceased person, in order to make them more conscious. Spiritualism as a collective phenomenon thus pursues the same goals as medical psychology, and in so doing produces, as in this case, the same basic ideas and image – styling themselves the 'teachings of the spirits' – which are characteristic of the nature of the collective unconscious. Such things, however baffling they may be, prove nothing either for or against the hypothesis of spirits. But it is a very different matter when we come to proven cases of identity. I shall not commit the

fashionable stupidity of regarding everything I cannot explain as a fraud. There are probably very few proofs of this kind which could stand up to the test of cryptomnesia and, above all, of extra-sensory perception. Science cannot afford the luxury of naïveté in these matters. Nevertheless, I would recommend anyone who is interested in the psychology of the unconscious to read the books of Stewart White.[7] The most interesting to my mind is *The Unobstructed Universe* (1940). *The Road I Know* (1942) is also remarkable in that it serves as an admirable introduction to the method of 'active imagination' which I have been using for more than thirty years in the treatment of neurosis, as a means to bringing un-conscious contents to consciousness.[8] In all these books you still find the primitive equation: spirit-land = dreamland (the unconscious).

600   These parapsychic phenomena seem to be connected as a rule with the presence of a medium. They are, so far as my experience goes, the exteriorized effects of unconscious complexes. I for one am certainly convinced that they are exteriorizations. I have repeatedly observed the telepathic effects of unconscious complexes, and also a number of parapsychic phenomena. But in all this I see no proof whatever of the existence of real spirits, and until such proof is forthcoming I must regard this whole territory as an appendix of psychology.[9] I think science has to impose this restriction on itself. Yet one should never forget that science is simply a matter of intellect, and that the intellect is only one among several fundamental psychic functions and therefore does not suffice to give a complete picture of the world. For this another function – feeling – is needed too. Feeling often arrives at convictions that are different from those of the intellect, and we cannot always prove that the convictions of feeling are necessarily inferior. We also have subliminal perceptions of the unconscious which are not at the disposal of the intellect and are therefore missing in a purely intellectual picture of the world. So we have every reason to grant our intellect only a limited validity. But when we work with the intellect, we must proceed scientifically and adhere to empirical principles until irrefutable evidence against their validity is forthcoming.

From: *Memories, Dreams, Reflections* (1963), pp. 175–6, 182–3

Soon after this fantasy another figure rose out of the unconscious. He developed out of the Elijah figure. I called him Philemon. Philemon was a pagan and brought with him an Egypto-Hellenistic atmosphere with a Gnostic colouration. His figure first appeared to me in the following dream.

There was a blue sky, like the sea, covered not by clouds but by flat brown clods of earth. It looked as if the clods were breaking apart and the blue water of the sea were becoming visible between them. But the water was the blue sky. Suddenly there appeared from the right a winged being sailing across the sky. I saw that it was an old man with the horns of a bull. He held a bunch of four keys, one of which he clutched as if he were about to open a lock. He had the wings of the kingfisher with its characteristic colours.

Since I did not understand this dream-image, I painted it in order to impress it upon my memory. During the days when I was occupied with the painting, I found in my garden, by the lake shore, a dead kingfisher! I was thunderstruck, for kingfishers are quite rare in the vicinity of Zurich and I have never since found a dead one. The body was recently dead – at the most, two or three days – and showed no external injuries.

Very gradually the outlines of an inner change began making their appearance within me. In 1916 I felt an urge to give shape to something. I was compelled from within, as it were, to formulate and express what might have been said by Philemon. This was how the *Septem Sermones ad Mortuos*[10] with its peculiar language came into being.

It began with a restlessness, but I did not know what it meant or what 'they' wanted of me. There was an ominous atmosphere all around me. I had the strange feeling that the air was filled with ghostly entities. Then it was as if my house began to be haunted. My eldest daughter saw a white figure passing through the room. My second daughter, independently of her elder sister, related that twice in the night her blanket had been snatched away; and that same night my nine-year-old son had an anxiety dream. In the morning he asked his mother for crayons, and he, who ordinarily never drew, now made a picture of his dream. He called it 'The Picture of the Fisherman'. Through the middle of the picture ran a river, and a fisherman with a rod was standing on the shore. He had caught a fish. On the fisherman's head was a chimney from which flames were leaping and smoke rising. From the other side of the river the devil came flying through the air. He was cursing because his fish had been stolen. But above the fisherman hovered an angel who said, 'You cannot do anything to him; he only catches the bad fish!' My son drew this picture on a Saturday.

Around five o'clock in the afternoon on Sunday the front-door bell began ringing frantically. It was a bright summer day; the two maids were in the kitchen, from which the open square outside the front door could be seen. Everyone immediately looked to see who was there, but there was no one in sight. I was sitting near the door bell, and not only heard it but saw it moving. We all simply stared at one another. The atmosphere was thick, believe me! Then I knew that something had to happen. The whole house was filled as if there were a crowd present, crammed full of spirits. They were packed deep right up to the door, and the air was so thick it was scarcely possible to breathe. As for myself, I was all a-quiver with the question: 'For God's sake, what in the world is this?' Then they cried out in chorus, 'We have come back from Jerusalem where we found not what we sought'. That is the beginning of the *Septem Sermones*.

Then it began to flow out of me, and in the course of three evenings the thing was written. As soon as I took up the pen, the whole ghostly assemblage evaporated. The room quieted and the atmosphere cleared. The haunting was over.

The experience has to be taken for what it was, or as it seems to have been. No doubt it was connected with the state of emotion I was in at the time, and which was favourable to parapsychological phenomena. It was an unconscious constellation whose peculiar atmosphere I recognised as the *numen* of an archetype. 'It walks abroad, it's in the air!'[11] The intellect, of course, would like to arrogate to itself some scientific, physical knowledge of the affair, or, preferably, to write the whole thing off as a violation of the rules. But what a dreary world it would be if the rules were not violated sometimes!

From: 'Foreword to Moser: "Spuk: Irrglaube oder Wahrglaube?"' (1950) (*CW* 18)[12]

757 The author has asked me for a few introductory words to her book. It gives me all the more pleasure to comply with her request as her previous book on occultism,[13] written with great care and knowledge of the subject, is still fresh in my memory. I welcome the appearance of this new book, a copiously documented collection of parapsychological experiences, as a valuable contribution to psychological literature in general. Extraordinary and mysterious stories are not necessarily always lies and fantasies. Many 'ingenious, curious and edifying tales' were known to previous centuries, among them observations whose scientific validity has since been confirmed. The modern psychological description of man as a totality had its precursors in the numerous biographical accounts of unusual people such as somnambulists and the like at the beginning of the nineteenth century. Indeed, though we owe the discovery of the unconscious to these old prescientific observations, our investigation of parapsychological phenomena is still in its infancy. We do not yet know the full range of the territory under discussion. Hence a collection of observations and of reliable material performs a very valuable service. The collector must certainly have courage and an unshakable purpose if he is not to be intimidated by the difficulties, handicaps, and possibilities of error that beset such an undertaking, and the reader, too, must summon up sufficient interest and patience to allow this sometimes disconcerting material to work upon him objectively, regardless of his prejudices. In this vast and shadowy region, where everything seems possible and nothing believable, one must oneself have observed many strange happenings and in addition heard, read, and if possible tested many stories by examining their witnesses in order to form an even moderately sure judgment.

758 In spite of such advances as the founding of the British and American Society for Psychical Research and the existence of a considerable and in

part well-documented literature, a prejudice is still rampant even in the best informed circles, and reports of this kind meet with a mistrust which is only partially justified. It looks as though Kant will be proved right for a long time to come when he wrote nearly two hundred years ago: 'Stories of this kind will have at any time only secret believers, while publicly they are rejected by the prevalent fashion of disbelief.'[14] He himself reserved judgment in the following words: 'The same ignorance makes me so bold as to absolutely deny the truth of the various ghost stories, and yet with the common, although queer, reservation that while I doubt any one of them, still I have a certain faith in the whole of them taken together.'[15] One could wish that very many of our bigots would take note of this wise position adopted by a great thinker.

759   I am afraid this will not come about so easily, for our rationalistic prejudice is grounded – *lucus a non lucendo* – not on reason but on something far deeper and more archaic, namely on a primitive instinct to which Goethe referred when he said in *Faust*: 'Summon not the well-known throng . . .'. I once had a valuable opportunity to observe this instinct at work. It was while I was with a tribe on Mount Elgon, in East Africa, most of whom had never come into contact with the white man. Once, during a palaver, I incautiously uttered the word *seleteni*, which means 'ghosts'. Suddenly a deathly silence fell on the assembly. The men glanced away, looked in all directions, and some of them made off. My Somali headman and the chief confabulated together, and then the head-man whispered in my ear: 'What did you say that for? Now you'll have to break up the palaver'. This taught me that one must never mention ghosts on any account. The same primitive fear of ghosts is still deep in our bones, but it is unconscious. Rationalism and superstition are complementary. It is a psychological rule that the brighter the light, the blacker the shadow; in other words, the more rationalistic we are in our conscious minds, the more alive becomes the spectral world of the unconscious. And it is indeed obvious that rationality is in large measure an apotropaic defence against superstition, which is everpresent and unavoidable. The daemonic world of primitives is only a few generations away from us, and the things that have happened and still go on happening in the dictator states teach us how terrifyingly close it is. I must constantly remind myself that the last witch was burned in Europe in the year my grandfather was born.

760   The widespread prejudice against the factual reports discussed in this book shows all the symptoms of the primitive fear of ghosts. Even educated people who should know better often advance the most nonsensical arguments, tie themselves in knots and deny the evidence of their own eyes. They will put their names to reports of séances and then – as has actually happened more than once – withdraw their signatures afterwards, because what they have witnessed and corroborated is nevertheless impossible – as though anyone knew exactly what is impossible and what is not!

761   Ghost stories and spiritualistic phenomena practically never prove what

they seem to. They offer no proof of the immortality of the soul, which for obvious reasons is incapable of proof. But they are of interest to the psychologist from several points of view. They provide information about things the layman knows nothing of, such as the exteriorization of unconscious processes, about their content, and about the possible sources of parapsychological phenomena. They are of particular importance in investigating the localization of the unconscious and the phenomenon of synchronicity, which points to a relativization of space and time and hence also of matter. It is true that with the help of the statistical method existence of such effects can be proved, as Rhine and other investigators have done. But the individual nature of the more complex phenomena of this kind forbids the use of the statistical method, since this stands in a complementary relation to synchronicity and necessarily destroys the latter phenomenon, which the statistician is bound to discount as due to chance. We are thus entirely dependent on well observed and well authenticated individual cases. The psychologist can only bid a hearty welcome to any new crop of objective reports.

762   The author has put together an impressive collection of factual material in this book. It differs from other collections of the kind by its careful and detailed documentation, and thus gives the reader a total impression of the situation which he often looks for in vain in other reports of this nature. Although ghosts exhibit certain universal features they nevertheless appear in individual forms and under conditions which are infinitely varied and of especial importance for the investigator. The present collection provides the most valuable information in just this respect.

763   The question discussed here is a weighty one for the future. Science has only just begun to take a serious interest in the human psyche and, more particularly, in the unconscious. The wide realm of psychic phenomena also includes parapsychology, which is opening undreamt-of vistas before our eyes. It is high time humanity took cognizance of the nature of the psyche, for it is becoming more and more evident that the greatest danger which threatens man comes from his own psyche and hence from that part of the empirical world we know the least about. Psychology needs a tremendous widening of its horizon. The present book is a milestone on the long road to knowledge of the psychic nature of man.

April 1950

Jung's Contribution[16]

764   In the summer of 1920 I went to London, at the invitation of Dr X, to give some lectures. My colleague told me that, in expectation of my visit, he had found a suitable weekend place for the summer. This, he said, had not been so easy, because everything had already been let for the summer holidays, or else was so exorbitantly expensive or unattractive that he had almost given up hope. But finally, by a lucky chance, he had found a

charming cottage that was just right for us, and at a ridiculously low price. In actual fact it turned out to be a most attractive old farmhouse in Buckinghamshire, as we saw when we went there at the end of our first week of work, on a Friday evening. Dr X had engaged a girl from the neighbouring village to cook for us, and a friend of hers would come in the afternoons as a voluntary help. The house was roomy, two-storeyed, and built in the shape of a right angle. One of these wings was quite sufficient for us. On the ground floor there was a conservatory leading into the garden; then a kitchen, dining-room and drawing-room. On the top floor a corridor ran from the conservatory steps through the middle of the house to a large bedroom, which took up the whole front of the wing. This was my room. It had windows facing east and west, and a fireplace in the front wall (north). To the left of the door stood a bed, opposite the fireplace a big old-fashioned chest of drawers, and to the right a wardrobe and a table. This, together with a few chairs, was all the furniture. On either side of the corridor was a row of bedrooms, which were used by Dr X and occasional guests.

765   The first night, tired from the strenuous work of the week, I slept well. We spent the next day walking and talking. That evening, feeling rather tired, I went to bed at eleven o'clock, but did not get beyond the point of drowsing. I only fell into a kind of torpor, which was unpleasant because I felt I was unable to move. Also it seemed to me that the air had become stuffy, and that there was an indefinable, nasty smell in the room. I thought I had forgotten to open the windows. Finally, in spite of my torpor, I was driven to light a candle: both windows were open, and a night wind blew softly through the room, filling it with the flowery scents of high summer. There was no trace of the bad smell. I remained half awake in my peculiar condition, until I glimpsed the first pale light of dawn through the east window. At this moment the torpor dropped away from me like magic, and I fell into a deep sleep from which I awoke only towards nine o'clock.

766   On Sunday evening I mentioned in passing to Dr X that I had slept remarkably badly the night before. He recommended me to drink a bottle of beer, which I did. But when I went to bed the same thing happened: I could not get beyond the point of drowsing. Both windows were open. The air was fresh to begin with, but after about half an hour it seemed to turn bad; it became stale and fuggy and finally somehow repulsive. It was hard to identify the smell, despite my efforts to establish its nature. The only thing that came into my head was that there was something sickly about it. I pursued this clue through all the memories of smells that a man can collect in eight years of work at a psychiatric clinic. Suddenly I hit on the memory of an old woman who was suffering from an open carcinoma. This was quite unmistakably the same sickly smell I had so often noticed in her room.

767   As a psychologist, I wondered what might be the cause of this peculiar olfactory hallucination. But I was unable to discover any convincing connection between it and my present state of consciousness. I only felt very uncomfortable because my torpor seemed to paralyze me. In the end

I could not think any more, and fell into a torpid doze. Suddenly I heard the noise of water dripping. 'Didn't I turn off the tap properly?' I thought. 'But of course, there's no running water in the room – so it's obviously raining – yet today was so fine'. Meanwhile the dripping went on regularly, one drop every two seconds. I imagined a little pool of water to the left of my bed, near the chest of drawers. 'Then the roof must leak', I thought. Finally, with a heroic effort, so it seemed to me, I lit the candle and went over to the chest of drawers. There was no water on the floor, and no damp spot on the plaster ceiling. Only then did I look out of the window: it was a clear, starry night. The dripping still continued. I could make out a place on the floor, about eighteen inches from the chest of drawers, where the sound came from. I could have touched it with my hand. All at once the dripping stopped and did not come back. Towards three o'clock, at the first light of dawn, I fell into a deep sleep. No – I have heard death-watch beetles. The ticking noise they make is sharper. This was a duller sound, exactly what would be made by drops of water falling from the ceiling.

768   I was annoyed with myself, and not exactly refreshed by this weekend. But I said nothing to Dr X. The next weekend, after a busy and eventful week, I did not think at all about my previous experience. Yet hardly had I been in bed for half an hour than everything was there as before: the torpor, the repulsive smell, the dripping. And this time there was something else: something brushed along the walls, the furniture creaked now here and now there, there were rustlings in the corners. A strange restlessness was in the air. I thought it was the wind, lit the candle and went to shut the windows. But the night was still, there was no breath of wind. So long as the light was on, the air was fresh and no noise could be heard. But the moment I blew out the candle, the torpor slowly returned, the air became fuggy, and the creakings and rustlings began again. I thought I must have noises in my ear, but at three o'clock in the morning they stopped as promptly as before.

769   The next evening I tried my luck again with a bottle of beer. I had always slept well in London and could not imagine what could give me insomnia in this quiet and peaceful spot. During the night the same phenomena were repeated, but in intensified form. The thought now occurred to me that they must be parapsychological. I knew that problems of which people are unconscious can give rise to exteriorization phenomena, because constellated unconscious contents often have a tendency to manifest themselves outwardly somehow or other. But I knew the problems of the present occupants of the house very well, and could discover nothing that would account for the exteriorizations. The next day I asked the others how they had slept. They all said they had slept wonderfully.

770   The third night it was even worse. There were loud knocking noises, and I had the impression that an animal, about the size of a dog, was rushing round the room in a panic. As usual, the hubbub stopped abruptly with the first streak of light in the east.

771   The phenomena grew still more intense during the following weekend. The rustling became a fearful racket, like the roaring of a storm. Sounds of knocking came also from outside in the form of dull blows, as though somebody were banging on the brick walls with a muffled hammer. Several times I had to assure myself that there was no storm, and that nobody was banging on the walls from outside.

772   The next weekend, the fourth, I cautiously suggested to my host that the house might be haunted, and that this would explain the surprisingly low rent. Naturally he laughed at me, although he was as much at a loss as I about my insomnia. It had also struck me how quickly the two girls cleared away after dinner every evening, and always left the house long before sundown. By eight o'clock there was no girl to be seen. I jokingly remarked to the girl who did the cooking that she must be afraid of us if she had herself fetched every evening by her friend and was then in such a hurry to get home. She laughed and said that she wasn't at all afraid of the gentlemen, but that nothing would induce her to stay a moment in this house alone, and certainly not after sunset. 'What's the matter with it?' I asked. 'Why, it's haunted, didn't you know? That's the reason why it was going so cheap. Nobody's ever stuck it here'. It had been like that as long as she could remember. But I could get nothing out of her about the origin of the rumour. Her friend emphatically confirmed everything she had said.

773   As I was a guest, I naturally couldn't make further inquiries in the village. My host was sceptical, but he was willing to give the house a thorough looking over. We found nothing remarkable until we came to the attic. There, between the two wings of the house, we discovered a dividing wall, and in it a comparatively new door, about half an inch thick, with a heavy lock and two huge bolts, that shut off our wing from the unoccupied part. The girls did not know of the existence of this door. It presented something of a puzzle because the two wings communicated with one another both on the ground floor and on the first floor. There were no rooms in the attic to be shut off, and no signs of use. The purpose of the door seemed inexplicable.

774   The fifth weekend was so unbearable that I asked my host to give me another room. This is what had happened: it was a beautiful moonlight night, with no wind; in the room there were rustlings, creakings, and bangings; from outside, blows rained on the walls. I had the feeling there was something near me, and opened my eyes. There, beside me on the pillow, I saw the head of an old woman, and the right eye, wide open, glared at me. The left half of the face was missing below the eye. The sight of it was so sudden and unexpected that I leapt out of bed with one bound, lit the candle, and spent the rest of the night in an armchair. The next day I moved into the adjoining room, where I slept splendidly and was no longer disturbed during this or the following weekend.

775   I told my host that I was convinced the house was haunted, but he dismissed this explanation with smiling scepticism. His attitude, under-

standable though it was, annoyed me somewhat, for I had to admit that my health had suffered under these experiences. I felt unnaturally fatigued, as I had never felt before. I therefore challenged Dr X to try sleeping in the haunted room himself. He agreed to this, and gave me his word that he would send me an honest report of his observations. He would go to the house alone and spend the weekend there so as to give me a 'fair chance'.

776   Next morning I left. Ten days later I had a letter from Dr X. He had spent the weekend alone in the cottage. In the evening it was very quiet, and he thought it was not absolutely necessary to go up to the first floor. The ghost, after all, could manifest itself anywhere in the house, if there was one. So he set up his camp bed in the conservatory, and as the cottage really was rather lonely, he took a loaded shotgun to bed with him. Everything was deathly still. He did not feel altogether at ease, but nevertheless almost succeeded in falling asleep after a time. Suddenly it seemed to him that he heard footsteps in the corridor. He immediately struck a light and flung open the door, but there was nothing to be seen. He went back grumpily to bed, thinking I had been a fool. But it was not long before he again heard footsteps, and to his discomfiture he discovered that the door lacked a key. He rammed a chair against the door, with its back under the lock, and returned to bed. Soon afterwards he again heard footsteps, which stopped just in front of the door; the chair creaked, as though somebody was pushing against the door from the other side. He then set up his bed in the garden, and there he slept very well. The next night he again put his bed in the garden, but at one o'clock it started to rain, so he shoved the head of the bed under the eaves of the conservatory and covered the foot with a waterproof blanket. In this way he slept peacefully. But nothing in the world would induce him to sleep again in the conservatory. He had now given up the cottage.

777   A little later I heard from Dr X that the owner had had the cottage pulled down, since it was unsaleable and scared away all tenants. Unfortunately I no longer have the original report, but its contents are stamped indelibly on my mind. It gave me considerable satisfaction after my colleague had laughed so loudly at my fear of ghosts.

778 I would like to make the following remarks by way of summing up. I can find no explanation of the dripping noise. I was fully awake and examined the floor carefully. I consider it out of the question that it was a delusion of the senses. As to the rustling and creaking, I think they were probably not objective noises, but noises in the ear which seemed to me to be occurring objectively in the room. In my peculiar hypnoid state they appeared exaggeratedly loud. I am not at all sure that the knocking noises, either, were objective. They could just as well have been heartbeats that seemed to me to come from outside. My torpor was associated with an inner excitation probably corresponding to fear. Of this fear I was unconscious until the moment of the vision – only then did it break through into consciousness. The vision had the character of a hypnagogic

hallucination and was probably a reconstruction of the memory of the old woman with carcinoma.

779   Coming now to the olfactory hallucination, I had the impression that my presence in the room gradually activated something that was somehow connected with the walls. It seemed to me that the dog rushing round in a panic represented my intuition. Common speech links intuition with the nose: I had 'smelt' something. If the olfactory organ in man were not so hopelessly degenerate, but as highly developed as a dog's, I would have undoubtedly have had a clearer idea of the persons who had lived in the room earlier. Primitive medicine-men can not only smell out a thief, they also 'smell' spirits and ghosts.

780   The hypnoid catalepsy that each time was associated with these phenomena was the equivalent of intense concentration, the object of which was a subliminal and therefore 'fascinating' olfactory perception. The two things together bear some resemblance to the physical and psychic state of a pointer that has picked up the scent. The source of the fascination, however, seems to me to have been of a peculiar nature, which is not sufficiently explained by any substance emitting a smell. The smell may have 'embodied' a psychic situation of an excitatory nature and carried it across to the percipient. This is by no means impossible when we consider the extraordinary importance of the sense of smell in animals. It is also conceivable that intuition in man has taken the place of the world of smells that were lost to him with the degeneration of the olfactory organ. The effect of intuition on man is indeed very similar to the instant fascination which smells have for animals. I myself have had a number of experiences in which 'psychic smells', or olfactory hallucinations, turned out to be subliminal intuitions which I was able to verify afterwards.

781   This hypothesis naturally does not pretend to explain all ghost phenomena, but at most a certain category of them. I have heard and read a great many ghost stories, and among them are a few that could very well be explained in this way. For instance, there are all those stories of ghosts haunting rooms where a murder was committed. In one case, bloodstains were still visible under the carpet. A dog would surely have smelt the blood and perhaps recognized it as human, and if he possessed a human imagination he would also have been able to reconstruct the essential features of the crime. Our unconscious, which possesses very much more subtle powers of perception and reconstruction than our conscious minds, could do the same thing and project a visionary picture of the psychic situation that excited it. For example, a relative once told me that, when stopping at a hotel on a journey abroad, he had a fearful nightmare of a woman being murdered in his room. The next morning he discovered that on the night before his arrival a woman had in fact been murdered there. These remarks are only meant to show that parapsychology would do well to take account of the modern psychology of the unconscious.

From: *Memories, Dreams, Reflections* (1963), pp. 217–19

On another such still night when I was alone in Bollingen (it was in the late winter or early spring of 1924) I awoke to the sound of soft footsteps going round the Tower. Distant music sounded, coming closer and closer, and then I heard voices laughing and talking. I thought, 'Who can be prowling around? What is this all about? There is only the little footpath along the lake, and scarcely anybody ever walks on it!' While I was thinking these things I became wide awake, and went to the window. I opened the shutters – all was still. There was no one in sight, nothing to be heard – no wind – nothing – nothing at all.

'This is really strange', I thought. I was certain that the footsteps, the laughter and talk, had been real. But apparently I had only been dreaming. I returned to bed and mulled over the way we can deceive ourselves after all, and what might have been the cause of such a strange dream. In the midst of this, I fell asleep again – and at once the same dream began: once more I heard footsteps, talk, laughter, music. At the same time I had a visual image of several hundred dark-clad figures, possibly peasant boys in their Sunday clothes, who had come down from the mountains and were pouring in around the Tower, on both sides, with a great deal of loud trampling, laughing, singing, and playing of accordions. Irritably, I thought, 'This is really the limit! I thought it was a dream and now it turns out to be reality!' At this point, I woke up. Once again I jumped up, opened the window and shutters, and found everything just the same as before: a deathly still moonlit night. Then I thought: 'Why, this is simply a case of haunting!'

Naturally I asked myself what it meant when a dream was so insistent on its reality and at the same time on my being awake. Usually we experience that only when we see a ghost. Being awake means perceiving reality. The dream therefore represented a situation equivalent to reality, in which it created a kind of wakened state. In this sort of dream, as opposed to ordinary dreams, the unconscious seems bent on conveying a powerful impression of reality to the dreamer, an impression which is emphasized by repetition. The sources of such realities are known to be physical sensations on the one hand, and archetypal figures on the other.

That night everything was so completely real, or at least seemed to be so, that I could scarcely sort out the two realities. Nor could I make anything of the dream itself. What was the meaning of these music-making peasant boys passing by in a long procession? It seemed to me they had come out of curiosity, in order to look at the Tower.

Never again did I experience or dream anything similar, and I cannot recall ever having heard of a parallel to it. It was only much later that I found an explanation. This was when I came across the seventeenth-century Lucerne chronicle by Rennward Cysat. He tells the following story: On a high pasture of Mount Pilatus, which is particularly notorious for apparitions – it is said

that Wotan to this day practises his magic arts there – Cysat, while climbing
the mountain, was disturbed one night by a procession of men who poured
past his hut on both sides, playing music and singing – precisely what I had
experienced at the Tower.

The next morning Cysat asked the herdsman with whom he had spent that
night what could have been the meaning of it. The man had a ready
explanation: those must be the departed folk – *sälig Lüt*, in Swiss dialect; the
phrase also means blessed folk – namely, Wotan's army of departed souls.
These, he said, were in the habit of walking abroad and showing themselves.

It may be suggested that this is a phenomenon of solitude, the outward
emptiness and silence being compensated by the image of a crowd of people.
This would put it in the same class with the hallucinations of hermits, which
are likewise compensatory. But do we know what realities such stories may
be founded on? It is also possible that I had been so sensitized by the solitude
that I was able to perceive the procession of 'departed folk' who passed by.

The explanation of this experience as a psychic compensation never
entirely satisfied me, and to say that it was an hallucination seemed to
me to beg the question. I felt obliged to consider the possibility of its
reality, especially in view of the seventeenth-century account which had
come my way.

It would seem most likely to have been a synchronistic phenomenon. Such
phenomena demonstrate that premonitions or visions very often have some
correspondence in external reality. There actually existed, as I discovered, a
real parallel to my experience. These were the *Reisläufer* (mercenaries) who
usually assembled in spring, marched from Central Switzerland to Locarno,
met at the Casa di Ferro in Minusio and then marched on together to Milan.
In Italy they served as soldiers, fighting for foreign princes. My visions,
therefore, might have been one of these gatherings which took place regularly
each spring when the young men, with singing and jollity, bade farewell to
their native land.

NOTES

1 This should not be misconstrued as a metaphysical statement. The question of
whether spirits exist *in themselves* is far from having been settled. Psychology is
not concerned with things as they are 'in themselves', but only with what people
think about them.

2 By this I do not mean the existing form of the motif but its preconscious, invisible
'ground plan'. This might be compared to the crystal lattice which is preformed
in the crystalline solution. It should not be confused with the variously structured
axial system of the individual crystal.

3 Cf., my *Symbols of Transformation*; also Spielrein, 'Über den psychischen Inhalt
eines Falles von Schizophrenie'; Nelken, 'Analytische Beobachtungen über
Phantasien eines Schizophrenen'; C.A. Meier, 'Spontanmanifestationen des
kollektiven Unbewussten'.

4 This is not always a pleasant feeling, for the patient was quite content to lose the
complex so long as he did not feel the disagreeable consequences of the loss.

5 Those who are familiar with this material will object that my description is one-sided, because they know that the archetype, the autonomous collective content, does not have only the negative aspect described here. I have merely restricted myself to the common symptomatology that can be found in every text-book of psychiatry, and to the equally common defensive attitude towards anything extraordinary. Naturally the archetype also has a positive numinosity which I have repeatedly mentioned elsewhere.

6 [The rest of this paragraph was added in the 1948 Swiss edition.]

7 I am indebted to Dr Fritz Künkel, of Los Angeles, for drawing my attention to this author.

8 Cf., 'The Transcendent Function', supra, pars. 166ff., and *Two Essays*, pars. 343ff. (Also *Mysterium Coniunctionis*, pars. 706, 752ff.)

9 After collecting psychological experiences from many people and many countries for fifty years, I no longer feel as certain as I did in 1919, when I wrote this sentence. To put it bluntly, I doubt whether an exclusively psychological approach can do justice to the phenomena in question. Not only the findings of para-psychology, but my own theoretical reflections, outlined in 'On the Nature of the Psyche', have led me to certain postulates which touch on the realm of nuclear physics and the conception of the space-time continuum. This opens up the whole question of the transpsychic reality immediately underlying the psyche.

10 Privately printed (n.d.) and pseudonymously subtitled 'The Seven Sermons to the Dead written by Basilides in Alexandria, the City where the East toucheth the West'.

11 *Faust*, Part Two.

12 [Baden, 1950. By Fanny Moser. ('Ghost: False Belief or True?')]

13 [*Okkultismus: Täuschungen und Tatsachen* (1935).]

14 [*Dreams of a Spirit-Seer*, trans. by Goerwitz, p. 92.]

15 [Ibid., p. 88.]

16 [Pp. 253ff.]

3 Analytical psychology

From: *Memories, Dreams, Reflections* (1963),
pp. 152, 188–9

It interested me to hear Freud's views on precognition and on parapsychology in general. When I visited him in Vienna in 1909 I asked him what he thought of these matters. Because of his materialistic prejudice, he rejected this entire complex of questions as nonsensical, and did so in terms of so shallow a positivism that I had difficulty in checking the sharp retort on the tip of my tongue. It was some years before he recognized the seriousness of parapsychology and acknowledged the factuality of 'occult' phenomena.

While Freud was going on this way, I had a curious sensation. It was as if my diaphragm were made of iron and were becoming red-hot – a glowing vault. And at that moment there was such a loud report in the bookcase, which stood right next to us, that we both started up in alarm, fearing the thing was going to topple over on us. I said to Freud: 'There, that is an example of a so-called catalytic exteriorization phenomenon'.

'Oh come', he exclaimed. 'That is sheer bosh'.

'It is not', I replied. 'You are mistaken, Herr Professor. And to prove my point I now predict that in a moment there will be another loud report!' Sure enough, no sooner had I said the words than the same detonation went off in the bookcase.

To this day I do not know what gave me this certainty. But I knew beyond all doubt that the report would come again. Freud only stared aghast at me. I do not know what was in his mind, or what his look meant. In any case, this incident aroused his mistrust of me, and I had the feeling that I had done something against him. I never afterwards discussed the incident with him.[1]

During those years, between 1918 and 1920, I began to understand that the goal of psychic development is the self. There is no linear evolution; there is only a circumambulation of the self. Uniform development exists, at most, only at the beginning; later, everything points towards the centre. This insight gave me stability, and gradually my inner peace returned. I knew that in finding the mandala as an expression of the self I had attained what was for me the ultimate. Perhaps someone else knows more, but not I.

Some years later (in 1927) I obtained confirmation of my ideas about the centre and the self by way of a dream. I represented its essence in a mandala which I called 'Window on Eternity'. The picture is reproduced in *The Secret of the Golden Flower* (Fig. 3).[2] A year later I painted a second picture, likewise a mandala,[3] with a golden castle in the centre. When it was finished, I asked myself, 'Why is this so Chinese?' I was impressed by the form and choice of colours, which seemed to me Chinese, although there was nothing outwardly Chinese about it. Yet that was how it affected me. It was a strange coincidence that shortly afterwards I received a letter from Richard Wilhelm enclosing the manuscript of a Taoist-alchemical treatise entitled *The Secret of the Golden Flower*, with a request that I write a commentary on it. I devoured the manuscript at once, for the text gave me undreamed-of confirmation of my ideas about the mandala and the circumambulation of the centre. That was the first event which broke through my isolation. I became aware of an affinity; I could establish ties with something and someone.[4]

In remembrance of this coincidence, this 'synchronicity,' I wrote underneath the picture which had made so Chinese an impression upon me: 'In 1928, when I was painting this picture, showing the golden, well-fortified castle, Richard Wilhelm in Frankfurt sent me the thousand-year-old Chinese text on the yellow castle, the germ of the immortal body'.

From: *Dream Analysis: Notes of the Seminar Given in 1928–1930* (1984), pp. 43–5 (28 November 1928)

Before continuing our dream, I must tell you about certain things which have happened in the meantime. Those of you who are intuitive probably observed that the mood in our second meeting was somewhat upset. We had the bull dream with its community aspect, and so we lived through a little scene which we might have watched in ancient Athens – I mentioned the fact that important men used to tell their dreams, and illustrated it by the dream of the senator's daughter and the dream of the Greek poet. Or we might have watched such a scene in the market-place of some primitive village, where a man gets up and says: 'In the night I saw a vision, a spirit spoke,' and then everybody gathers round and is dreadfully impressed. All this has brought interesting coincidences to light.

You remember that on 21 November we spoke of the bull and the meaning of the bull-fight. The dreamer is a man whom I occasionally still see – that means analysis has not killed him yet! Now from the 20th to the 24th he spent four days making a picture which he could not understand, and which astonished him so much that he came to me to ask for an explanation. He had to draw a bull's head, and it must be a very sacred bull because he holds the disc of the sun between the horns. Unfortunately I cannot show you the picture because the man thinks we have already been very indiscreet in discussing his dreams here in the seminar. I get my examples from my patients – from you too! I told him that we were talking of the bull in connection with his dream, and that his drawing synchronizes with that, and then I explained to him the meaning of his drawing.

Then after our last meeting, after Dr Shaw's dream, when I commented on the antique meaning of the bull-fight, I got another letter from Mexico, from the friend who had just actually been to a bull-fight. This letter came about two days after the last seminar, it would have been about two weeks on the way, so she must have written it just about the day when we first spoke of the bull in the seminar. She does not describe the fighting. I will quote what she says: 'The one point of supreme art in the whole thing is the moment when the bull stops still, confused, and faces the matador, and the matador standing in front of him makes the gesture of scorn to show his complete mastery'. 'The matador is the point of perfect conscious control in that weltering mass of unconsciousness, in that black background of barbarism'. And it seemed to me that that was the meaning of the symbol: one must have perfect conscious control, perfect style and consummate grace and daring, to live in the bosom of barbarism; if one weakens anywhere one is done for. That is why the bull-fight was the symbol of the divine. And the toreador is the hero because he is the only shining light in that dark mass of passion and rage, that lack of control and discipline. He personifies the perfect discipline. My friend is a quite independent observer, but she got the gist of it and in that moment found it necessary to convey it to me.

This is what we call just a coincidence. I mention it to show how the dream is a living thing, by no means a dead thing that rustles like dry paper. It is a living situation, it is like an animal with feelers, or with many umbilical cords. We don't realize that while we are talking of it, it is producing. This is why primitives talk of their dreams, and why I talk of dreams. We are moved by the dreams, they express us and we express them, and there are coincidences connected with them. We decline to take coincidences seriously because we cannot consider them as causal. True, we would make a mistake to consider them as causal; events don't come about *because* of dreams, that would be absurd, we can never demonstrate that; they just happen. But it is wise to consider the fact that they do happen. We would not notice them if they were not of a peculiar regularity, not like that of laboratory experiments, it is only a sort of irrational regularity. The East bases much of its science on this irregularity and considers coincidences as the reliable basis of the world rather than causality. Synchronism[5] is the prejudice of the East; causality is the modern prejudice of the West. The more we busy ourselves with dreams, the more we shall see such coincidences – chances. Remember that the oldest Chinese scientific book is about the possible chances of life.[6]

From: *Memories, Dreams, Reflections* (1963), p. 60

I too have this archaic nature, and in me it is linked with the gift – not always pleasant – of seeing people and things as they are. I can let myself be deceived from here to Tipperary when I don't want to recognise something, and yet at

bottom I know quite well how matters really stand. In this I am like a dog –
he can be tricked, but he always smells it out in the end. This 'insight' is
based on instinct, or on a *participation mystique* with others. It is as if the
'eyes of the background' do the seeing in an impersonal act of perception.

This was something I did not realise until much later, when some very
strange things happened to me. For instance, there was the time when I
recounted the life story of a man without knowing him. It was at the wedding
of a friend of my wife's; the bride and her family were all entirely unknown
to me. During the meal I was sitting opposite a middle-aged gentleman with
a long, handsome beard, who had been introduced to me as a barrister. We
were having an animated conversation about criminal psychology. In order
to answer a particular question of his, I made up a story to illustrate it,
embellishing it with all sorts of details. While I was telling my story, I noticed
that a quite different expression came over the man's face, and a silence fell
on the table. Very much abashed, I stopped speaking. Thank heavens we were
already at the dessert, so I soon stood up and went into the lounge of the
hotel. There I withdrew into a corner, lit a cigar, and tried to think over the
situation. At this moment one of the other guests who had been sitting at my
table came over and asked reproachfully, 'How did you ever come to commit
such a frightful indiscretion?' 'Indiscretion?' 'Why yes, that story you told'.
'But I made it all up!'

To my amazement and horror it turned out that I had told the story of the
man opposite me, exactly and in all its details. I also discovered, at this
moment, that I could no longer remember a single word of the story – even
to this day I have been unable to recall it.

From: 'A Psychological View of Conscience' (1958) (*CW* 10)

850 As with all archetypal phenomena, the synchronicity factor must be taken
into account in considering conscience. For although the voice of genuine
conscience (and not just the recollection of the moral code) may make
itself heard in the context of an archetypal situation, it is by no means
certain that the reason for this is always a subjective moral reaction. It
sometimes happens that a person suffers from a decidedly bad conscience
for no demonstrable reason. Naturally there are any number of cases where
ignorance and self-deception offer a sufficient explanation. But this does
not alter the fact that one can suddenly have a bad conscience when one
is conversing with an unknown person who would have every reason to
feel a bad conscience but is unconscious of it. The same is true of fear and
other emotions arising from a collision with an archetype. When one is
talking with somebody whose unconscious contents are 'constellated', a
parallel constellation arises in one's own unconscious. The same or a
similar archetype is activated, and since one is less unconscious than the

other person and has no reason for repression, one becomes increasingly aware of its feeling-tone in the form of a growing uneasiness of conscience. When this happens, we naturally tend to ascribe the moral reaction to ourselves, the more easily since no one, actually, has reason to enjoy a perfectly good conscience. But in the case we are discussing the self-criticism, laudable in itself, goes too far. We discover that, as soon as the conversation is ended, the bad conscience stops as suddenly as it began, and after a while it turns out that it is the other person who should take note of his bad conscience. By way of example, one thinks of cases like the one described by Heinrich Zschokke.[7] While in Brugg, he visited an inn, where he ate lunch. Opposite him sat a young man. Suddenly Zschokke saw in his mind's eye this young man standing at a desk, breaking it open, and pocketing the money he found. Zschokke even knew the exact amount and was so sure of it that he took the young man to task. The latter was so flabbergasted by Zschokke's knowledge that he made a confession on the spot.

From: Memories, Dreams, Reflections (1963), pp. 136–7

The relationship between doctor and patient, especially when a tranference on the part of the patient occurs, or a more or less unconscious identification of doctor and patient, can lead to parapsychological phenomena. I have frequently run into this. One such case which was particularly impressive was that of a patient whom I had pulled out of a psychogenic depression. He went back home and married; but I did not care for his wife. The first time I saw her, I had an uneasy feeling. Her husband was grateful to me, and I observed that I was a thorn in her side because of my influence over him. It frequently happens that women who do not really love their husbands are jealous and destroy their friendships. They want the husband to belong entirely to them because they themselves do not belong to him. The kernel of all jealousy is lack of love.

   The wife's attitude placed a tremendous burden on the patient which he was incapable of coping with. Under its pressure he relapsed, after a year of marriage, into a new depression. Foreseeing this possibility, I had arranged with him that he was to get in touch with me at once if he observed his spirits sinking. He neglected to do so, partly because of his wife, who scoffed at his moods. I heard not a word from him.

   At that time I had to deliver a lecture in B. I returned to my hotel around midnight. I sat with some friends for a while after the lecture, then went to bed, but I lay awake for a long time. At about two o'clock – I must have just fallen asleep – I awoke with a start, and had the feeling that someone had come into the room; I even had the impression that the door had been hastily opened. I instantly turned on the light, but there was nothing. Someone might have mistaken the door, I thought, and I looked into the corridor. But it was still as death. 'Odd', I thought, 'someone did come into the room!' Then I tried to recall exactly what had happened, and it occurred to me that I had been awakened by a feeling of dull pain, as though something had struck my forehead and then the back of my skull. The following day I received a telegram saying that my patient had committed suicide. He had shot himself. Later, I learned that the bullet had come to rest in the back of the skull.

This experience was a genuine synchronistic phenomenon such as is quite often observed in connection with an archetypal situation – in this case, death. By means of a relativization of time and space in the unconscious it could well be that I had perceived something which in reality was taking place elsewhere. The collective unconscious is common to all; it is the foundation of what the ancients called the 'sympathy of all things'. In this case the unconscious had knowledge of my patient's condition. All that evening, in fact, I had felt curiously restive and nervous, very much in contrast to my usual mood.

From: Letter to L. Kling (14 January 1958), *Letters*, vol. 2, pp. 409–10[8]

Your question concerning synchronicity and ideas of reference[9] is very interesting indeed. I have often found that synchronistic experiences were interpreted by schizophrenics as delusions. Since archetypal situations are not uncommon in schizophrenia, we must also suppose that corresponding synchronistic phenomena will occur which follow exactly the same course as with so-called normal persons. The difference lies simply and solely in the interpretation. The schizophrenic's interpretation is morbidly narrow because it is mostly restricted to the intentions of other people and to his own ego-importance. The normal interpretation, so far as this is possible at all, is based on the philosophic premise of the sympathy of all things,[10] or something of that kind. Your patient is obviously someone who would need either to pay his tribute to Nature or to make some correspondingly meaningful sacrifice. What this might be is provisionally indicated by the dreams. We certainly shouldn't think we know what good advice to offer or what, if anything, ought to be done. On the contrary we must endeavour to find out what the unconscious thinks and adjust our attitude accordingly. If synchronicities occur in these cases it is because an archetypal situation is present, for whenever archetypes are constellated we find manifestations of the prim-ordial unity. Thus the synchronistic effect should be understood not as a psychotic but as a normal phenomenon.

Ideas of reference arise as a concomitant symptom of the patient's wrong understanding, and consequent repression, of his psychic situation. Then what should normally have been an expression of the sympathy of all things turns into a pseudo-rationalistic attempt to explain the missing sympathy, so in place of the uniting Eros he feels a divisive fear or a hatred which is its opposite. The pathological factor is that the original participation in all things is perverted into a negation on rational or other plausible grounds which seem obvious enough to the average intelligence. Not only is no account taken of the significance of this sympathy, but the religious attitude is also lacking which sees in it a divine will that has to be served accordingly. Thus the erotic relationship, no matter how unconventional it may be, would have to be understood as an *opus divinum,* and the perhaps necessary sacrifice of this relationship as a *thysia,* a 'ritual slaughter'.[11]

NOTES

1 For Freud's reaction to the incident, see *Memories, Dreams, Reflections,* Appendix I, pp. 333–4
2 Cf., 'Concerning Mandala Symbolism', in *The Archetypes and the Collective Unconscious (CW* 9, i), figs. 5 ff. and pp. 363 ff.
3 *The Secret of the Golden Flower,* fig. 10. See also 'Concerning Mandala Symbolism', fig. 36 and p. 377.
4 On Richard Wilhelm, see *Memories, Dreams, Reflections,* Appendix IV, pp. 342–5.
5 [Apparently Jung's first use of this term in the sense of 'synchronicity', or meaningful coincidence, as an explanatory principle of parallel physical and psychic events, equal in importance and complementary to the principle of causality. Also see *Dream Analysis,* 27 Nov. 1929, n. 6, and 4 Dec. 1929, p. 417. Jung first published the term 'synchronicity' in 1930, in his memorial address for Richard Wilhelm *(CW* 15, par. 81). The concept is fully developed in the monograph 'Synchronicity: An Acausal Connecting Principle' (1952; *CW* 8).]
6 [*The I Ching, or Book of Changes,* trans Cary F. Baynes (1950) from the German trans of Richard Wilhelm (1924). Jung wrote a foreword especially for the English trans; it is also in *CW* 11, pars. 964ff. Cf. *Dream Analysis,* 6 Feb. 1929, n. 8.]
7 *Eine Selbstschau* (1843).
8 [M.D., analytical psychologist, of Strasbourg.]
9 [Ideas of reference frequently occur in schizophrenia when the patient interprets quite ordinary events as having some special reference to him.]
10 [The 'sympathy of all things', the harmonious interdependence and interaction of the elements of the universe, is a concept largely developed by the Stoic philosophers Chrysippus (c. 280–207 BC) and Poseidonius (c. 135–50 BC). It greatly influenced the thought of the Middle Ages (cf., 'Synchronicity', *CW* 8, pars. 924ff.).]
11 [The symbolic meaning of the *thysia* is discussed in 'Transformation Symbolism in the Mass', *CW* 11, pars. 302ff., 324f., 345f.]

4   Astrology and the *I Ching*

From: Letter to Sigmund Freud (12 June 1911), *Letters*, vol. 1, p. 24

My evenings are taken up very largely with astrology. I make horoscopic calculations in order to find a clue to the core of psychological truth. Some remarkable things have turned up which will certainly appear incredible to you. In the case of one lady, the calculation of the position of the stars at her nativity produced a quite definite character picture, with several biographical details which did not belong to her but to her mother – and the characteristics fitted the mother to a T. The lady suffers from an extraordinary mother complex. I dare say that we shall one day discover in astrology a good deal of knowledge that has been intuitively projected into the heavens. For instance, it appears that the signs of the zodiac are character pictures, in other words libido symbols which depict the typical qualities of the libido at a given moment.

From: *Dream Analysis: Notes of the Seminar Given in 1928–1930* (1984), p. 412.

Astrology consists of all these little tricks that help to make the diagnosis more accurate. So the astrologer, though he does not know the year or the month of your birth, may guess by your qualities. Now, the unfortunate thing is that we can designate the condition of energy, universal energy, in no other way than by time. Instead of saying the time of the falling stone, we say it was ten seconds ago that the stone has fallen. We call this year 1929, because once upon a time we began counting, assuming that we knew when Christ was born – though there is a controversy about that, Christ may have been born 100 BC. Mead has written a very interesting book about that.[1] In China the years have names. In Rome they were named for the consuls, reckoned from the beginning of Rome in 750 BC. After the French Revolution, they began to count the years as if it were the beginning of a new epoch. We indicate the conditions of the times by a number. For instance, 1875 might be called the time of crinolines, the first railways, newspapers twice a week with pages, corsets for ladies, top-hats for men, bad taste generally. They knew nothing of Nietzsche, Schopenhauer was the most recent news. Chicago was then the most ridiculous little place, and imagine New York in 1875! Four years after the Franco-German

War, everything was moving in a different way, the way that was characteristic for that year, and nothing before or after will be like it.

So, in 1929, everything has the cast and brand of this year. And the children born in this year will be recognizable as part of a great process and marked by a particular condition.[2]

From: Letter to B. Baur[3] (29 January 1934), *Letters*, vol. 1, pp. 138–9

Dear Dr Baur,

Best thanks for your kind information. So far as the argument of the precession[4] is concerned, this is no objection to the validity of astrology but rather to the primitive theory that the stars themselves radiate certain effects. The precession argument says that a person born today in Aries 1, when ostensibly Aries has risen one degree over the Eastern horizon, is not born at this point of time at all but in Pisces 1. The secret powers of the sun are in Aries 1. Moon for instance in Cancer 7, Venus, Jupiter in similar positions, are therefore not right astronomically and so cannot be derived from these merely apparent and arbitrarily fixed positions. Choisnard quite correctly says: 'Le bélier reste toujours à la 12ème partie du zodiaque',[5] etc., obviously meaning that 'sun in Aries' is not an astronomical statement but an indication of time. It is 'springtime' that contains the active forces no matter in which real astronomical zodion the sun is standing. In a few thousand years, when we say it is Aries time, the sun will be in reality in Capricorn, a deep winter sign, though the spring will not have lost its powers.

The fact that astrology nevertheless yields valid results proves that it is not the apparent positions of the stars which work, but rather the times which are measured or determined by arbitrarily named stellar positions. Time thus proves to be a stream of energy filled with qualities and not, as our philosophy would have it, an abstract concept or precondition of knowledge.

The validity of the results of the *I Ching* oracle points to the same peculiar fact. Careful investigation of the unconscious shows that there is a peculiar coincidence with time, which is also the reason why the ancients were able to project the succession of unconsciously perceived inner contents into the outer astronomical determinants of time. This is the basis for the connection of psychic events with temporal determinants. So it is not a matter of an indirect connection, as you suppose, but of a direct one. Conjunctions, oppositions, etc. Are not in the least affected by the fact that we arbitrarily designate Pisces 1 as Aries 1.

With best regards,

Yours sincerely, C.G. JUNG

Letter to B.V. Raman (6 September 1947), *Letters*, vol. 1, pp. 475–6

[Original in English]

Dear Prof. Raman,

I haven't yet received *The Astrological Magazine*,[6] but I will answer your letter nevertheless.

Since you want to know my opinion about astrology I can tell you that I've been interested in this particular activity of the human mind for more than 30 years.[7] As I am a psychologist I'm chiefly interested in the particular light the horoscope sheds on certain complications in the character. In cases of difficult psychological diagnosis I usually get a horoscope in order to have a further point of view from an entirely different angle. I must say that I very often found that the astrological data elucidated certain points which I otherwise would have been unable to understand. From such experiences I formed the opinion that astrology is of particular interest to the psychologist, since it contains a sort of psychological experience which we call 'projected' – this means that we find the psychological facts as it were in the constellations. This originally gave rise to the idea that these factors derive from the stars, whereas they are merely in a relation of synchronicity with them. I admit that this is a very curious fact which throws a peculiar light on the structure of the human mind.

What I miss in astrological literature is chiefly the statistical method by which certain fundamental facts could be scientifically established.

Hoping that this answer meets your request, I remain,

Yours sincerely, C.G. JUNG

From: *Memories, Dreams, Reflections* (1963), pp. 342–3

I first met Richard Wilhelm at Count Keyserling's during a meeting of the 'School of Wisdom' in Darmstadt. That was in the early twenties. In 1923 we invited him to Zurich and he spoke on the *I Ching*[8] at the Psychology Club.

Even before meeting him I had been interested in oriental philosophy, and around 1920 had begun experimenting with the *I Ching*. One summer in Bollingen I resolved to make an all-out attack on the riddle of this book. Instead of traditional stalks of yarrow required by the classical method, I cut myself a bunch of reeds. I would sit for hours on the ground beneath the hundred-year-old pear tree, the *I Ching* beside me, practising the technique by referring the resultant oracles to one another in the interplay of questions and answers. All sorts of undeniably remarkable results emerged – meaningful connections with my own thought processes which I could not explain to myself.

The only subjective intervention in this experiment consists in the experimenter's arbitrarily – that is, without counting – dividing up the bundle of forty-nine stalks at a single swoop. He does not know how many stalks are contained in each bundle, and yet the result depends upon their numerical relationship. All other manipulations proceed mechanically and leave no room for interference by the will. If a psychic causal connection is present at all, it can only consist in the chance division of the bundle (or, in the other method, the chance fall of the coins).

During the whole of those summer holidays I was preoccupied with the question: Are the *I Ching*'s answers meaningful or not? If they are, how does the connection between the psychic and the physical sequence of events come about? Time and again I encountered amazing coincidences which seemed to suggest the idea of an acausal parallelism (a synchronicity, as I later called it). So fascinated was I by these experiments that I altogether forgot to take notes, which I afterwards greatly regretted. Later, however, when I often used to carry out the experiment with my patients, it became quite clear that a significant number of answers did indeed hit the mark. I remember, for example, the case of a young man with a strong mother complex. He wanted to marry, and had made the acquaintance of a seemingly suitable girl. However, he felt uncertain, fearing that under the influence of his complex he might once more find himself in the power of an overwhelming mother. I conducted the experiment with him. The text of his hexagram read: 'The maiden is powerful. One should not marry such a maiden'.

In the mid-thirties I met the Chinese philosopher Hu Shih. I asked him his opinion of the *I Ching*, and received the reply: 'Oh, that's nothing but an old collection of magic spells, without significance'. He had no experience with it – or so he said. Only once, he remembered, had he come across it in practice. One day on a walk with a friend, the friend told him about his unhappy love affair. They were just passing by a Taoist temple. As a joke, he had said to his friend: 'Here you can consult the oracle!' No sooner said than done. They went into the temple together and asked the priest for an *I Ching* oracle. But he had not the slightest faith in this nonsense.

I asked him whether the oracle had been correct. Whereupon he replied reluctantly, 'Oh yes, it was, of course'. Remembering the well-known story of the 'good friend' who does everything one does not wish to do oneself, I cautiously asked him whether he had not profited by this opportunity. 'Yes', he replied, 'as a joke I asked a question too'.

'And did the oracle give you a sensible answer?' I asked.

He hesitated. 'Oh well, yes, if you wish to put it that way'. The subject obviously made him uncomfortable.

A few years after my first experiments with the reeds, the *I Ching* was published with Wilhelm's commentary. I instantly obtained the book, and found to my gratification that Wilhelm took much the same view of the meaningful connections as I had. But he knew the entire literature and could therefore fill in the gaps which had been outside my competence. When

Wilhelm came to Zurich, I had the opportunity to discuss the matter with him at length, and we talked a great deal about Chinese philosophy and religion. What he told me, out of his wealth of knowledge of the Chinese mentality, clarified some of the most difficult problems that the European unconscious had posed for me. On the other hand, what I had to tell him about the results of my investigations of the unconscious caused him no little surprise; for he recognized in them things he had considered to be the exclusive possession of the Chinese philosophical tradition.

From: 'Richard Wilhelm: In Memoriam' (1930) (*CW* 15)

77   To me the greatest of his achievements is his translation of, and commentary on, the *I Ching*.[9] Before I came to know Wilhelm's translation, I had worked for years with Legge's inadequate rendering,[10] and I was therefore fully able to appreciate the extraordinary difference between the two. Wilhelm has succeeded in bringing to life again, in new form, this ancient work in which not only many sinologists but most of the modern Chinese see nothing more than a collection of absurd magical spells. This book embodies, as perhaps no other, the living spirit of Chinese civilization, for the best minds of China have collaborated on it and contributed to it for thousands of years. Despite its fabulous age it has never grown old, but still lives and works, at least for those who seek to understand its meaning. That we too belong to this favoured group we owe to the creative achievement of Wilhelm. He has brought the book closer to us by his careful translation and personal experience both as a pupil of a Chinese master of the old school and as an initiate in the psychology of Chinese yoga, who made constant use of the *I Ching* in practice.

78   But together with these rich gifts, Wilhelm has bequeathed to us a task whose magnitude we can only surmise at present, but cannot fully apprehend. Anyone who, like myself, has had the rare good fortune to experience in association with Wilhelm the divinatory power of the *I Ching* cannot remain ignorant of the fact that we have here an Archimedean point from which our Western attitude of mind could be lifted off its foundations. It is no small service to have given us, as Wilhelm did, such a comprehensive and richly coloured picture of a foreign culture. What is even more important is that he has inoculated us with the living germ of the Chinese spirit, capable of working a fundamental change in our view of the world. We are no longer reduced to being admiring or critical observers, but find ourselves partaking of the spirit of the East to the extent that we succeed in experiencing the living power of the *I Ching*.

79   The principle on which the use of the *I Ching* is based appears at first sight to be in complete contradiction to our scientific and causal thinking. For us it is unscientific in the extreme, almost taboo, and therefore outside the scope of our scientific judgment, indeed incomprehensible to it.

80   Some years ago, the then president of the British Anthropological Society asked me how it was that so highly intelligent a people as the Chinese had produced no science. I replied that this must be an optical illusion, since the Chinese did have a science whose standard text-book was the *I Ching*, but that the principle of this science, like so much else in China, was altogether different from the principle of our science.

81   The science of the *I Ching* is based not on the causality principle but on one which – hitherto unnamed because not familiar to us – I have tentatively called the *synchronistic* principle. My researches into the psychology of unconscious processes long ago compelled me to look around for another principle of explanation, since the causality principle seemed to me insufficient to explain certain remarkable manifestations of the unconscious. I found that there are psychic parallelisms which simply cannot be related to each other causally, but must be connected by another kind of principle altogether. This connection seemed to lie essentially in the relative simultaneity of the events, hence the term 'synchronistic.' It seems as though time, far from being an abstraction, is a concrete continuum which possesses qualities or basic conditions capable of manifesting themselves simultaneously in different places by means of an acausal parallelism, such as we find, for instance, in the simultaneous occurrence of identical thoughts, symbols, or psychic states. Another example, pointed out by Wilhelm, would be the coincidence of Chinese and European periods of style, which cannot have been causally related to one another. Astrology would be an example of synchronicity on a grand scale if only there were enough thoroughly tested findings to support it. But at least we have at our disposal a number of well-tested and statistically verifiable facts which make the problem of astrology seem worthy of scientific investigation. Its value is obvious enough to the psychologist, since astrology represents the sum of all the psychological knowledge of antiquity.

82   The fact that it is possible to reconstruct a person's character fairly accurately from his birth data shows the relative validity of astrology. It must be remembered, however, that the birth data are in no way dependent on the actual astronomical constellations, but are based on an arbitrary, purely conceptual time system. Owing to the precession of the equinoxes, the spring-point has long since moved out of the constellation of Aries into Pisces, so that the astrological zodiac on which horoscopes are calculated no longer corresponds to the heavenly one. If there are any astrological diagnoses of character that are in fact correct, this is due not to the influence of the stars but to our own hypothetical time qualities. In other words, whatever is born or done at this particular moment of time has the quality of this moment of time.

83   Here we have the basic formula for the use of the *I Ching*. As you know, the hexagram that characterizes the moment of time, and gives us insight into it, is obtained by manipulating a bundle of yarrow stalks or by

throwing three coins. The division of the yarrow stalks or the fall of the coins depends on pure chance. The runic stalks or coins fall into the pattern of the moment. The only question is: Did King Wen and the Duke of Chou, who lived a thousand years before the birth of Christ, interpret these chance patterns correctly? Experience alone can decide.

84   At his first lecture at the Psychological Club in Zurich, Wilhelm, at my request, demonstrated the use of the *I Ching* and at the same time made a prognosis which, in less than two years, was fulfilled to the letter and with the utmost clarity. Predictions of this kind could be further confirmed by numerous parallel experiences. However, I am not concerned with establishing objectively the validity of the *I Ching*'s statements, but take it simply as a premise, just as Wilhelm did. I am concerned only with the astonishing fact that the hidden qualities of the moment become legible in the hexagram. The interconnection of events made evident by the *I Ching* is essentially analogous to what we find in astrology. There the moment of birth corresponds to the fall of the coins, the constellation to the hexagram, and the astrological interpretation of the birth data corresponds to the text assigned to the hexagram.

85   The type of thinking based on the synchronistic principle, which reached its climax in the *I Ching*, is the purest expression of Chinese thinking in general. In the West it has been absent from the history of philosophy since the time of Heraclitus, and reappears only as a faint echo in Leibniz.[11] However, in the interim it was not altogether extinguished, but lingered on in the twilight of astrological speculation, and it still remains on that level today.

From: 'Foreword to the "I Ching"' (1950) (*CW* 11)

966 I am greatly indebted to Wilhelm for the light he has thrown upon the complicated problem of the *I Ching*, and for insight into its practical application. For more than thirty years I have interested myself in this oracle technique, for it seemed to me of uncommon significance as a method of exploring the unconscious. I was already fairly familiar with the *I Ching* when I first met Wilhelm in the early 1920s; he confirmed then what I already knew, and taught me many things more.

967 I do not know Chinese and have never been in China. I can assure my reader that it is not altogether easy to find the right approach to this monument of Chinese thought, which departs so completely from our ways of thinking. In order to understand what such a book is all about, it is imperative to cast off certain of our Western prejudices. It is a curious fact that such a gifted and intelligent people as the Chinese has never developed what we call science. Our science, however, is based upon the principle of causality, and causality is considered to be an axiomatic truth. But a

great change in our standpoint is setting in. What Kant's *Critique of Pure Reason* failed to do is being accomplished by modern physics. The axioms of causality are being shaken to their foundations: we know now that what we term natural laws are merely statistical truths and thus must necessarily allow for exceptions. We have not sufficiently taken into account as yet that we need the laboratory with its incisive restrictions in order to demonstrate the invariable validity of natural law. If we leave things to nature, we see a very different picture: every process is partially or totally interfered with by chance, so much so that under natural circumstances a course of events absolutely conforming to specific laws is almost an exception.

968   The Chinese mind, as I see it at work in the *I Ching*, seems to be exclusively preoccupied with the chance aspect of events. What we call coincidence seems to be the chief concern of this peculiar mind, and what we worship as causality passes almost unnoticed. We must admit that there is something to be said for the immense importance of chance. An incalculable amount of human effort is directed to combatting and restricting the nuisance or danger that chance represents. Theoretical considerations of cause and effect often look pale and dusty in comparison with the practical results of chance. It is all very well to say that the crystal of quartz is a hexagonal prism. The statement is quite true in so far as an ideal crystal is envisaged. But in nature one finds no two crystals exactly alike, although all are unmistakably hexagonal. The actual form, however, seems to appeal more to the Chinese sage than the ideal one. The jumble of natural laws constituting empirical reality holds more significance for him than a causal explanation of events that, in addition, must usually be separated from one another in order to be properly dealt with.

969   The manner in which the *I Ching* tends to look upon reality seems to disfavour our causal procedures. The moment under actual observation appears to the ancient Chinese view more of a chance hit than a clearly defined result of concurrent causal chains. The matter of interest seems to be the configuration formed by chance events at the moment of observation, and not at all the hypothetical reasons that seemingly account for the coincidence. While the Western mind carefully sifts, weighs, selects, classifies, isolates, the Chinese picture of the moment encompasses everything down to the minutest nonsensical detail, because all of the ingredients make up the observed moment.

970   Thus it happens that when one throws the three coins, or counts through the forty-nine yarrow-stalks, these chance details enter into the picture of the moment of observation and form a part of it – a part that is insignificant to us, yet most meaningful to the Chinese mind. With us it would be a banal and almost meaningless statement (at least on the face of it) to say that whatever happens in a given moment has inevitably the quality peculiar to that moment. This is not an abstract argument but a very

practical one. There are certain connoisseurs who can tell you merely from the appearance, taste and behaviour of a wine the site of its vineyard and the year of its origin. There are antiquarians who with almost uncanny accuracy will name the time and place of origin and the maker of an *objet d'art* or piece of furniture on merely looking at it. And there are even astrologers who can tell you, without any previous knowledge of your nativity, what the position of sun and moon was and what zodiacal sign rose above the horizon at the moment of your birth. In the face of such facts, it must be admitted that moments can leave long-lasting traces.

971   In other words, whoever invented the *I Ching* was convinced that the hexagram worked out in a certain moment coincided with the latter in quality no less than in time. To him the hexagram was the exponent of the moment in which it was cast − even more so than the hours of the clock or the divisions of the calendar could be − inasmuch as the hexagram was understood to be an indicator of the essential situation prevailing at the moment of its origin.

972   This assumption involves a certain curious principle which I have termed synchronicity,[12] a concept that formulates a point of view diametrically opposed to that of causality. Since the latter is a merely statistical truth and not absolute, it is a sort of working hypothesis of how events evolve one out of another, whereas synchronicity takes the coincidence of events in space and time as meaning something more than mere chance, namely, a peculiar interdependence of objective events among themselves as well as with the subjective (psychic) states of the observer or observers.

973   The ancient Chinese mind contemplates the cosmos in a way comparable to that of the modern physicist, who cannot deny that his model of the world is a decidedly psychophysical structure. The microphysical event includes the observer just as much as the reality underlying the *I Ching* comprises subjective, i.e., psychic conditions in the totality of the momentary situation. Just as causality describes the sequence of events, so synchronicity to the Chinese mind deals with the coincidence of events. The causal point of view tells us a dramatic story about how D came into existence: it took its origin from C, which existed before D, and C in its turn had a father, B, etc. The synchronistic view on the other hand tries to produce an equally meaningful picture of coincidence. How does it happen that A', B', C', D', etc., all appear at the same moment and in the same place? It happens in the first place because the physical events A' and B' are of the same quality as the psychic events C' and D', and further because all are the exponents of one and the same momentary situation. The situation is assumed to represent a legible or understandable picture.

974   Now the sixty-four hexagrams of the *I Ching* are the instrument by which the meaning of sixty-four different yet typical situations can be determined. These interpretations are equivalent to causal explanations.

Causal connection can be determined statistically and can be subjected to experiment. Inasmuch as situations are unique and cannot be repeated, experimenting with synchronicity seems to be impossible under ordinary conditions.[13] In the *I Ching*, the only criterion of the validity of synchronicity is the observer's opinion that the text of the hexagram amounts to a true rendering of his psychic condition. It is assumed that the fall of the coins or the result of the division of the bundle of yarrow-stalks is what it necessarily must be in a given 'situation', inasmuch as anything happening at that moment belongs to it as an indispensable part of the picture. If a handful of matches is thrown to the floor, they form the pattern characteristic of that moment. But such an obvious truth as this, reveals its meaningful nature only if it is possible to read the pattern and to verify its interpretation, partly by the observer's knowledge of the subjective and objective situation, partly by the character of subsequent events. It is obviously not a procedure that appeals to a critical mind used to experimental verification of facts or to factual evidence. But for someone who likes to look at the world at the angle from which ancient China saw it, the *I Ching* may have some attraction.

From: Letter to the Rev. W.P. Witcutt (24 August 1960), *Letters*, vol. 2, p. 584

As you have found out for yourself, the *I Ching* consists of readable archetypes, and it very often presents not only a picture of the actual situation but also of the future, exactly like dreams. One could even define the *I Ching* oracle as an experimental dream, just as one can define a dream as an experiment of a four-dimensional nature. I have never tried even to describe this aspect of dreams, not to speak of the hexagrams, because I have found that our public today is incapable of understanding. I considered it therefore my first duty to talk and write of the things that might be understandable and would thus prepare the ground upon which one could later on explain the more complicated things. I quite agree that the *I Ching* symbolism can be interpreted like that of dreams.

From: Letter to André Barbault (26 May 1954), *Letters*, vol. 2, p. 176

Qualitative time. This is a notion I used formerly[14] but I have replaced it with the idea of synchronicity, which is analogous to sympathy or *correspondentia* (the συμπάθεια of antiquity), or to Leibniz's *pre-established harmony*. Time in itself consists of nothing. It is only a *modus cogitandi* that is used to express

12 [Cf., Jung's 'Synchronicity: An Acausal Connecting Principle'. In that work (pp. 450–3) he is concerned with the synchronistic aspects of the *I Ching*.]
13 [Cf., J.B. Rhine, *The Reach of the Mind*.]
14 [Cf., 'Richard Wilhelm: In Memoriam', *CW* 15, par. 82: 'Whatever is born or done at this particular moment of time has the quality of this moment of time'. Also 'Foreword to the *I Ching*', *CW* 11, pars. 970f.]

Part II

The theory of synchronicity

5   Synchronicity

'On Synchronicity' (1951) (*CW* 8)[1]

969   It might seem appropriate to begin my exposition by defining the concept with which it deals. But I would rather approach the subject the other way and first give you a brief description of the facts which the concept of synchronicity is intended to cover. As its etymology shows, this term has something to do with time or, to be more accurate, with a kind of simultaneity. Instead of simultaneity we could also use the concept of a *meaningful coincidence* of two or more events, where something other than the probability of chance is involved. A statistical – that is, a probable – concurrence of events, such as the 'duplication of cases' found in hospitals, falls within the category of chance. Groupings of this kind can consist of any number of terms and still remain within the framework of the probable and rationally possible. Thus, for instance, someone chances to notice the number on his street-car ticket. On arriving home he receives a telephone call during which the same number is mentioned. In the evening he buys a theatre ticket that again has the same number. The three events form a chance grouping that, although not likely to occur often, nevertheless lies well within the framework of probability owing to the frequency of each of its terms. I would like to recount from my own experience the following chance grouping, made up of no fewer than six terms:

970   On April 1, 1949, I made a note in the morning of an inscription containing a figure that was half man and half fish. There was fish for lunch. Somebody mentioned the custom of making an 'April fish' of someone. In the afternoon, a former patient of mine, whom I had not seen for months, showed me some impressive pictures of fish. In the evening, I was shown a piece of embroidery with sea monsters and fishes in it. The next morning, I saw a former patient, who was visiting me for the first time in ten years. She had dreamed of a large fish the night before. A few months later, when I was using this series for a larger work and had just finished writing it down, I walked over to a spot by the lake in front of the house, where I had already been several times that morning. This time a fish a foot long lay on the sea-wall. Since no one else was present, I have no idea how the fish could have got there.

971   When coincidences pile up in this way one cannot help being impressed by them – for the greater the number of terms in such a series, or the more unusual its character, the more improbable it becomes. For reasons that I have mentioned elsewhere and will not discuss now, I assume that this was a chance grouping. It must be admitted, though, that it is more improbable than a mere duplication.

972   In the above-mentioned case of the street-car ticket, I said that the observer 'chanced' to notice the number and retain it in his memory, which ordinarily he would never have done. This formed the basis for the series of chance events, but I do not know what caused him to notice the number. It seems to me that in judging such a series a factor of uncertainty enters in at this point and requires attention. I have observed something similar in other cases, without, however, being able to draw any reliable conclusions. But it is sometimes difficult to avoid the impression that there is a sort of foreknowledge of the coming series of events. This feeling becomes irresistible when, as so frequently happens, one thinks one is about to meet an old friend in the street, only to find to one's disappointment that it is a stranger. On turning the next corner one then runs into him in person. Cases of this kind occur in every conceivable form and by no means infrequently, but after the first momentary astonishment they are as a rule quickly forgotten.

973   Now, the more the foreseen details of an event pile up, the more definite is the impression of an existing foreknowledge, and the more improbable does chance become. I remember the story of a student friend whose father had promised him a trip to Spain if he passed his final examinations satisfactorily. My friend thereupon dreamed that he was walking through a Spanish city. The street led to a square, where there was a Gothic cathedral. He then turned right, around a corner, into another street. There he was met by an elegant carriage drawn by two cream-coloured horses. Then he woke up. He told us about the dream as we were sitting round a table drinking beer. Shortly afterwards, having successfully passed his examinations, he went to Spain, and there, in one of the streets, he recognized the city of his dream. He found the square and the cathedral, which exactly corresponded to the dream-image. He wanted to go straight to the cathedral, but then remembered that in the dream he had turned right, at the corner, into another street. He was curious to find out whether his dream would be corroborated further. Hardly had he turned the corner when he saw in reality the carriage with the two cream-coloured horses.

974   The *sentiment du déjà-vu* is based, as I have found in a number of cases, on a foreknowledge in dreams, but we saw that this foreknowledge can also occur in the waking state. In such cases mere chance becomes highly improbable because the coincidence is known in advance. It thus loses its chance character not only psychologically and subjectively, but objectively too, since the accumulation of details that coincide immeasurably increases the improbability of chance as a determining factor. (For correct

precognitions of death, Dariex and Flammarion have computed probabilities ranging from 1 in 4,000,000 to 1 in 8,000,000.)[2] So in these cases it would be incongruous to speak of 'chance' happenings. It is rather a question of meaningful coincidences. Usually they are explained by precognition – in other words, foreknowledge. People also talk of clairvoyance, telepathy, etc., without, however, being able to explain what these faculties consist of or what means of transmission they use in order to render events distant in space and time accessible to our perception. All these ideas are mere names; they are not scientific concepts which could be taken as statements of principle, for no one has yet succeeded in constructing a causal bridge between the elements making up a meaningful coincidence.

975   Great credit is due to J.B. Rhine for having established a reliable basis for work in the vast field of these phenomena by his experiments in extrasensory perception, or ESP. He used a pack of twenty-five cards divided into five groups of five, each with its special sign (star, square, circle, cross, two wavy lines). The experiment was carried out as follows. In each series of experiments the pack is laid out 800 times, in such a way that the subject cannot see the cards. He is then asked to guess the cards as they are turned up. The probability of a correct answer is one in five. The result, computed from very high figures, showed an average of 6.5 hits. The probability of a chance deviation of 1.5 amounts to only one in 250,000. Some individuals scored more than twice the probable number of hits. On one occasion all twenty-five cards were guessed correctly, which gives a probability of one in 298,023,223,876,953,125. The spatial distance between experimenter and subject was increased from a few yards to about 4,000 miles, with no effect on the result.

976   A second type of experiment consisted in asking the subject to guess a series of cards that was still to be laid out in the near or more distant future. The time factor was increased from a few minutes to two weeks. The result of these experiments showed a probability of one in 400,000.

977   In a third type of experiment, the subject had to try to influence the fall of mechanically thrown dice by wishing for a certain number. The results of this so-called psychokinetic (PK) experiment were the more positive the more dice were used at a time.

978   The result of the spatial experiment proves with tolerable certainty that the psyche can, to some extent, eliminate the space factor. The time experiment proves that the time factor (at any rate, in the dimension of the future) can become psychically relative. The experiment with dice proves that moving bodies, too, can be influenced psychically – a result that could have been predicted from the psychic relativity of space and time.

979   The energy postulate shows itself to be inapplicable to the Rhine experiments, and thus rules out all ideas about the transmission of force. Equally, the law of causality does not hold – a fact that I pointed out thirty years ago. For we cannot conceive how a future event could bring about

an event in the present. Since for the time being there is no possibility whatever of a causal explanation, we must assume provisionally that improbable accidents of an acausal nature – that is, meaningful co-incidences – have entered the picture.

980   In considering these remarkable results we must take into account a fact discovered by Rhine, namely that in each series of experiments the first attempts yielded a better result than the later ones. The falling off in the number of hits scored was connected with the mood of the subject. An initial mood of faith and optimism makes for good results. Scepticism and resistance have the opposite effect, that is, they create an unfavourable disposition. As the energic, and hence also the causal, approach to these experiments has shown itself to be inapplicable, it follows that the affective factor has the significance simply of a *condition* which makes it possible for the phenomenon to occur, though it need not. According to Rhine's results, we may nevertheless expect 6.5 hits instead of only five. But it cannot be predicted in advance when the hit will come. Could we do so, we would be dealing with a law, and this would contradict the entire nature of the phenomenon. It has, as said, the improbable character of a 'lucky hit' or accident that occurs with a more than merely probable frequency and is as a rule dependent on a certain state of affectivity.

981   This observation has been thoroughly confirmed, and it suggests that the psychic factor which modifies or even eliminates the principles underlying the physicist's picture of the world is connected with the affective state of the subject. Although the phenomenology of the ESP and PK experiments could be considerably enriched by further experiments of the kind described above, deeper investigation of its bases will have to concern itself with the nature of the affectivity involved. I have therefore directed my attention to certain observations and experiences which, I can fairly say, have forced themselves upon me during the course of my long medical practice. They have to do with spontaneous, meaningful coincidences of so high a degree of improbability as to appear flatly unbelievable. I shall therefore describe to you only one case of this kind, simply to give an example characteristic of a whole category of phenomena. It makes no difference whether you refuse to believe this particular case or whether you dispose of it with an *ad hoc* explanation. I could tell you a great many such stories, which are in principle no more surprising or incredible than the irrefutable results arrived at by Rhine, and you would soon see that almost every case calls for its own explanation. But the causal explanation, the only possible one from the standpoint of natural science, breaks down owing to the psychic relativization of space and time, which together form the indispensable premises for the cause-and-effect relationship.

982   My example concerns a young woman patient who, in spite of efforts made on both sides, proved to be psychologically inaccessible. The difficulty lay in the fact that she always knew better about everything. Her excellent education had provided her with a weapon ideally suited to this

purpose, namely a highly polished Cartesian rationalism with an impeccably 'geometrical'[3] idea of reality. After several fruitless attempts to sweeten her rationalism with a somewhat more human understanding, I had to confine myself to the hope that something unexpected and irrational would turn up, something that would burst the intellectual retort into which she had sealed herself. Well, I was sitting opposite her one day, with my back to the window, listening to her flow of rhetoric. She had had an impressive dream the night before, in which someone had given her a golden scarab – a costly piece of jewellery. While she was still telling me this dream, I heard something behind me gently tapping on the window. I turned round and saw that it was a fairly large flying insect that was knocking against the window-pane from outside in the obvious effort to get into the dark room. This seemed to me very strange. I opened the window immediately and caught the insect in the air as it flew in. It was a scarabaeid beetle, or common rose-chafer (*Cetonia aurata*), whose gold-green colour most nearly resembles that of a golden scarab. I handed the beetle to my patient with the words, 'Here is your scarab.' This experience punctured the desired hole in her rationalism and broke the ice of her intellectual resistance. The treatment could now be continued with satisfactory results.

983   This story is meant only as a paradigm of the innumerable cases of meaningful coincidence that have been observed not only by me but by many others, and recorded in large collections. They include everything that goes by the name of clairvoyance, telepathy, etc., from Swedenborg's well-attested vision of the great fire in Stockholm to the recent report by Air Marshal Sir Victor Goddard about the dream of an unknown officer, which predicted the subsequent accident to Goddard's plane.[4]

984   All the phenomena I have mentioned can be grouped under three categories:

1 The coincidence of a psychic state in the observer with a simultaneous, objective, external event that corresponds to the psychic state or content (e.g., the scarab), where there is no evidence of a causal connection between the psychic state and the external event, and where, considering the psychic relativity of space and time, such a connection is not even conceivable.
2 The coincidence of a psychic state with a corresponding (more or less simultaneous) external event taking place outside the observer's field of perception, i.e., at a distance, and only verifiable afterward (e.g., the Stockholm fire).
3 The coincidence of a psychic state with a corresponding, not yet existent future event that is distant in time and can likewise only be verified afterward.

985   In groups 2 and 3 the coinciding events are not yet present in the

observer's field of perception, but have been anticipated in time in so far as they can only be verified afterward. For this reason I call such events *synchronistic*, which is not to be confused with *synchronous*.

986   Our survey of this wide field of experience would be incomplete if we failed to take into account the so-called mantic methods. Manticism lays claim, if not actually to producing synchronistic events, then at least to making them serve its ends. An example of this is the oracle method of the *I Ching*, which Dr Hellmut Wilhelm has described in detail.[5] The *I Ching* presupposes that there is a synchronistic correspondence between the psychic state of the questioner and the answering hexagram. The hexagram is formed either by the random division of the forty-nine yarrow stalks or by the equally random throw of three coins. The result of this method is, incontestably, very interesting, but so far as I can see it does not provide any tool for an objective determination of the facts, that is to say a statistical evaluation, since the psychic state in question is much too indefinite and indefinable. The same holds true of the geomantic experiment, which is based on similar principles.

987   We are in a somewhat more favourable situation when we turn to the astrological method, as it presupposes a meaningful coincidence of planetary aspects and positions with the character or the existing psychic state of the questioner. In the light of the most recent astrophysical research, astrological correspondence is probably not a matter of synchronicity but, very largely, of a causal relationship. As Professor Max Knoll has demonstrated,[6] the solar proton radiation is influenced to such a degree by planetary conjunctions, oppositions and quartile aspects that the appearance of magnetic storms can be predicted with a fair amount of probability. Relationships can be established between the curve of the earth's magnetic disturbances and the mortality rate that confirm the unfavourable influence of conjunctions, oppositions, and quartile aspects and the favourable influence of trine and sextile aspects. So it is probably a question here of a causal relationship, i.e., of a natural law that excludes synchronicity or restricts it. At the same time, the zodiacal qualification of the houses, which plays a large part in the horoscope, creates a complication in that the astrological zodiac, although agreeing with the calendar, does not coincide with the actual constellations themselves. These have shifted their positions by almost a whole platonic month as a result of the precession of the equinoxes since the time when the spring-point was in zero Aries, about the beginning of our era. Therefore, anyone born in Aries today (according to the calendar) is actually born in Pisces. It is simply that his birth took place at a time which, for approximately 2,000 years, has been called 'Aries'. Astrology presupposes that this time has a determining quality. It is possible that this quality, like the disturbances in the earth's magnetic field, is connected with the seasonal fluctuations to which solar proton radiation is subject. It is therefore not

beyond the realm of possibility that the zodiacal positions may also represent a causal factor.

988 Although the psychological interpretation of horoscopes is still a very uncertain matter, there is nevertheless some prospect today of a causal explanation in conformity with natural law. Consequently, we are no longer justified in describing astrology as a mantic method. Astrology is in the process of becoming a science. But as there are still large areas of uncertainty, I decided some time ago to make a test and find out how far an accepted astrological tradition would stand up to statistical investigation. For this purpose it was necessary to select a definite and indisputable fact. My choice fell on marriage. Since antiquity, the traditional belief in regard to marriage has been that there is a conjunction of sun and moon in the horoscope of the marriage partners, that is, ☉ (sun) with an orbit of 8 degrees in the case of one partner, in ☌ (conjunction) with ☾ (moon) in the case of the other. A second, equally old, tradition takes ☾ ☌ ☾ as another marriage characteristic. Of like importance are the conjunctions of the ascendent (*Asc.*) with the large luminaries.

989 Together with my co-worker, Mrs Liliane Frey-Rohn, I first proceeded to collect 180 marriages, that is to say, 360 horoscopes,[7] and compared the 50 most important aspects that might possibly be characteristic of marriage, namely the conjunctions and oppositions of ☉ ☾ ♂ (Mars) ♀ (Venus) *Asc.* and *Desc.* This resulted in a maximum of 10 per cent for ☉ ☌ ☾. As Professor Markus Fierz, of Basel, who kindly went to the trouble of computing the probability of my result, informed me, my figure has a probability of 1 : 10,000. The opinion of several mathematical physicists whom I consulted about the significance of this figure is divided: some find it considerable, others find it of questionable value. Our figure is inconclusive inasmuch as a total of 360 horoscopes is far too small from a statistical point of view.

990 While the aspects of these 180 marriages were being worked out statistically, our collection was enlarged, and when we had collected 220 more marriages, this batch was subjected to separate investigation. As on the first occasion, the material was evaluated just as it came in. It was not selected from any special point of view and was drawn from the most varied sources. Evaluation of this second batch yielded a maximum figure of 10.9 per cent for ☾ ☌ ☾. The probability of this figure is also about 1 : 10,000.

991 Finally, 83 more marriages arrived, and these in turn were investigated separately. The result was a maximum figure of 9.6 per cent for ☾ ☌ *Asc.* The probability of this figure is approximately 1: 3,000.[8]

992 One is immediately struck by the fact that the conjunctions are all *moon conjunctions*, which is in accord with astrological expectations. But the strange thing is that what has turned up here are the three basic positions of the horoscope, ☉ ☾ and *Asc.* The probability of a concurrence of ☉ ☌ ☾ and ☾ ☌ ☾ amounts to 1 : 100,000,000. The concurrence

of the three moon conjunctions with $\odot$ $\mathbb{C}$ *Asc.* has a probability of $1 : 3 \times 10^{11}$; in other words, the improbability of its being due to mere chance is so enormous that we are forced to take into account the existence of some factor responsible for it. The three batches were so small that little or no theoretical significance can be attached to the individual probabilities of $1 : 10,000$ and $1 : 3,000$. Their concurrence, however, is so improbable that one cannot help assuming the existence of an impelling factor that produced this result.

993   The possibility of there being a scientifically valid connection between astrological data and proton radiation cannot be held responsible for this, since the individual probabilities of $1 : 10,000$ and $1 : 3,000$ are too great for us to be able, with any degree of certainty, to view our result as other than mere chance. Besides, the maxima cancel each other out as soon as one divides up the marriages into a larger number of batches. It would require hundreds of thousands of marriage horoscopes to establish the statistical regularity of occurrences like the sun, moon and ascendent conjunctions, and even then the result would be questionable. That anything so improbable as the turning up of the three classical moon conjunctions should occur at all, however, can only be explained either as the result of an intentional or unintentional fraud, or else as precisely such a meaningful coincidence, that is, as synchronicity.

994   Although I was obliged to express doubt, earlier, about the mantic character of astrology, I am now forced as a result of my astrological experiment to recognize it again. The chance arrangement of the marriage horoscopes, which were simply piled on top of one another as they came in from the most diverse sources, and the equally fortuitous way they were divided into three unequal batches, suited the sanguine expectations of the research workers and produced an overall picture that could scarcely have been improved upon from the standpoint of the astrological hypothesis. The success of the experiment is entirely in accord with Rhine's ESP results, which were also favourably affected by expectation, hope and faith. However, there was no definite expectation of any one result. Our selection of fifty aspects is proof of this. After we got the result of the first batch, a slight expectation did exist that the $\odot$ σ $\mathbb{C}$ would be confirmed. But we were disappointed. The second time, we made up a larger batch from the newly added horoscopes in order to increase the element of certainty. But the result was $\mathbb{C}$ σ $\mathbb{C}$. With the third batch, there was only a faint expectation that $\mathbb{C}$ σ $\mathbb{C}$ would be confirmed, but again this was not the case.

995   What happened in this case was admittedly a curiosity, apparently a unique instance of meaningful coincidence. If one is impressed by such things, one could call it a minor miracle. Today, however, we are obliged to view the miraculous in a somewhat different light. The Rhine experiments have demonstrated that space and time, and hence causality, are factors that can be eliminated, with the result that acausal phenomena,

otherwise called miracles, appear possible. All natural phenomena of this kind are unique and exceedingly curious combinations of chance, held together by the common meaning of their parts to form an unmistakable whole. Although meaningful coincidences are infinitely varied in their phenomenology, as acausal events they nevertheless form an element that is part of the scientific picture of the world. Causality is the way we explain the link between two successive events. Synchronicity designates the parallelism of time and meaning between psychic and psychophysical events, which scientific knowledge so far has been unable to reduce to a common principle. The term explains nothing, it simply formulates the occurrence of meaningful coincidences which, in themselves, are chance happenings, but are so improbable that we must assume them to be based on some kind of principle, or on some property of the empirical world. No reciprocal causal connection can be shown to obtain between parallel events, which is just what gives them their chance character. The only recognizable and demonstrable link between them is a common meaning, or equivalence. The old theory of correspondence was based on the experience of such connections – a theory that reached its culminating point and also its provisional end in Leibniz' idea of pre-established harmony, and was then replaced by causality. Synchronicity is a modern differentiation of the obsolete concept of correspondence, sympathy, and harmony. It is based not on philosophical assumptions but on empirical experience and experimentation.

996   Synchronistic phenomena prove the simultaneous occurrence of meaningful equivalences in heterogeneous, causally unrelated processes; in other words, they prove that a content perceived by an observer can, at the same time, be represented by an outside event, without any causal connection. From this is follows either that the psyche cannot be localized in space, or that space is relative to the psyche. The same applies to the temporal determination of the psyche and the psychic relativity of time. I do not need to emphasize that the verification of these findings must have far-reaching consequences.

997   In the short space of a lecture I cannot, unfortunately, do more than give a very cursory sketch of the vast problem of synchronicity. For those of you who would care to go into this question more deeply, I would mention that a more extensive work of mine is soon to appear under the title 'Synchronicity: An Acausal Connecting Principle'. It will be published together with a work by Professor W. Pauli in a book called *The Interpretation of Nature and the Psyche*.[9]

NOTES

1 [Originally given as a lecture, 'Über Synchronizität', at the 1951 Eranos conference, Ascona, Switzerland, and published in the *Eranos-Jahrbuch 1951* (Zurich, 1952). The present translation was published in *Man and Time* (Papers from the

Eranos Yearbooks, 3: New York and London, 1957); it is republished with minor revisions. The essay was, in the main, drawn from the preceding monograph in *CW* 8.]

2 [For documentation, see *CW* 8, par. 830.]

3 [Descartes demonstrated his propositions by the 'Geometrical Method'.]

4 [This case was the subject of an English film, *The Night My Number Came Up*.]

5 ['The Concept of Time in the Book of Changes', originally a lecture at the 1951 Eranos conference.]

6 ['Transformations of Science in Our Age', ibid.]

7 This material stemmed from different sources. They were simply horoscopes of married people. There was no selection of any kind. We took at random all the marriage horoscopes we could lay hands on.

8 [These and the following figures were later revised by Professor Fierz and considerably reduced. See *CW* 8, pars. 901ff.]

9 [See *CW*8, pars. 816–968.]

6   Parapsychology

From: Letter to L.M. Boyers (30 September 1932), *Letters*, vol. 1, p. 100

I'm personally convinced of the existence of connections between our psychological observations and the parapsychological phenomena, but the connection is just as evasive as for instance the management of a Bank and the dreams of a philosopher, or better still: childbirth and mythological images. I know, however, that certain archetypal figures of the unconscious literally appear as ghostly controls with materialization mediums. I can't deny the possibility that certain figures that might appear in our dreams could materialize just as well as ghosts, though I'm in no way capable of proving such a possibility. From my experience with unconscious phenomena I must even admit that what we call thoughts or emotions could be in a way independent psychic agencies of which we perceive only the psychological aspect, but not their potentially physical nature. Analytical psychology is full of unsolved riddles and is teeming with mysteries. I'm therefore following up very closely the facts of parapsychology, because it is quite conceivable that these phenomena will throw a new light on the psychology of the unconscious, perhaps in the near future already.

Letter to J.B. Rhine (18 September 1945), *Letters*, vol. 1, pp. 378–9

[Original in English]

Dear Dr Rhine,

Your letter[1] was a great joy to me. I have often thought of you in these last years and I also often mentioned your name and your experiments to many people.

I wish I could fulfil your wish[2] but having a scientific conscience I feel very hesitant about it since, being a doctor, my observations are all of a clinical kind, which means that they are unavoidably subjective to a certain extent, and never systematic as they are all isolated cases and facts which form a rather incoherent mass that would look like a collection of anecdotes. I despise such a way of dealing with this matter and I would much prefer to be in a position to deal with coherent material collected along certain scientific lines. Of course, I have had quite a number of noteworthy experiences, and you know how it is: the circumstances and persons involved, though indispensably important for the explanation of the facts, cannot be described in a way that would convince the outsider. It would all look hopelessly haphazard and pretty flimsy. As you assume, I have thought a great deal about parapsychological facts and I tried to establish certain connections, but I always refrain from talking publicly about such matters for the above-mentioned reasons. But, seeing your point of view, I'm quite willing to tell you whatever I have thought if that is of any value to you. In this case I should propose that you put certain questions to me[3] about things that interest you and I will try to formulate my answers so far as I am able to do so. It might give me a certain lead to talk about matters which otherwise wouldn't occur to me.

Parapsychology plays a subtle part in psychology because it lurks everywhere behind the surface of things. But, as the facts are difficult to catch, their theoretical aspect is still more elusive on account of its transcendent character. When certain people hold that it is something like a fourth dimension, they don't seem to be very far off the truth.

During the war my health wasn't too good. As a matter of fact I was seriously ill and having reached the biblical age of seventy, I'm none too efficient any more, though I have done a decent amount of scientific work lately. I can't omit to warn you that I perhaps don't know so much about parapsychology as you suspect me to do. It is not exactly my field, and therefore I don't feel very competent to talk much about it. There is only a faint possibility that you will find something of value in the maze of my thoughts.

Hoping you are always in good health, I remain,

Yours sincerely, C.G. JUNG

From: Letter to J.B. Rhine (November 1945), *Letters*, vol. 1, pp. 393–5

Answers to Rhine's Questions[4]   [Original in English]

1 I consider parapsychology as a branch or discipline of general psychology, more especially of the psychology of the unconscious.
2 The psychology of the unconscious has much to say about the mind-body relation (psychogenic disturbances of the physiological functions). Parapsychology is apt to demonstrate the existence of phenomena of a psychic nature, which influence material objects or create physical bodies in a place where no such or similar matter was before. Thus parapsychology

may elucidate the problem of how the living is shaped and continuously reshaped through the unconscious psyche.

3 Parapsychology has shown above all that the psyche has an aspect of a relative-temporal and relative-spatial character. It has shown, moreover, that the unconscious psyche has a faculty to influence matter detached from bodily contact and to assemble matter beyond the reach of the body to such a degree that it appears as a physical body perceptible to our senses as well as to the photographic plate.

4 I see, for the time being at least, no 'useful' connection between parapsychology and psychiatry. It is as yet a merely scientific problem, but as such of the highest importance. Parapsychological phenomena appear not infrequently in the beginning of psychoses, perhaps less frequently during the course of such diseases.

5 I can explain extra-sensory perception only through the working hypothesis of the relativity of time and space. They seem to be *psychically* relative, i.e., what one calls absolute space, for instance, only exists in the world of macrophysical aspects. In the microphysical world the relativity of space and time is an established fact. The psyche, inasmuch as it produces phenomena of a non-spatial or a non-temporal character, seems to belong to the microphysical world. This would also explain the obvious non-spatial nature of psychic existences such as thought etc. And the fact of precognition. In so far as the psyche is an energic phenomenon, it has mass, but mass of microphysical extension or weight. From this fact we can derive material effects of the psyche.

As the relativity of time and space includes the relativity of causality, and as the psyche partakes of relative time-space, it also relativizes causality and therefore enjoys, in so far as it is microphysical, an at least relative independence of absolute causality. (Chinese philosophy says that as long as things are in the North-East, i.e., before they have risen, they can be altered. When they have entered the East, they take their unalterable course.) The fact that the future can be occasionally foreseen does not exclude freedom in general, but only in this particular case. Freedom could become doubtful only if everything could be foreseen.

Viewed from the psychological standpoint, extra-sensory perception appears as a manifestation of the *collective unconscious*. This particular psyche behaves as if it were *one* and not as if it were split up into many individuals. It is *non-personal*. (I call it the 'objective psyche'.) It is the same everywhere and at all times. (If it were not so, comparative psychology would be impossible.) As it is not limited to the person, it is also not limited to the body. It manifests itself therefore not only in human beings but also at the same time in animals and even in physical circumstances. (Cf. the oracle technique of the *I Ching* and character horoscopes.) I call these latter phenomena the synchronicity of archetypal events. For instance, I walk with a woman patient in a wood. She tells me about the first dream in her life that had made an everlasting impression upon her. She had seen a spectral fox coming down the stairs in her parental home. At this moment a real fox comes out of the trees not 40 yards away and walks quietly on the path ahead of us for several minutes. The animal behaves as if it were a partner in the human situation. (One fact is no fact, but when you have seen many, you begin to sit up.)

The bread-knife is still in my possession.[5] The table is gone.

Letter to A.D. Cornell (9 February 1960), *Letters*, vol. 2, pp. 537–43

Dear Mr Cornell,[6]

Your interest in the origin of Psi-activity brings you face-to-face with a problem of the first order. The only thing we know positively in this respect is that experimentally verifiable Psi-phenomena are conditioned by a psychological factor, namely the stimulus of *novelty*, which is responsible for the good results obtained in the beginning of Rhine's laboratory experiments and their decrease upon repetition. It is important to remember that novelty represents an emotional situation (beginner's luck).

Outside the laboratory, too, synchronistic phenomena occur for the most part in emotional situations; for instance, in cases of death, sickness, accident and so on. During the psychotherapeutic treatment of neuroses and psychoses we observe them relatively frequently at moments of heightened emotional tension, which need not however be conscious. Emotions have a typical 'pattern' (fear, anger, sorrow, hatred, etc.); that is, they follow an inborn archetype which is universally human and arouses the same ideas and feelings in everyone. These 'patterns' appear as archetypal motifs chiefly in dreams. The majority of synchronistic phenomena thus occur in *archetypal situations* such as are connected with risks, dangers, fateful developments, etc., and they manifest themselves in the form of telepathy, clairvoyance, precognition, and so forth.

In Rhine's case the experimental set-up is influenced by the expectation of a *miracle*. A miracle is an archetypal situation which is accompanied by a corresponding emotion.

The investigation of a great number of synchronistic phenomena has convinced me that at least one of their most frequent prerequisites is the presence of an active archetype. An archetypal dream may follow the critical event or even precede it (without being its cause in the latter case). In cases of telepathy it might be possible under some circumstances to give a causal explanation, but in the case of precognition this is out of the question. 'Telepathy', 'precognition', etc. are mere concepts (words) and explain nothing. The only explanatory factor we can establish with some certainty is the almost regular, or at least very frequent, simultaneous emergence of an archetype, or rather, of an emotion corresponding to it. One of the commonest symptoms of the presence of an archetype is its connection with religious ideas and convictions.

Two roads for further investigation exist: 1 experiment, and 2 the study of case material.

1 Under certain conditions it is possible to experiment with archetypes, as my 'astrological experiment' has shown.[7] As a matter of fact we had begun such experiments at the C.G. Jung Institute in Zurich, using the historically known intuitive, i.e., synchronistic methods (astrology, geomancy, Tarot cards, and the *I Ching*). But we had too few co-workers and too little means, so we could not go on and had to stop.
2 This would require the observation of individual cases of death, severe illness, and serious accidents, together with a careful analysis of the concomitant psychological situations. Some work along these lines has already been done in Zurich but it is far from sufficient.

Research of this kind requires teamwork and money, and we have neither at present. Above all, superior intelligence and psychological competence are needed. Both are hard to find.

Paranormal psychic phenomena have interested me all my life. Usually, as I have said, they occur in acute psychological states (emotionality, depression, shock, etc.), or, more frequently, with individuals characterized by a peculiar or pathological personality structure, where the threshold to the collective unconscious is habitually lowered. People with a creative genius also belong to this type.

Experience has shown that the so-called Psi-faculty occurs as a spontaneous phenomenon and is not a regular function or quality of the psyche. One can count on its 'regularity' only when the observations are based on very large numbers of cases, as in Rhine's experiments. In Psi-phenomena the psyche apperceives definite impressions through the usual channels of the senses: seeing, hearing, touch, and endopsychic perception (intuition). The 'miracle' does not consist in the process of perception itself but rather in the event perceived. In other words, I perceive with my normal senses and the object of my perception is an objective event. Nevertheless it is an inexplicable event, for within the framework of our physical premises we could not have counted upon its happening. The problem has already been posed in this form by Geulincx, Leibniz and Schopenhauer.

What I mean is that a telepathically perceived event – a vision, let us say – is not the product of a telepathic faculty but rather that the outer event *occurs simultaneously inside the psyche* and reaches consciousness by the usual pathways of inner perception. However, it is not always possible to determine whether a primary inner process is accompanied by an outer one or whether, conversely, a primary outer event is being reflected in a secondary inner process.

To give an example: two English society ladies, sisters, were sitting by the fire one evening. Both were indignant and filled with hatred because of an inheritance which, contrary to their expectations, had not been left to them. It was a matter of an old family mansion with a title attached and a large landed estate. The inheritance had gone instead to a distant cousin, and both sisters were convinced that this was unjust. Suddenly one of them proposed that they should make an 'image' of the heir. This they did together. They shaped it like a wax doll and then, in accordance with ancient custom, threw it into the fire. That same night the mansion was burned to the ground. If we disregard the hypothesis that this was 'chance' (which explains nothing), we have here an example of synchronicity in which the *inner* image was probably primary, though it could easily be the other way round. But in either case there was no observable causality. Hence the 'magical' hypothesis arises: Either the doll set fire to the mansion (but how?), or the fire kindled the fantasy of the sisters (but how?)

My emphasis – as in all such cases – lies on the *reality of the event*, not on its having been perceived. This point of view accords with the hypothesis of an *acausal connection*, i.e., a non-spatial and non-temporal conditioning of events.

Since causality is not an axiomatic but a statistical truth, there must be exceptions in which time and space appear to be relative, otherwise the truth would not be statistical. On this epistemological basis one *must* conclude that the possibility does exist of observing non-spatial and non-temporal events – the very phenomena which we actually do observe contrary to all expectations and which we are now discussing.

In my view, therefore, it is not our perception which is necessarily para- or supranormal but the *event itself*. This, however, is not 'miraculous' but merely 'extra-ordinary' and unexpected, and then only from our biased standpoint which takes causality as axiomatic. From the statistical standpoint, of course, it is simply a matter of random phenomena, but from a truly realistic standpoint they are actual and significant facts. Exceptions are just as real as probabilities. The premise of probability simultaneously postulates the existence of the improbable.

Wherever and whenever the collective unconscious (the basis of our psyche) comes into play, the possibility arises that something will happen which contradicts our rationalistic prejudices. Our consciousness performs a selective function and is in itself the product of selection, whereas the collective unconscious is simply Nature – and since Nature contains everything it also contains the unknown. It is beyond truth and error, independent of the interference of consciousness, and therefore often completely at odds with the intentions and attitudes of the ego.

So far as we can see, the collective unconscious is identical with Nature to the extent that Nature herself, including matter, is unknown to us. I have nothing against the assumption that the psyche is a quality of matter or matter the concrete aspect of the psyche, provided that 'psyche' is defined as the collective unconscious. In my opinion the collective unconscious is the preconscious aspect of things on the 'animal' or instinctive level of the psyche. Everything that is stated or manifested by the psyche is an expression of the nature of things, whereof man is a part.

Just as in physics we cannot observe nuclear processes directly, so there can be no direct observation of the contents of the collective unconscious. In both cases their actual nature can be inferred only from their effects – just as the trajectory of a nuclear particle in a Wilson chamber[8] can be traced only by observing the condensation trail that follows its movement and thus makes it visible.

In practice we observe the archetypal 'traces' primarily in dreams, where they become perceptible as psychic forms. But this is not the only way they reach perception: they can appear objectively and concretely in the form of physical facts just as well. In this case the observation is not an endopsychic perception (fantasy, intuition, vision, hallucination, etc.) but a real outer object which behaves as if it were motivated or evoked by, or as if it were expressing, a thought corresponding to the archetype. Take for instance my case of the scarab: at the moment my patient was telling me her dream a real 'scarab' tried to get into the room, as if it had understood that it must play its mythological role as a symbol of rebirth.[9] Even inanimate objects behave occasionally in the same way – meteorological phenomena, for instance.

Since I assume that our instincts (i.e., archetypes) are biological facts and not arbitrary opinions, I do not believe that synchronistic (or Psi-) phenomena are due to any supranormal (psychic) faculties but rather that they are *bound to occur* under certain conditions if space, time, and causality are not axiomatic but merely statistical truths. They occur spontaneously and not because we think we possess a special faculty for perceiving them. For this reason I do not think in terms of concepts like 'telepathy', 'precognition', or 'psychokinesis'.

In the same way, the archetype is not evoked by a conscious act of the will; experience shows that it is activated, independently of the will, in a psychic situation that needs compensating by an archetype. One might even speak of a spontaneous archetypal intervention. The language of religion calls these happenings 'God's will' – quite correctly in so far as this refers to the peculiar behaviour of the archetype, its spontaneity and its functional relation to the actual situation.

The situation may be indicative of illness or danger to life, for instance. Consciousness feels such a situation to be overwhelming in so far as it knows no way of meeting it effectively. In this predicament, even people who can boast of no particular religious belief find themselves compelled by fear to utter a fervent prayer: the archetype of a 'helpful divine being' is constellated by their submission and may eventually intervene with an unexpected influx of strength, or an unforeseen saving impulse, producing at the last moment a turn in the threatening situation which is felt to be miraculous. Such crises have occurred countless times in human history. They are the lot of man, who is exposed to the vicissitudes of Nature and constantly gets into situations where he must call on instinct because his reason fails. Instinct appears in myths and in dreams as the motif of the helpful animal, the guardian spirit, the good angel, the helper in need, the saint, saviour, etc. 'God is nearest where the need is greatest'. An 'instinct' warns birds and quadrupeds of impending catastrophes, and even humans are sometimes gifted with second sight. Emergencies of other kinds, as we know from experience, evoke the archetypes that correspond to them.

Hence the archetype has a compensatory effect, as do most of our more important dreams. Because of its ubiquity, the archetype can by its very nature manifest itself not only in the individual directly concerned but in another person or even in several people at once – for instance, in parallel dreams, the 'transmission' of which should be regarded more as a Psi-phenomenon than anything else. Similarly, collective psychoses are based on a constellated archetype, though of course this fact is not taken into account at all. In this respect our attitude is still characterized by a prodigious unconsciousness.

I must add, however, that I have observed and also partially analysed people who seemed to possess a supranormal faculty and were able to make use of it at will. But the apparently supranormal faculty consisted in their already being in, or voluntarily putting themselves into, a state corresponding to an archetypal constellation – a state of numinous possession in which synchronistic phenomena become possible and even, to some extent, probable. This faculty was clearly coupled with a religious attitude which enabled them to give suitable expression to their sense of the ego's subordination to the archetype. In one such case I predicted a catastrophic end if the patient abandoned this attitude. He did and he actually lost his life.[10] The religious tendency is obvious enough in nearly all serious-minded mediums. As a rule they cannot exploit their 'art' for egoistic purposes; and this proves that their faculty is not subject to the will of the ego but owes its existence rather to the overriding dominance of the unconscious.

I therefore think it would be advisable to consider Psi-phenomena in the first place as *sua sponte* facts and not as supranormal perceptions. The uncertainty of their relation to time and space does not necessarily depend on a supranormality of our perceptions but rather on the relativity and only partial validity of time and space categories. Most of the cases of Psi-perception are due to the presence of a constellated archetype, which produces an *abaissement du niveau mental* (numinosity, emotion). Under such a condition unconscious contents become manifest, i.e., can be perceived by the normal sense organs. Thus, for example, psychokinesis or extrusions of ectoplasm are objective facts and not intuitions or hallucinations. The medium producing these effects is in a markedly passive state (trance), which shows that an *abaissement* – the elimination of consciously controlled psychic activity – is needed in order to give spontaneous phenomena a chance. Hence the universal belief that 'spiritual agencies' are at work – agents that do not coincide with the conscious psyche. The phenomena may be purely psychic or of a material nature too. This latter fact is an indication that 'psyche' and 'matter' are not basically incommensurable, but may perhaps be qualities of one and the same existential being.

Hoping I have made myself understandable, I remain,

Yours sincerely, C.G. JUNG

NOTES

1 [R. Recalled 'the delightful occasion of the luncheon party in New York'. It took place in the summer of 1937 when Jung was in the US for his Terry Lectures at Yale, and was the only time he and Rhine met personally.]

2 [That Jung write down his observations and reflections on parapsychological problems. He did so to some extent in 'Synchronicity: An Acausally Connecting Principle' (orig. 1952), and also in *Memories*, esp. Ch. XI: 'On Life After Death'.]

3 [R. Took up this suggestion in a letter of 30 Oct; Jung's answers appear in his letter to Rhine of Nov. 45.]

4 [As suggested by Jung (Rhine, 18 Sept. 45) R. submitted the following questions:
   a What do you think is the proper relation of parapsychology to the general science of psychology?
   b What is your view of the mind-body relation, and to what extent is parapsychology of help on this question?
   c What, in your judgment, has parapsychology taught us regarding the character of the human psyche?
   d To what extent do you see a useful relation between parapsychology and psychiatry?
   e Can you interpret the experimental findings of parapsychology in extrasensory perception and its apparent reach beyond the limits of space and time as we think of them, in terms of your views of the human personality? I would particularly appreciate having your account of how precognition can be explained in your terms. Does this allow for volitional freedom?
   Jung's answers give his preliminary formulations which were clarified seven years later in his work on synchronicity.]

5 [Cf., Rhine, 27 Nov. 34.]

6 [President, Cambridge University Society for Research in Parapsychology. – The original English version of this letter was translated into German by H. Bender (cf., Bender, 12 Jan. 58) for publication in his *Zeitschrift für Parapsychologie* and appeared in V:1 (1961), with corrections and additions by Jung. The German version was subsequently translated into English by Hildegard Nagel and was published in *Spring*, 1961, which version is reproduced here with minor modifications.]

7 ['Synchronicity', *CW* 8, ch. 2.]

8 [The 'cloud chamber', developed by the English physicist C.T.R. Wilson, is an apparatus for observing the tracks made by electrically charged particles. For this discovery he received the Nobel Prize for Physics in 1927.]

9 ['Synchronicity', par. 843, and Appendix, par. 982.]

10 [The case of the mountaineer dreaming of stepping off into empty space, described in 'Child Development and Education', *CW* 17, pars. 117ff., and in 'The Practical Use of Dream Analysis', *CW* 16, pars. 323f.]

7   Jung's astrological experiment

'An Astrological Experiment' (1958)[1] (*CW* 18)

1174   In the Swiss edition[2] I purposely set out the results of the astrological statistics in tabular form in this chapter, so that the reader could gain some insight into the behaviour of the figures – in other words, see for himself how fortuitous these results were. Subsequently, I wanted to suppress that account of the experiment in the English edition and for a very peculiar reason indeed. That is, it has been forcibly borne in on me that practically nobody has understood it the right way, despite – or perhaps because – of the fact that I took the trouble to describe the experiment in great detail and in all its vicissitudes. Since it involved the use of statistics and comparative frequencies, I had the (as it now seems) unlucky idea that it would be helpful to present the resultant figures in tabular form. But evidently the suggestive effect emanating from statistical tables is so strong that nobody can rid himself of the notion that such an array of figures is somehow connected with the tendentious desire to *prove* something. Nothing could have been further from my mind, because all I intended to do was to describe a certain sequence of events in all its aspects. This altogether too unassuming intention was misunderstood all round, with the consequence that the meaning of the whole exposition went by the board.

1175   I am not going to commit this mistake again, but shall make my point at once by anticipating the result: the experiment shows how synchronicity plays havoc with statistical material. Even the choice of my material seems to have thrown my readers into confusion, since it is concerned with *astrological* statistics. One can easily imagine how obnoxious such a choice must be to a prudish intellectualism. Astrology, we are told, is unscientific, absolute nonsense, and everything to do with it is branded as rank superstition. In such a dubious context, how could columns of figures mean anything except an attempt to furnish proofs in favour of astrology, proofs whose invalidity is a foregone conclusion? I have already said that there was never any question of that – but what can words do against numerical tables?

1176   We hear so much of astrology nowadays that I determined to inquire a little more closely into the empirical foundations of this intuitive method.

For this reason I picked on the following question: *How do the conjunctions and oppositions of the sun, moon, Mars, Venus, ascendant and descendant behave in the horoscopes of married people?* The sum of all these aspects amounts to fifty.

1177   The material to be examined, namely, marriage horoscopes, was obtained from friendly donors in Zurich, London, Rome and Vienna. The horoscopes, or rather the birth data, were piled up in chronological order just as the post brought them in. The misunderstanding already began here, as several astrological authorities informed me that my procedure was quite unsuited to evaluating the marriage relationship. I thank these amiable counsellors, but on my side there was never any intention of evaluating marriage astrologically but only of investigating the question raised above. As the material only trickled in very slowly I was unable to restrain my curiosity any longer, and I also wanted to test out the methods to be employed. I therefore took the 360 horoscopes (i.e., 180 pairs) that had so far accumulated and gave the material to my co-worker, Dr Liliane Frey-Rohn, to be analysed. I called these 180 pairs the 'first batch'.

1178   Examination of this batch showed that the conjunction of sun (masculine) and moon (feminine) was the most frequent of all the 50 aspects, occurring in 10 per cent of all cases. The second batch, evaluated later, consisted of 440 additional horoscopes (220 pairs) and showed as the most frequent aspect a moon-moon conjunction (10.9 per cent). A third batch, consisting of 166 horoscopes (83 pairs), showed as the most frequent aspect the ascendant-moon conjunction (9.6 per cent).

1179   What interested me most to begin with was, of course, the question of probability: were the maximum results obtained 'significant' figures or not; that is, were they improbable or not? Calculations undertaken by a mathematician showed unmistakably that the average frequency of 10 per cent in all three batches is far from representing a significant figure. Its probability is much too great; in other words, there is no ground for assuming that our maximum frequencies are more than mere dispersions due to chance. Thus far the result of our statistics (which nevertheless cover nearly one thousand horoscopes) is disappointing for astrology. The material is, however, much too scanty for us to be able to draw from it any conclusions either for or against.

1180   But if we look at the results qualitatively, we are immediately struck by the fact that in all three batches it is a *moon conjunction*, and what is more – a point which the astrologer will doubtless appreciate – a conjunction of moon and sun, moon and moon, moon and ascendant, respectively. The sun indicates the month, the moon the day, and the ascendant the 'moment' of birth. The positions of sun, moon and ascendant form the three main pillars of the horoscope. It is altogether probable that a moon conjunction should occur once, but that it should occur three times is extremely improbable (the improbability increases by the square each time), and that it should single out precisely the three main positions of the horoscope from among forty-seven other possibilities is something supranormal and looks like the most gorgeous falsification in favour of astrology.

1181   These results, as simple as they are unexpected, were consistently misunderstood by the statisticians. They thought I wanted to prove something with my set of figures, whereas I only wished to give an ocular demonstration of their 'chance' nature. It is naturally a little unexpected that a set of figures, meaningless in themselves, should 'arrange' a result which everybody agrees to be improbable. It seems in fact to be an instance of that possibility which Spencer-Brown has in mind when he says that 'the results of the best-designed and most rigorously observed experiments in psychical research are chance results after all', and that 'the concept of chance can cover a wider natural field than we previously suspected'.[3] In other words what the previous statistical view obliged us to regard as 'significant', that is, as a quasi-intentional grouping or arrangement, must be regarded equally as belonging to the realm of chance, which means nothing less than that the whole concept of probability must be revised. One can also interpret Spencer-Brown's view as meaning that under certain circumstances the quality of 'pseudo-intention' attaches to chance, or – if we wish to avoid a negative formulation – that chance can 'create' meaningful arrangements that look as if a causal intention had been at work. But that is precisely what I mean by 'synchronicity', and is what I wanted to demonstrate in the report on my astrological experiment. Naturally I did not embark on the experiment for the purpose of achieving, or in anticipation of, this unexpected result, which no one could have foreseen; I was only curious to find out what sort of numbers would turn up in an investigation of this kind. This wish seemed suspicious not only to certain astrologers but also to my friendly mathematical adviser, who saw fit to warn me against thinking that my maximal figures would be a proof of the astrological thesis. Neither before nor afterwards was there any thought of such proof, besides which my experiment was arranged in a way most unsuited to that purpose, as my astrological critics had already pointed out.

1182   Since most people believe that numbers have been *invented* or thought out by man, and are therefore nothing but concepts of quantities, containing nothing that was not previously put into them by the human intellect, it was naturally very difficult for me to put my question in any other form. But it is equally possible that numbers were *found* or discovered. In that case they are not only concepts but something more – autonomous entities which somehow contain more than just quantities. Unlike concepts they are based not on any psychic assumption but on the quality of being themselves, on a 'so-ness' that cannot be expressed by an intellectual concept. Under these circumstances they might easily be endowed with qualities that have still to be discovered. Also one could, as with all autonomous beings, raise the question of their behaviour; for instance one could ask what numbers do when they are intended to express something as archetypal as astrology. For astrology is the last remnant, now applied

to the stars, of that fateful assemblage of gods whose numinosity can still
be felt despite the critical procedures of our scientific age. In no previous
age, however 'superstitious', was astrology so widespread and so highly
esteemed as it is today.

1183   I must confess that I incline to the view that numbers were as much
found as invented, and that in consequence they possess a relative
autonomy analogous to that of the archetypes. They would then have, in
common with the latter, the quality of being pre-existent to consciousness,
and hence, on occasion, of conditioning it rather than being conditioned
by it. The archetypes too, as *a priori* forms of representation, are as much
found as invented: they are *discovered* inasmuch as one did not know of
their unconscious autonomous existence, and *invented* by the mind inasmuch as their presence was inferred from analogous representational
structures. Accordingly it would seem that natural numbers must possess
an archetypal character. If that is so, then not only would certain numbers
have a relation to and an effect on certain archetypes, but the reverse would
also be true. The first case is equivalent to number magic, but the second
is equivalent to my question whether numbers, in conjunction with the
numinous assemblage of gods which the horoscope represents, would
show a tendency to behave in a special way.

1184   All reasonable people, especially mathematicians, are acutely concerned with the question of what we can do by means of numbers. Only
a few devote any attention to the question of what, in so far as they are
autonomous, numbers do in themselves. The question sounds so absurd
that one hardly dares to utter it in decent intellectual society. I could not
predict what result my scandalous statistics would show. I had to wait
and see. And as a matter of fact my figures behaved in so obliging a
fashion that an astrologer can probably appreciate them far better than a
mathematician. Owing to their excessively strict adherence to reason,
mathematicians seem unable to see beyond the fact that in each separate
case my result has too great a probability to prove anything about
astrology. Of course it doesn't, because it was never intended to do any
such thing, and I never for a moment believed that the maximum, falling
each time on a moon conjunction, represented a so-called significant
figure. Yet in spite of this critical attitude a number of mistakes were
made in working out and computing the statistics, which all without
exception contrived to bring about the most favourable possible result for
astrology. As though to punish him for his well-meaning warning, the
worst mistake of all fell to the lot of my mathematician, who at first
calculated far too small a probability for the individual maxima, and was
thus unwittingly deceived by the unconscious in the interests of astrological prestige.

1185   Such lapses can easily be explained by a secret support for astrology in
face of the violently prejudiced attitude of the conscious mind. But this
explanation does not suffice in the case of the extremely significant overall

result, which with the help of quite fortuitous numbers produced the picture of the classical marriage tradition in astrology, namely the conjunction of the moon with the three principal positions of the horoscope, when there were forty-seven other possibilities to choose from. Tradition since the time of Ptolemy predicts that the moon conjunction with the sun or moon of the partner is the marriage characteristic. Because of its position in the horoscope, the ascendant has just as much importance as the sun and moon. In view of this tradition one could not have wished for a better result. The figure giving the probability of this predicted concurrence, unlike the first-obtained maximum of 10 per cent, is indeed highly significant and deserves emphasizing, although we are no more able to account for its occurrence and for its apparent meaningfulness than we can account for the results of Rhine's experiments, which prove the existence of a perception independent of the space-time barrier.

1186   Naturally I do not think that this experiment or any other report on happenings of this kind proves anything; it merely points to something that even science can no longer overlook – namely, that its truths are in essence statistical and are therefore not absolute. Hence there is in nature a background of acausality, freedom, and meaningfulness which behaves complementarily to determinism, mechanism and meaninglessness; and it is to be assumed that such phenomena are observable. Owing to their peculiar nature, however, they will hardly be prevailed upon to lay aside the chance character that makes them so questionable. If they did this they would no longer be what they are – acausal, undetermined, meaningful.[4]

1187   [Pure causality is only meaningful when used for the creation and functioning of an efficient instrument or machine by an intelligence standing outside this process and independent of it. A self-running process that operates entirely by its own causality, i.e., by absolute necessity, is meaningless. One of my critics accuses me of having too rigid a conception of causality. He has obviously not considered that if cause and effect were not necessarily[5] connected there would hardly be any meaning in speaking of causality at all. My critic makes the same mistake as the famous scientist[6] who refuses to believe that God played dice when he created the world. He fails to see that if God did not play dice he had no choice but to create a (from the human point of view) meaningless machine. Since this question involves a transcendental judgment there can be no final answer to it, only a paradoxical one. *Meaning arises not from causality but from freedom, i.e., from acausality.*]

1188   [Modern physics has deprived causality of its axiomatic character. Thus, when we explain natural events we do so by means of an instrument which is not quite reliable. Hence an element of uncertainty always attaches to our judgment, because – theoretically, at least – we might always be dealing with an exception to the rule which can only be registered negatively by the statistical method. No matter how small this chance is, it nevertheless exists. Since causality is our only means of explanation and since it is only relatively valid, we explain the world by applying causality in a paradoxical way, both positively and negatively: A is the cause of B and possibly not. The negation can be omitted in the great majority of cases. But it is my contention that it cannot be omitted in the case of phenomena which are relatively independent of space and time. As the time-factor is indispensable to the concept of causality, one cannot speak of causality in a case where the time-factor is eliminated (as in precognition). *Statistical truth leaves a gap open for acausal phenomena.* And since our causalistic explanation of nature contains the possibility of its own negation, it belongs to the category *of transcendental judgments*, which are paradoxical or antinomian. That is so because nature is still beyond us and because science gives us only an average picture of the world, but not a true one. If human society consisted of average individuals only, it would be a sad sight indeed.]

1189   From a rational point of view, an experiment like the one I conducted is completely valueless, for the oftener it is repeated the more probable becomes its lack of results. But that this is also *not* so is proved by the very old tradition, which would hardly have come about had not these 'lucky hits' often happened in the past. They behave like Rhine's results: they are exceedingly improbable, and yet they happen so persistently that they even compel us to criticize the foundations of our probability calculus, or at least its applicability to certain kinds of material.

1190   When analysing unconscious processes I often had occasion to observe synchronistic or ESP phenomena, and I therefore turned my attention to the psychic conditions underlying them. I believe I have found that they nearly always occur in the region of archetypal constellations, that is, in situations which have either activated an archetype or were evoked by the autonomous activity of an archetype. It is these observations which led me to the idea of getting the combination of archetypes found in astrology to give a quantitatively measurable answer. In this I succeeded, as the result shows; indeed one could say that the organizing factor responded with enthusiasm to my prompting. The reader must pardon this anthropomorphism, which I know positively invites misinterpretation; it fits in excellently well with the psychological facts and aptly describes the emotional background from which synchronistic phenomena emerge.

1191   I am aware that I ought at this point to discuss the psychology of the archetype, but this has been done so often and in such detail elsewhere[7] that I do not wish to repeat myself now.

1192   I am also aware of the enormous impression of improbability made by events of this kind, and that their comparative rarity does not make them any more probable. The statistical method therefore excludes them, as they do not belong to the average run of events.

From: 'Letters on Synchronicity' (1950–55) (*CW* 18)

2 March 1950

Dear Professor Fierz,

1197   My best thanks for all the trouble you have taken. You have given me just what I hoped for from you – an objective opinion as to the significance of the statistical figures obtained from my material of now 400 marriages. Only I am amazed that my statistics have amply confirmed the traditional view that the sun-moon aspects are marriage characteristics, which is further underlined by the value you give for the moon-moon conjunction, namely 0.125 per cent.

For myself I regard the result as very unsatisfactory and have therefore stopped collecting further material, as the approximation to the probable mean with increasing material seems to me suspicious.

1198   Although the figure of 0.125 per cent is still entirely within the bounds of possibility, I would nevertheless like to ask you, for the sake of clarity, whether one may regard this value as 'significant' in so far as its represents a relatively low probability that coincides with the historical tradition? May one at least *conjecture* that it argues for rather than against the tradition (since Ptolemy)? I fully share your view of divinatory methods as *catalysts* of intuition. But the result of these statistics has made me somewhat sceptical, especially in connection with the latest ESP experiments which have obtained probabilities of 10^{-31}. These experiments and the whole experience of ESP are sufficient proof that meaningful coincidences do exist. There is thus some probability that the divinatory methods actually produce synchronistic phenomena. These seem to me most clearly discernible in astrology. The statistical findings undoubtedly show that the astrological correspondences are nothing more than chance. The statistical method is based on the assumption of a continuum of uniform objects. But synchronicity is a qualified individual event which is ruined by the statistical method; conversely, synchronicity abolishes the assumption of [a continuum of] uniform objects and so ruins the statistical method. It seems, therefore, that a *complementarity relationship* exists between synchronicity and causality. Rhine's statistics have proved the existence of synchronicity *in spite of unsuitable methods*. This aroused false hopes in me as regards astrology. In Rhine's experiments the phenomenon of synchronicity is an extremely simple matter. The situation in astrology is incomparably more complicated and is therefore more sensitive to the statistical method, which emphasizes just what is least characteristic of synchronicity, that is, uniformity. Now my results, mischievously enough, exactly confirm the old tradition although they are as much due to chance as were the results in the old days. So again something has happened that shows all the signs of synchronicity, namely a 'meaningful coincidence' or 'Just So' story. Obviously the ancients must have experienced the same thing quite by chance, otherwise no such tradition could ever have arisen. I don't believe any ancient astrologer statistically examined 800 horoscopes for marriage characteristics. He always had only small batches at his disposal, which did not ruin the synchronistic phenomenon and could therefore, as in my case, establish the prevalence of moon-moon and moon-sun conjunctions, although these are bound to diminish with a higher range of numbers. All synchronistic phenomena, which are more highly qualified than ESP, are as such unprovable, that is to say a single authenticated instance is sufficient proof in principle, just as one does not need to produce ten thousand duckbilled platypi in order to prove they exist. It seems to me synchronicity represents a *direct act of creation* which manifests itself as chance. The statistical proof of natural conformity to law is therefore only a very limited way of describing nature, since it grasps only uniform events. But nature is essentially discontinuous, i.e., subject to chance. To describe it we need a principle of discontinuity. In psychology this is the drive to individuation, in biology it is differentiation, but in nature it is the 'meaningful coincidence', that is to say synchronicity.

1199   Forgive me for putting forward these somewhat abstruse-looking re-flections. They are new to me too and for that reason are still rather chaotic like everything *in statu nascendi*.

Thanks again for your trouble! I should be glad to have your impressions.

Best regards, C.G. JUNG

Letter to Hans Bender[8] (12 February 1958), *Letters*, vol. 2, pp. 414–16

Dear Colleague,

Your prefatory note[9] on synchronicity is perfectly adequate up to the point where you speak of the 'synchronistic effect that was sought'. This effect was, if I may be permitted the remark, not sought at all but found, and it was found probably because the experiment was so arranged that the restrictions were reduced to a minimum; in other words, wide room was left for the play of chance. If you give the 'synchronistic arrangement' the smallest possible play, the play of chance is obviously restricted and the synchronistic 'effect' thereby hindered. The synchronistic phenomenon in my experiment consists in the fact that the classical expectations of astrology were confirmed in all three batches [of marriage horoscopes], which is extremely improbable, although taken individually the figures are not significant. Such a result has in principle nothing whatever to do with astrology, but could occur just as well in any other set of statistics. The astrological experiment is by its very nature a lucky hit; were it not so it would have to be causal. But presumably it is causal only in the most minimal degree. You could therefore dismiss it as a mere *lusus naturae* if nobody wondered about the so-called chance. The psychologist, who is concerned with the processes in the unconscious, knows that these remarkable 'chances' happen chiefly when archetypal conditions are present, and it often looks as if the inner psychic disposition were reflected either in another person or in an animal or in circumstances generally, thanks to a simultaneous and causally independent parallel disposition. Hence the accompanying phenomena in cases of death: the clock stops, a picture falls off the wall, a glass cracks, etc. Until now such phenomena were furnished with *ad hoc* explanations and with names like telepathy, clairvoyance, precognition, psychokinesis, and so on. But that explains nothing, even when certain of these phenomena are compared with radar. I have never yet heard of a radar beam that could pick up a point in the future. It is probably better, therefore, not to put forward any such *ad hoc* analogies or special fantasy hypotheses of this kind, but to lump together all these phenomena, which exceed the range of physical probability, under the uniform aspect of the meaningful 'lucky hit' and to investigate under what emotional conditions these coincidences occur; and then, following Rhine, to demonstrate the existence of these phenomena with the largest possible numbers. My line of enquiry aimed at the psychic conditions of their occurrence, and I rejected any semi-physicistic explanations in terms of energy.

I hope I have expressed myself clearly. There is, if I may be permitted the further remark, no particular meaning in investigating marriages. You could just as well observe a beehive and then, under a particular psychic condition, statistically determine the number of bees flying in and out, or watch a stony slope and see how many pebbles roll down. It is obvious that, if you choose an experimental set-up that allows chance the least possible play, you will, if you conduct it skilfully, also get the least possible chances out of it; that is, you have effectively prevented a synchronistic 'effect' from taking place.

It seems to be very difficult to form a picture of the Geulincx-Leibniz lateral connection of events[10] and to rid oneself of the causal hypothesis. Chance is an event, too, and if it didn't exist causality would be axiomatic. Meaningful coincidences present a tremendous problem which it is impossible to overestimate. Leibniz as well as Schopenhauer[11] had inklings of it, but they gave a false answer because they started with an axiomatic causality. With friendly greetings and best thanks,

Yours sincerely, C.G. JUNG

NOTES

1 [A condensed version of ch. II of 'Synchronicity: An Acausal Connecting Principle' (*CW* 8). Published as 'Ein astrologisches Experiment', *Zeitschrift für Parapsychologie und Grenzgebiete der Psychologie* (Bern), I:2/3 (May 1958), 81–92. A long prefatory note by the editor, Hans Bender, quoted a letter to him from Jung, 12 Feb. 1958, in further clarification; it is in *Letters*, ed. G. Adler, vol. 2. [See above, pp. 119–20.–*RM*]].

2 Jung and Pauli, *Naturerklärung und Psyche*, 1952.

3 [G. Spencer-Brown, 'Statistical Significance in Psychical Research', *Nature*, vol. 172, 25 July 1953, p. 154.]

4 [The following two paragraphs, not represented in the *Zeitschrift* version, were added by Jung respectively to the German MS and to a letter containing queries sent to him by the translator, 23 April 1954.]

5 With all due respect to their statistical nature! (C.G.J.)

6 [Albert Einstein.]

7 [Cf., 'On the Nature of the Psyche', *CW* 8, pars. 397ff.]

8 [Professor of psychology, U. Of Freiburg im Breslau, Germany. Director of the Institut für Grenzgebiete der Psychologie und Psychohygiene and editor of the *Zeitschrift für Parapsychologie und Grenzgebiete der Psychologie* (Bern).]

9 [B. had drafted a prefatory note to Jung's 'Ein astrologisches Experiment', later published in the above *Zeitschrift*, 1:2/3 (May 1958), 81–92. (In *CW* 18 [See above, pp. 112–17.–*RM*].) The note appeared together with Jung's letter. The article was written as a simplified explanation of ch. 2 of 'Synchronicity', *CW* 8. This chapter had led to many misunderstandings, as if it were meant to confirm astrological causality. Cf., Metman, 27 Mar. 54, n. 2.]

10 [The lateral connection of events refers to Leibniz's 'System of Communication between Substances' according to which 'From the beginning God has made each of these two substances [body and soul] of such a nature that merely by following its own peculiar laws, received with its being, it nevertheless accords with the other . . .'. He compares body and soul to two synchronized clocks, an idea Leibniz may have taken over from Geulincx. Cf., 'Synchronicity', par. 937 and n. 58, also par. 948.]

11 [Cf., Bender, 10 Apr. 58, n. 2.]

8   Physics

Letter to Carl Seelig[1] (25 February 1953), *Letters*, vol. 2, pp. 108–9

Dear Dr Seelig

I got to know Albert Einstein[2] through one of his pupils, a Dr Hopf[3] if I remember correctly. Professor Einstein was my guest on several occasions at dinner, when, as you have heard, Adolf Keller[4] was present on one of them and on others Professor Eugen Bleuler, a psychiatrist and my former chief. These were very early days when Einstein was developing his first theory of relativity.[5] He tried to instil into us the elements of it, more or less successfully. As non-mathematicians we psychiatrists had difficulty in following his argument. Even so, I understood enough to form a powerful impression of him. It was above all the simplicity and directness of his genius as a thinker that impressed me mightily and exerted a lasting influence on my own intellectual work. It was Einstein who first started me off thinking about a possible relativity of time as well as space, and their psychic conditionality. More than thirty years later this stimulus led to my relation with the physicist Professor W. Pauli and to my thesis of psychic synchronicity. With Einstein's departure from Zurich my relation with him ceased, and I hardly think he has any recollection of me. One can scarcely imagine a greater contrast than that between the mathematical and the psychological mentality. The one is extremely quantitative and the other just as extremely qualitative.

With kind regards,

Yours sincerely, C.G. JUNG

Letter to Wolfgang Pauli[6] (29 October 1934), *Letters*, vol. 1, pp. 174–6

Dear Professor Pauli,

Best thanks for kindly sending me Jordan's paper.[7] I think this paper should be published, as it is concerned with the actual changeover of the physicist's mode of observation to the psychological field. This paper was inevitable. Having come to the conclusion that the observed is also a disturbance by the observer, the consistent investigator of the unknown interior of the atom could not help seeing that the nature of the observing process becomes perceptible in the disturbance caused by the observation. To put it more simply, if you look long enough into a dark hole you perceive what is looking in. This is also the principle of cognition in yoga, which derives all cognition from the absolute emptiness of consciousness. This method of cognition is thus a special instance of the introspective investigation of the psyche in general.

With regard to Jordan's reference to parapsychological phenomena, clairvoyance in space is of course one of the most obvious phenomena that demonstrate the relative non-existence of our empirical space picture. In order to supplement this argument, he would also have to adduce clairvoyance in time, which would demonstrate the relativity of our time picture. Jordan naturally sees these phenomena from the standpoint of the physicist, whereas I start from that of the psychologist, namely, from the fact of the collective unconscious, as you have so rightly noted, which represents a layer of the psyche in which individual differences of consciousness are more or less obliterated. But if individual consciousnesses are blotted out in the unconscious, then all perception in the unconscious takes place as though in a single person. Jordan says that senders and receivers in the same conscious space simultaneously observe the same object. One could invert this proposition and say that in unconscious 'space' senders and receivers are the same perceiving subject. As you see, I as a psychologist would speak from the standpoint of the common space in which two or more observers are present. Jordan's view, carried to its logical conclusion, would lead to the assumption of an absolutely unconscious space in which an infinity of observers observe the same object. The psychological version would be: in the unconscious there is only one observer who observes an infinity of objects.

If you should draw Jordan's attention to my writings, perhaps I may recommend you to mention – besides the essay already cited by you[8] – 'Basic Postulates of Analytical Psychology' in the same volume.[9] As regards the collective unconscious, there is in an earlier volume, *Seelenprobleme der Gegenwart*, an essay where I treat this theme in greater detail, namely 'The Structure of the Psyche'.[10] I would be grateful if I could keep Jordan's paper a while longer.

It has just occurred to me that with regard to the relativity of time there is a book by one of Eddington's pupils, Dunne, *An Experiment with Time*,[11] in which he treats clairvoyance in time in the same way as Jordan treats clairvoyance in space. He postulates an infinite number of time dimensions roughly corresponding to Jordan's 'intermediate stages'. It would interest me very much to hear what your attitude is to Dunne's arguments.

I also thank you for your personal news and wish you further progress. With kindest regards,

Yours sincerely, C.G. JUNG

Letter to Pascual Jordan[12] (10 November 1934), *Letters*, vol. 1, pp. 176–8

Dear Professor Jordan,

Thank you very much for kindly sending me your offprints,[13] some of which I already knew.

Although I am no mathematician, I am interested in the advances of modern physics, which is coming ever closer to the nature of the psyche, as I have seen for a long time. I have often talked about it with Pauli. One is, to be sure, concerned here with aspects of the psyche which can be mentioned only with the greatest caution, as one is exposed to too many misunderstandings. Probably you will get a taste of them in time. So long as you keep to the physical side of the world, you can say pretty well anything that is more or less provable without incurring the prejudice of being unscientific, but if you touch on the psychological problem the little man, who also goes in for science, gets mad.

With respect to your paper[14] I can only tell you that I have read it with the greatest interest. It marks an extremely memorable moment in the history of the mind, the moment when the circle closes,[15] or when the cutting of the tunnel from opposite sides of the mountain is complete. I don't know whether Pauli has told you of the letter I wrote him after reading your MS. If not, I am taking the liberty of sending you a carbon copy. At the same time I would like to tell you that I have asked my bookseller to send you the book containing my essay 'The Structure of the Psyche'.

As to the hypothesis of the collective unconscious, not nearly all the material bearing on this matter has yet been published. For the reasons mentioned above, I must restrict myself at present wholly to the parallelism of psychic phenomena. With this in mind, I have also brought out a little book with the late Richard Wilhelm, which deals with a Taoist text called *The Secret of the Golden Flower*. There you will find those parallels of which I speak. The strange cases of parallelism in time, which are commonly called coincidences but which I call synchronistic phenomena,[16] are very frequent in the observation of the unconscious. In this connection there is a rather crazy book by Kammerer, *Das Gesetz der Serie*,[17] which may be known to you. It may be said in passing that Chinese science is based on the principle of synchronicity,[18] or parallelism in time, which is naturally regarded by us as superstition. The standard work on this subject is the *I Ching*, of which Richard Wilhelm brought out a translation with an excellent commentary.

Again with best thanks and kindest regards,

Yours sincerely, C.G. JUNG

From: 'On the Nature of the Psyche' (1947/1954) (*CW* 8)

439 The application of statistical laws to processes of atomic magnitude in physics has a noteworthy correspondence in psychology, so far as psychology investigates the bases of consciousness by pursuing the conscious processes until they lose themselves in darkness and unintelligibility, and nothing more can be seen but effects which have an *organizing* influence on the contents of consciousness.[19] Investigation of these effects yields the singular fact that they proceed from an unconscious, i.e., objective, reality which behaves at the same time like a subjective one – in other words, like a consciousness. Hence the reality underlying the unconscious effects includes the observing subject and is therefore constituted in a way that we cannot conceive. It is, at one and the same time, absolute subjectivity and universal truth, for in principle it can be shown to be present everywhere, which certainly cannot be said of conscious contents of a personalistic nature. The elusiveness, capriciousness, haziness, and uniqueness that the lay mind always associates with the idea of the psyche applies only to consciousness, and not to the absolute unconscious. The qualitatively rather than quantitatively definable units with which the unconscious works, namely the archetypes, therefore have a nature that *cannot with certainty be designated as psychic.*

440 Although I have been led by purely psychological considerations to doubt the exclusively psychic nature of the archetypes, psychology sees itself obliged to revise its 'only psychic' assumptions in the light of the physical findings too. Physics has demonstrated, as plainly as could be wished, that in the realm of atomic magnitudes an observer is postulated in objective reality, and that only on this condition is a satisfactory scheme of explanation possible. This means that a subjective element attaches to the physicist's world picture, and secondly that a connection necessarily exists between the psyche to be explained and the objective space-time continuum. Since the physical continuum is inconceivable it follows that we can form no picture of its psychic aspect either, which also necessarily exists. Nevertheless, the relative or partial identity of psyche and physical continuum is of the greatest importance theoretically, because it brings with it a tremendous simplification by bridging over the seeming incommensurability between the physical world and the psychic, not of course in any concrete way, but from the physical side by means of mathematical equations, and from the psychological side by means of empirically derived postulates – archetypes – whose content, if any, cannot be represented to the mind. Archetypes, so far as we can observe and experience them at all, manifest themselves only through their ability to *organize* images and ideas, and this is always an unconscious process which cannot be detected until afterwards. By assimilating ideational material whose provenance in the phenomenal world is not to be contested, they become visible and *psychic*. Therefore they are recognized at first

only as psychic entities and are conceived as such, with the same right with which we base the physical phenomena of immediate perception on Euclidean space. Only when it comes to explaining psychic phenomena of a minimal degree of clarity are we driven to assume that archetypes must have a nonpsychic aspect. Grounds for such a conclusion are supplied by the phenomena of synchronicity, which are associated with the activity of unconscious operators and have hitherto been regarded, or repudiated, as 'telepathy', etc.[20] Scepticism should, however, be levelled only at incorrect theories and not at facts which exist in their own right. No unbiased observer can deny them. Resistance to the recognition of such facts rests principally on the repugnance people feel for an allegedly supernatural faculty tacked on to the psyche, like 'clairvoyance'. The very diverse and confusing aspects of these phenomena are, so far as I can see at present, completely explicable on the assumption of a psychically relative space-time continuum. As soon as a psychic content crosses the threshold of consciousness, the synchronistic marginal phenomena disappear, time and space resume their accustomed sway, and consciousness is once more isolated in its subjectivity. We have here one of those instances which can best be understood in terms of the physicist's idea of 'complementarity'. When an unconscious content passes over into consciousness its synchronistic manifestation ceases; conversely, synchronistic phenomena can be evoked by putting the subject into an unconscious state (trance). The same relationship of complementarity can be observed just as easily in all those extremely common medical cases in which certain clinical symptoms disappear when the corresponding unconscious contents are made conscious. We also know that a number of psychosomatic phenomena which are otherwise outside the control of the will can be induced by hypnosis, that is, by this same restriction of consciousness. Professor Pauli formulates the physical side of the complementarity relationship here expressed, as follows: 'It rests with the free choice of the experimenter (or observer) to decide . . . which insights he will gain and which he will lose; or, to put it in popular language, whether he will measure A and ruin B or ruin A and measure B. It does *not* rest with him, however, to gain only insights and not lose any.' This is particularly true of the relation between the physical standpoint and the psychological. Physics determines qualities without being able to measure quantities. Despite that, both sciences arrive at ideas which come significantly close to one another. The parallelism of psychological and physical explanations has already been pointed out by C.A. Meier in his essay 'Modern Physik–Moderne Psychologie.'[21] He says:

> Both sciences have, in the course of many years of independent work, amassed observations and systems of thought to match them. Both sciences have come up against certain barriers which . . . display similar basic characteristics. The object to be investigated, and the

human investigator with his organs of sense and knowledge and their extensions (measuring instruments and procedures), are indissolubly bound together. That is complementarity in physics as well as in psychology.

Between physics and psychology there is in fact 'a genuine and authentic relationship of complementarity'.

441   Once we can rid ourselves of the highly unscientific pretence that it is merely a question of chance coincidence, we shall see that synchronistic phenomena are not unusual occurrences at all, but are relatively common. This fact is in entire agreement with Rhine's 'probability-exceeding' results. The psyche is not a chaos made up of random whims and accidents, but is an objective reality to which the investigator can gain access by the methods of natural science. There are indications that psychic processes stand in some sort of energy relation to the physiological substrate. In so far as they are objective events, they can hardly be interpreted as anything but energy processes,[22] or to put it another way: in spite of the non-measurability of psychic processes, the perceptible changes effected by the psyche cannot possibly be understood except as a phenomenon of energy. This places the psychologist in a situation which is highly repugnant to the physicist: the psychologist also talks of energy although he has nothing measurable to manipulate, besides which the concept of energy is a strictly defined mathematical quantity which cannot be applied as such to anything psychic. The formula for kinetic energy, $E = mv^2/2$, contains the factors m (mass) and v (velocity), and these would appear to be incommensurable with the nature of the empirical psyche. If psychology nevertheless insists on employing its own concept of energy for the purpose of expressing the activity (ἐνέργεια) of the psyche, it is not of course being used as a mathematical formula, but only as its analogy. But note: the analogy is itself an older intuitive idea from which the concept of physical energy originally developed. The latter rests on earlier applications of an ἐνέργεια not mathematically defined, which can be traced back to the primitive or archaic idea of the 'extraordinarily potent'. This mana concept is not confined to Melanesia, but can also be found in Indonesia and on the east coast of Africa; and it still echoes in the Latin *numen* and, more faintly, in *genius* (e.g., *genius loci*). The use of the term *libido* in the newer medical psychology has surprising affinities with the primitive mana.[23] This archetypal idea is therefore far from being only primitive, but differs from the physicist's conception of energy by the fact that it is essentially qualitative and not quantitative. In psychology the exact measurement of quantities is replaced by an approximate determination of intensities, for which purpose, in strictest contrast to physics, we enlist the function of *feeling* (valuation). The latter takes the place, in psychology, of concrete measurement in physics. The psychic intensities and their graduated differences point to quantitative processes

which are inaccessible to direct observation and measurement. While psychological data are essentially qualitative, they also have a sort of latent physical energy, since psychic phenomena exhibit a certain quantitative aspect. Could these quantities be measured, the psyche would be bound to appear as having motion in space, something to which the energy formula would be applicable. Therefore, since mass and energy are of the same nature, mass and velocity would be adequate concepts for characterizing the psyche so far as it has any observable effects in space: in other words, it must have an aspect under which it would appear as mass in motion. If one is unwilling to postulate a pre-established harmony of physical and psychic events, then they can only be in a state of interaction. But the latter hypothesis requires a psyche that touches matter at some point, and, conversely, a matter with a latent psyche, a postulate not so very far removed from certain formulations of modern physics (Eddington, Jeans, and others). In this connection I would remind the reader of the existence of parapsychic phenomena whose reality value can only be appreciated by those who have had occasion to satisfy themselves by personal observation.

442   If these reflections are justified, they must have weighty consequences with regard to the nature of the psyche, since as an objective fact it would then be intimately connected not only with physiological and biological phenomena but with physical events too – and, so it would appear, most intimately of all with those that pertain to the realm of atomic physics. As my remarks may have made clear, we are concerned first and foremost to establish certain analogies, and no more than that; the existence of such analogies does not entitle us to conclude that the connection is already proven. We must, in the present state of our physical and psychological knowledge, be content with the mere resemblance to one another of certain basic reflections. The existing analogies, however, are significant enough in themselves to warrant the prominence we have given them.

NOTES

1 [(1894–1962), Swiss author, journalist and theatre critic. Cf., his *Albert Einstein. Eine dokumentarische Biographie* (1952); *Albert Einstein, Leben und Werk eines Genies unserer Zeit* (1954). He asked Jung for his impressions of Einstein. – The letter was published in *Spring*, 1971.]

2 [Einstein (1879–1955) had been living in Bern until 1909 as an examiner of patents at the Patent Office, during which period he took his Ph.D. at the University of Zurich. After publishing several papers on physical subjects, he was appointed extraordinary professor of theoretical physics at the U. in 1909, and in 1912 professor at the Federal Polytechnic (E.T.H.). Cf., *The Freud/Jung Letters*, 230J, par. 1.]

3 [Ludwig Hopf, theoretical physicist.]

4 [Cf., Keller, 26 Mar 51.]

5 [In 1905 Einstein published his famous *On the Electrodynamics of Moving Bodies*, in which the principle of relativity is mentioned for the first time.]

6 [(1900–58), Austrian theoretical physicist, later in Zurich. He received the Nobel prize for physics in 1945 for his formulation of the 'exclusion principle' (also called the 'Pauli principle'). Lectured in Zurich (where he died) and frequently met Jung for a fruitful exchange of ideas on the relations between nuclear physics and psychology. Cf., Jung and Pauli, *The Interpretation of Nature and the Psyche* (orig. 1952). P.'s contribution was 'The Influence of Archetypal Ideas on the Scientific Theories of Kepler'; Jung's was 'Synchronicity: An Acausal Connecting Principle', (*CW* 8). This letter is published with the kind permission of Frau Franka Pauli.]

7 ['Positivistische Bemerkungen über die paraphysischen Erscheinungen', later published in *Zentralblatt für Psychotherapie*, IX (1936).]

8 ['The Soul and Death', *CW* 8.]

9 [Ibid.; orig. In *Wirklichkeit der Seele*.]

10 [In *CW* 8.]

11 [John William Dunne, *An Experiment with Time* (1927). Cf., Jung, 'Synchronicity', pars. 852f.]

12 [German physicist, professor in Rostock, Berlin, and Hamburg; made important contributions to quantum physics. Cf., Jung, 'On the Nature of the Psyche', *CW* 8, par. 440, n. 131, and 'Synchronicity', *CW* 8, par. 862, no. 55.]

13 [The exact titles are not identifiable, but from a letter of Jordan's to the editor, 18 Apr. 66, they dealt with general principles of quantum mechanics and their relations to causality.]

14 [In a letter of 2 Nov. 34 accompanying the above-mentioned offprints J. wrote of his 'Positivistische Bemerkungen über die paraphysischen Erscheinungen': 'I am very pleased to hear from Pauli that he sent you a copy of an MS in which I try to integrate telepathic etc. phenomena into our scientific picture of the world – or rather to integrate them into a fundamental extension of this picture. This extension seems to me necessary on the basis of the epistemological considerations resulting from the most recent discoveries in physics and of the modern psychology of the unconscious. Pauli also drew my attention to the relationship between the concepts presented in my MS and your concept of the "collective unconscious". I am trying to get two of your works which Pauli mentioned to me. I have read with great interest your essay 'The Soul and Death' which Pauli sent me'. For the telepathic phenomena see ibid., pars. 813ff.)]

15 [Cf., 'On the Nature of the Psyche', par 439, n. 130, quoting Pauli: 'As a matter of fact the physicist would expect a psychological correspondence at this point, because the epistemological situation with regard to the concepts "conscious" and "unconscious" seems to offer a pretty close analogy to the . . . "complementarity" situation in physics. . . . It is undeniable that the development of "microphysics" has brought the way in which nature is described in this science very much closer to that of the newer psychology.']

16 [Jung coined the term 'synchronicity' to characterize 'the simultaneous occurrence of a certain psychic state with one or more external events which appear as meaningful parallels to the momentary subjective state' ('Synchronicity', par. 850). One of the earliest formulations of synchronicity is to be found in the Seminar Notes on *Dream Analysis*, autumn 1929, p. 417: 'I have invented the word *synchronicity* as a term to cover these phenomena, that is, things happening at the same moment as an expression of the same time content'.]

17 [Paul Kammerer, *Das Gesetz der Serie* (1919). (Cf., 'Synchronicity', pars. 824f.) No further letter of Jung's to Jordan before that of 1 Apr. 48 has been preserved. That there must have been some intermediate correspondence is evident from a letter of Jordan's, 17 Feb. 36, in which he thanks Jung for sending him an offprint of 'Traumsymbole des Individuationsprozesses' (*Eranos Jahrbuch* 1935), now revised as Part II, 'Individual Dream Symbolism in Relation to Alchemy', in

Psychology and Alchemy. He writes: 'I am deeply impressed to see how a posthumous understanding of alchemy is opening up. I myself have felt for a long time that the utterly superficial assessment of alchemy, existent until now, ought to be liquidated. Up till now, however, I have sought in vain for a deeper understanding of this phenomenon, so significant in the history of civilization'.]

18 [Cf., 'Richard Wilhelm: In Memoriam', *CW* 15, par. 81.]

19 It may interest the reader to hear the opinion of a physicist on this point. Professor Pauli, who was good enough to glance through the ms. of this supplement, writes: 'As a matter of fact the physicist would expect a psychological correspondence at this point, because the epistemological situation with regard to the concepts "conscious" and "unconscious" seems to offer a pretty close analogy to the undermentioned "complementarity" situation in physics. On the one hand the unconscious can only be inferred indirectly from its (organizing) effects on conscious contents. On the other hand every "observation of the unconscious," i.e., every conscious realization of unconscious contents, has an uncontrollable reactive effect on these same contents (which as we know precludes in principle the possibility of "exhausting" the unconscious by making it conscious). Thus the physicist will conclude *per analogiam* that this uncontrollable reactive effect of the observing subject on the unconscious limits the objective character of the latter's reality and lends it at the same time a certain subjectivity. Although the *position* of the 'cut' between conscious and unconscious is (at least up to a point) left to the free choice of the "psychological experimenter," the *existence* of this "cut" remains an unavoidable necessity. Accordingly, from the standpoint of the psychologist, the "observed system" would consist not of physical objects only, but would also include the unconscious, while consciousness would be assigned the role of "observing medium." It is undeniable that the development of "microphysics" has brought the way in which nature is described in this science very much closer to that of the newer psychology: but whereas the former, on account of the basic "complementarity" situation, is faced with the impossibility of eliminating the effects of the observer by determinable correctives, and has therefore to abandon in principle any objective understanding of physical phenomena, the latter can supplement the purely subjective psychology of consciousness by postulating the existence of an unconscious that possesses a large measure of objective reality.'

20 The physicist Pascual Jordan ('Positivistische Bemerkungen über die parapsychischen Erscheinungen', pp. 14ff.) has already used the idea of relative space to explain telepathic phenomena.

21 *Die kulturelle Bedeutung der komplexen Psychologie*, p. 362.

22 By this I only mean that psychic phenomena have an energic aspect by virtue of which they can be described as 'phenomena'. I do not mean that the energic aspect embraces or explains the whole of the psyche.

23 Cf., the first paper in *CW* 8.

Part III
Outer limits

9 Visions and altered states

From: *Memories, Dreams, Reflections* (1963), pp. 169–70, 265–8, 270–6, 276–7

Towards the autumn of 1913 the pressure which I had felt was in *me* seemed to be moving outwards, as though there were something in the air. The atmosphere actually seemed to me darker than it had been. It was as though the sense of oppression no longer sprang exclusively from a psychic situation, but from concrete reality. This feeling grew more and more intense.

In October, while I was alone on a journey, I was suddenly seized by an overpowering vision: I saw a monstrous flood covering all the northern and low-lying lands between the North Sea and the Alps. When it came up to Switzerland I saw that the mountains grew higher and higher to protect our country. I realised that a frightful catastrophe was in progress. I saw the mighty yellow waves, the floating rubble of civilisation, and the drowned bodies of uncounted thousands. Then the whole sea turned to blood. This vision lasted about one hour. I was perplexed and nauseated, and ashamed of my weakness.

Two weeks passed; then the vision recurred, under the same conditions, even more vividly than before, and the blood was more emphasized. An inner voice spoke. 'Look at it well; it is wholly real and it will be so. You cannot doubt it'. That winter someone asked me what I thought were the political prospects of the world in the near future. I replied that I had no thoughts on the matter, but that I saw rivers of blood.

I asked myself whether these visions pointed to a revolution, but could not really imagine anything of the sort. And so I drew the conclusion that they had to do with myself, and decided that I was menaced by a psychosis. The idea of war did not occur to me at all.

Soon afterwards, in the spring and early summer of 1914, I had a thrice-repeated dream that in the middle of summer an Arctic cold wave descended and froze the land to ice. I saw, for example, the whole of Lorraine and its canals frozen and the entire region totally deserted by human beings. All living green things were killed by frost. This dream came in April and May, and for the last time in June, of 1914.

In the third dream frightful cold had again descended from out of the cosmos. This dream, however, had an unexpected end. There stood a leaf-bearing tree, but without fruit (my tree of life, I thought), whose leaves had been transformed by the effects of the frost into sweet grapes full of healing juices. I plucked the grapes and gave them to a large, waiting crowd.

At the end of July 1914 I was invited by the British Medical Association to deliver a lecture, 'On the Importance of the Unconscious in Psychopathology', at a congress in Aberdeen. I was prepared for something to happen, for such visions and dreams are fateful. In my state of mind just then, with the fears that were pursuing me, it seemed fateful to me that I should have to talk on the importance of the unconscious at such a time!

On 1st August the world war broke out. Now my task was clear: I had to try to understand what had happened and to what extent my own experience coincided with that of mankind in general. Therefore my first obligation was to probe the depths of my own psyche.

Even on the occasion of my first visit to Ravenna in 1913, the tomb of Galla Placidia seemed to me significant and unusually fascinating. The second time, twenty years later, I had the same feeling. Once more I fell into a strange mood in the tomb of Galla Placidia; once more I was deeply stirred. I was there with an acquaintance, and we went directly from the tomb into the Baptistery of the Orthodox.

Here, what struck me first was the mild blue light that filled the room; yet I did not wonder about this at all. I did not try to account for its source, and so the wonder of this light without any visible source did not trouble me. I was somewhat amazed because, in place of the windows I remembered having seen on my first visit, there were now four great mosaic frescoes of incredible beauty which, it seemed, I had entirely forgotten. I was vexed to find my memory so unreliable. The mosaic on the south side represented the baptism in the Jordan; the second picture, on the north, was of the passage of the Children of Israel through the Red Sea; the third, on the east, soon faded from my memory. It might have shown Naaman being cleansed of leprosy in the Jordan; there was a picture on this theme in the old Merian Bible in my library, which was much like the mosaic. The fourth mosaic on the west side of the baptistery, was the most impressive of all. We looked at this one last. It represented Christ holding out his hand to Peter, who was sinking beneath the waves. We stopped in front of this mosaic for at least twenty minutes and discussed the original ritual of baptism, especially the curious archaic conception of it as an initiation connected with real peril of death. Such initiations were often connected with the peril of death and so served to express the archetypal idea of death and rebirth. Baptism had originally been a real immersion which at least suggested the danger of drowning.

I retained the most distinct memory of the mosaic of Peter sinking, and to this day can see every detail before my eyes: the blue of the sea, individual chips of the mosaic, the inscribed scrolls proceeding from the mouths of Peter and Christ, which I attempted to decipher. After we left the baptistery, I went promptly to Alinari to buy photographs of the mosaics, but could not find any. Time was pressing – this was only a short visit – and so I postponed the purchase until later. I thought I might order the pictures from Zurich.

When I was back home, I asked an acquaintance who was going to Ravenna to obtain the pictures for me. He could not locate them, for he discovered that the mosaics I had described did not exist.

Meanwhile, I had already spoken at a seminar about the original conception of baptism, and on this occasion had also mentioned the mosaics that I had seen in the Baptistery of the Orthodox.[1] The memory of those pictures is still vivid to me. The lady who had been there with me long refused to believe that what she had 'seen with her own eyes' had not existed.

As we know, it is very difficult to determine whether, and to what extent, two persons simultaneously see the same thing. In this case, however, I was able to ascertain that at least the main features of what we both saw had been the same.

This experience in Ravenna is among the most curious events in my life. It can scarcely be explained. A certain light may possibly be cast on it by an incident in the story of Empress Galla Placidia (d. 450). During a stormy crossing from Byzantium to Ravenna in the worst of winter, she made a vow that if she came through safely, she would build a church and have the perils of the sea represented in it. She kept this vow by building the basilica of San Giovanni in Ravenna and having it adorned with mosaics. In the early Middle Ages, San Giovanni, together with its mosaics, was destroyed by fire; but in the Ambrosiana in Milan is still to be found a sketch representing Galla Placidia in a boat.

I had, from the first visit, been personally affected by the figure of Galla Placidia, and had often wondered how it must have been for this highly cultivated, fastidious woman to live at the side of a barbarian prince. Her tomb seemed to me a final legacy through which I might reach her personality. Her fate and her whole being were vivid presences to me; with her intense nature, she was a suitable embodiment for my anima.[2]

The anima of a man has a strongly historical character. As a personification of the unconscious she goes back into prehistory, and embodies the contents of the past. She provides the individual with those elements that he ought to know about his prehistory. To the individual, the anima is all life that has been in the past and is still alive in him. In comparison to her I have always felt myself to be a barbarian who really has no history – like a creature just sprung out of nothingness, with neither a past nor a future.

In the course of my confrontation with the anima I had actually had a brush with those perils which I saw represented in the mosaics. I had come close to drowning. The same thing happened to me as to Peter, who cried for help and was rescued by Jesus. What had been the fate of Pharaoh's army could have been mine. Like Peter and like Naaman, I came away unscathed, and the integration of the unconscious contents made an essential contribution to the completion of my personality.

What happens within oneself when one integrates previously unconscious contents with the consciousness is something which can scarcely be described in words. It can only be experienced. It is a subjective affair quite beyond discussion; we have a particular feeling about ourselves, about the way we are, and that is a fact which it is neither possible nor meaningful to doubt. Similarly, we convey a particular feeling to others, and that too is a fact that cannot be doubted. So far as we know, there is no higher authority which could eliminate the probable discrepancies between all these impressions and opinions. Whether a change has taken place as the result of integration, and what the nature of that change is, remains a matter of subjective conviction. To be sure, it is not a fact which can be scientifically verified and therefore finds no place in an official view of the world. Yet it nevertheless remains a fact which is in practice uncommonly important and fraught with consequences. Realistic psychotherapists, at any rate, and psychologists interested in therapy, can scarcely afford to overlook facts of this sort.

Since my experience in the baptistery in Ravenna, I know with certainty that something interior can seem to be exterior, and that something exterior can appear to be interior. The actual walls of the baptistery, though they must have been seen by my physical eyes, were covered over by a vision of some altogether different sight which was as completely real as the unchanged baptismal font. Which was real at that moment?

My case is by no means the only one of its kind. But when that sort of thing happens to oneself, one cannot help taking it more seriously than something heard or read about. In general, with anecdotes of that kind, one is quick to think of all sorts of explanations which dispose of the mystery. I have come to the conclusion that before we settle upon any theories in regard to the unconscious, we require many, many more experiences of it.

At the beginning of 1944 I broke my foot, and this misadventure was followed by a heart attack. In a state of unconsciousness I experienced deliriums and visions which must have begun when I hung on the edge of death and was being given oxygen and camphor injections. The images were so tremendous that I myself concluded that I was close to death. My nurse afterwards told me, 'It was as if you were surrounded by a bright glow'. That was a phenomenon she had sometimes observed in the dying, she added. I had reached the outermost limit, and do not know whether I was in a dream or an ecstasy. At any rate, extremely strange things began to happen to me.

It seemed to me that I was high up in space. Far below I saw the globe of the earth, bathed in a gloriously blue light. I saw the deep blue sea and the continents. Far below my feet lay Ceylon, and in the distance ahead of me the subcontinent of India. My field of vision did not include the whole earth, but its global shape was plainly distinguishable and its outlines shone with a silvery gleam through that wonderful blue light. In many places the globe seemed coloured, or spotted dark green like oxydised silver. Far away to the left lay a broad expanse – the reddish-yellow desert of Arabia; it was as though the silver of the earth had there assumed a reddish-gold hue. Then came the Red Sea, and far, far back – as if in the upper left of a map – I could just make out a bit of the Mediterranean. My gaze was directed chiefly towards that. Everything else appeared indistinct. I could also see the snow-covered Himalayas, but in that direction it was foggy or cloudy. I did not look to the right at all. I knew that I was on the point of departing from the earth.

Later I discovered how high in space one would have to be to have so extensive a view – approximately one thousand miles! The sight of the earth from this height was the most glorious thing I had ever seen.

After contemplating it for a while, I turned round. I had been standing with my back to the Indian Ocean, as it were, and my face to the north. Then it seemed to me that I made a turn to the south. Something new entered my field of vision. A short distance away I saw in space a tremendous dark block of stone, like a meteorite. It was about the size of my house, or even bigger. It was floating in space, and I myself was floating in space.

I had seen similar stones on the coast of the Gulf of Bengal. They were blocks of tawny granite, and some of them had been hollowed out into temples. My stone was one such gigantic dark block. An entrance led into a small antechamber. To the right of the entrance, a black Hindu sat silently in lotus posture upon a stone bench. He wore a white gown, and I knew that he expected me. Two steps led up to this antechamber, and inside, on the left, was the gate to the temple. Innumerable tiny niches, each with a saucer-like concavity filled with coconut oil and small burning wicks, surrounded the door with a wreath of bright flames. I had once actually seen this when I visited the Temple of the Holy Tooth at Kandy in Ceylon; the gate had been framed by several rows of burning oil lamps of this sort.

As I approached the steps leading up to the entrance into the rock, a strange thing happened: I had the feeling that everything was being sloughed away; everything I aimed at or wished for or thought, the whole phantasmagoria of earthly existence, fell away or was stripped from me – an extremely painful process. Nevertheless, something remained; it was as if I now carried along with me everything I had ever experienced or done, everything that had happened around me. I might also say: it was with me, and I was it. I consisted of all that, so to speak. I consisted of my own history, and I felt with great certainty: this is what I am. 'I am this bundle of what has been, and what has been accomplished'.

This experience gave me a feeling of extreme poverty, but at the same time of great fullness. There was no longer anything I wanted or desired. I existed in an objective form; I was what I had been and lived. At first the sense of annihilation predominated, of having been stripped or pillaged; but suddenly that became of no consequence. Everything seemed to be past; what remained was a *fait accompli*, without any reference back to what had been. There was no longer any regret that something had dropped away or been taken away. On the contrary: I had everything that I was, and that was everything.

Something else engaged my attention: as I approached the temple I had the certainty that I was about to enter an illuminated room and would meet there all those people to whom I belong in reality. There I would at last understand – this too was a certainty – what historical nexus I or my life fitted into. I would know what had been before me, why I had come into being, and where my life was flowing. My life as I lived it had often seemed to me like a story that has no beginning and no end. I had the feeling that I was a historical fragment, an excerpt for which the preceding and succeeding text was missing. My life seemed to have been snipped out of a long chain of events, and many questions had remained unanswered. Why had it taken this course? Why had I brought these particular assumptions with me? What had I made of them? What will follow? I felt sure that I would receive an answer to all these questions as soon as I entered the rock temple. There I would learn why everything had been thus and not otherwise. There I would meet the people who knew the answer to my question about what had been before and what would come after.

While I was thinking over these matters, something happened that caught my attention. From below, from the direction of Europe, an image floated up. It was my doctor, Dr H. – or, rather, his likeness – framed by a golden chain or a golden laurel wreath. I knew at once: 'Aha, this is my doctor, of course, the one who has been treating me. But now he is coming in his primal form, as a *basileus* of Kos.[3] In life he was an avatar of this *basileus*, the temporal embodiment of the primal form, which has existed from the beginning. Now he is appearing in that primal form.'

Presumably I too was in my primal form, though this was something I did not observe but simply took for granted. As he stood before me, a mute exchange of thought took place between us. Dr H. had been delegated by the earth to deliver a message to me, to tell me that there was a protest against my going away. I had no right to leave the earth and must return. The moment I heard that, the vision ceased.

I was profoundly disappointed, for now it all seemed to have been for nothing. The painful process of defoliation had been in vain, and I was not to be allowed to enter the temple, to join the people in whose company I belonged.

In reality, a good three weeks were still to pass before I could truly make up my mind to live again. I could not eat because all food repelled me. The view of city and mountains from my sick-bed seemed to me like a painted curtain with black holes in it, or a tattered sheet of newspaper full of photographs that meant nothing. Disappointed, I thought, 'Now I must return to the "box system" again'. For it seemed to me as if behind the horizon of the cosmos a three-dimensional world had been artificially built up, in which each person sat by himself in a little box. And now I should have to convince myself all over again that this was important! Life and the whole world struck me as a prison, and it bothered me beyond measure that I should again be finding all that quite in order. I had been so glad to shed it all, and now it had come about that I – along with everyone else – would again be hung up in a box by a thread. While I floated in space, I had been weightless, and there had been nothing tugging at me. And now all that was to be a thing of the past!

I felt violent resistance to my doctor because he had brought me back to life. At the same time, I was worried about him. 'His life is in danger, for heaven's sake! He has appeared to me in his primal form! When anybody attains this form it means he is going to die, for already he belongs to the "greater company"!' Suddenly the terrifying thought came to me that Dr H. Would have to die in my stead. I tried my best to talk to him about it, but he did not understand me. Then I became angry with him. 'Why does he always pretend he doesn't know he is a *basileus* of Kos? And that he has already assumed his primal form? He wants to make me believe that he doesn't know!' That irritated me. My wife reproved me for being so unfriendly to him. She was right; but at the time I was angry with him for stubbornly refusing to speak of all that had passed between us in my vision. 'Damn it all, he ought to watch his step. He has no right to be so reckless! I want to tell him to take care of himself'. I was firmly convinced that his life was in jeopardy.

In actual fact I was his last patient. On 4 April 1944 – I still remember the exact date – I was allowed to sit up on the edge of my bed for the first time since the beginning of my illness, and on this same day Dr H. took to his bed and did not leave it again. I heard that he was having intermittent attacks of fever. Soon afterwards he died of septicaemia. He was a good doctor; there was something of the genius about him. Otherwise he would not have appeared to me as a prince of Kos.

During those weeks I lived in a strange rhythm. By day I was usually depressed. I felt weak and wretched, and scarcely dared to stir. Gloomily, I thought, 'Now I must go back to this drab world'. Towards evening I would fall asleep, and my sleep would last until about midnight. Then I would come to myself and lie awake for about an hour, but in an utterly transformed state. It was as if I were in an ecstasy. I felt as though I were floating in space, as though I were safe in the womb of the universe – in a tremendous void, but filled with the highest possible feeling of happiness. 'This is eternal bliss', I thought. 'This cannot be described; it is far too wonderful!'

Everything around me seemed enchanted. At this hour of the night the nurse brought me some food she had warmed – for only then was I able to take any, and I ate with appetite. For a time it seemed to me that she was an old Jewish woman, much older than she actually was, and that she was preparing ritual kosher dishes for me. When I looked at her, she seemed to have a blue halo around her head. I myself was, so it seemed, in the Pardes Rimmonim, the garden of pomegranates,[4] and the wedding of Tifereth with Malchuth was taking place. Or else I was Rabbi Simon ben Jochai, whose wedding in the afterlife was being celebrated. It was the mystic marriage as it appears in the Cabbalistic tradition. I cannot tell you how wonderful it was. I could only think continually, 'Now this is the garden of pomegranates! Now this is the marriage of Malchuth with Tifereth!' I do not know exactly what part I played in it. At bottom it was I myself; I was the marriage. And my beatitude was that of a blissful wedding.

Gradually the garden of pomegranates faded away and changed. There followed the Marriage of the Lamb, in a Jerusalem festively bedecked. I cannot describe what it was like in detail. These were ineffable states of joy. Angels were present, and light. I myself was the 'Marriage of the Lamb'.

That, too, vanished, and there came a new image, the last vision. I walked up a wide valley to the end, where a gentle chain of hills began. The valley ended in a classical amphitheatre. It was magnificently situated in the green landscape. And there, in this theatre, the *hierosgamos* was being celebrated. Men and women dancers came on stage, and upon a flower-decked couch All-father Zeus and Hera consummated the mystic marriage, as it is described in the *Iliad*.

All these experiences were glorious. Night after night I floated in a state of purest bliss, 'thronged round with images of all creation'.[5] Gradually, the motifs mingled and paled. Usually the visions lasted for about an hour; then I would fall asleep again. By the time morning drew near, I would feel: Now grey morning is coming again; now comes the grey world with its boxes! What idiocy, what hideous nonsense! Those inner states were so fantastically beautiful that by comparison this world appeared downright ridiculous. As I approached closer to life again, they grew fainter, and scarcely three weeks after the first vision they ceased altogether.

It is impossible to convey the beauty and intensity of emotion during those visions. They were the most tremendous things I have ever experienced. And what a contrast the day was: I was tormented and on edge; everything irritated me; everything was too material, too crude and clumsy, terribly limited both spatially and spiritually. It was all an imprisonment, for reasons impossible to divine, and yet it had a kind of hypnotic power, a cogency, as if it were reality itself, for all that I had clearly perceived its emptiness. Although my belief in the world returned to me, I have never since entirely freed myself of the impression that this life is a segment of existence which is enacted in a three-dimensional boxlike universe especially set up for it.

There is something else I quite distinctly remember. At the beginning, when I was having the vision of the garden of pomegranates, I asked the nurse to forgive me if she were harmed. There was such sanctity in the room, I said, that it might be harmful to her. Of course she did not understand me. For me the presence of sanctity had a magical atmosphere; I feared it might be unendurable to others. I understood then why one speaks of the odour of sanctity, of the 'sweet smell' of the Holy Ghost. This was it. There was a *pneuma* of inexpressible sanctity in the room, whose manifestation was the *mysterium coniunctionis*.

I would never have imagined that any such experience was possible. It was not a product of imagination. The visions and experiences were utterly real;

there was nothing subjective about them; they all had a quality of absolute objectivity.

We shy away from the word 'eternal', but I can describe the experience only as the ecstasy of a non-temporal state in which present, past, and future are one. Everything that happens in time had been brought together into a concrete whole. Nothing was distributed over time, nothing could be measured by temporal concepts. The experience might best be defined as a state of feeling, but one which cannot be produced by imagination. How can I imagine that I exist simultaneously the day before yesterday, to-day and the day after to-morrow? There would be things which would not yet have begun, other things which would be indubitably present, and others again which would already be finished – and yet all this would be one. The only thing that feeling could grasp would be a sum, an iridescent whole, containing all at once expectation of a beginning, surprise at what is now happening, and satisfaction or disappointment with the result of what happened. One is interwoven into an indescribable whole and yet observes it with complete objectivity.

After the illness a fruitful period of work began for me. A good many of my principal works were written only then. The insight I had had, or the vision of the end of all things, gave me the courage to undertake new formulations. I no longer attempted to put forward my own opinion, but surrendered myself to the current of my thoughts. Thus one problem after the other revealed itself to me and took shape.

NOTES

1 Tantra Yoga Seminar, 1932.
2 [Jung himself explained the vision as a momentary new creation by the unconscious, arising out of his thoughts about archetypal initiation. The immediate cause of the concretization lay, in his opinion, in a projection of his anima upon Galla Placidia. – A.J.]
3 [*Basileus* = king. Kos was famous in antiquity as the site of the temple of Asklepios, and was the birthplace of Hippocrates. – A.J.]
4 *Pardes Rimmonim* is the title of an old Cabbalistic tract by Moses Cordovero (sixteenth century). In Cabbalistic doctrine Malchuth and Tifereth are two of the ten spheres of divine manifestation in which God emerges from his hidden state. They represent the female and male principles within the Godhead.
5 *Faust*, Part Two.

10 Life after death

From: 'The Soul and Death' (1934) (*CW* 8)

809 In my rather long psychological experience I have observed a great many people whose unconscious psychic activity I was able to follow into the immediate presence of death. As a rule the approaching end was indicated by those symbols which, in normal life also, proclaim changes of psychological condition – rebirth symbols such as changes of locality, journeys, and the like. I have frequently been able to trace back for over a year, in a dream-series, the indications of approaching death, even in cases where such thoughts were not prompted by the outward situation. Dying, therefore, has its onset long before actual death. Moreover, this often shows itself in peculiar changes of personality which may precede death by quite a long time. On the whole, I was astonished to see how little ado the unconscious psyche makes of death. It would seem as though death were something relatively unimportant, or perhaps our psyche does not bother about what happens to the individual. But it seems that the unconscious is all the more interested in *how* one dies; that is, whether the attitude of consciousness is adjusted to dying or not. For example, I once had to treat a woman of sixty-two. She was still hearty, and moderately intelligent. It was not for want of brains that she was unable to understand her dreams. It was unfortunately only too clear that she did not *want* to understand them. Her dreams were very plain, but also very disagreeable. She had got it fixed in her head that she was a faultless mother to her children, but the children did not share this view at all, and the dreams too displayed a conviction very much to the contrary. I was obliged to break off the treatment after some weeks of fruitless effort because I had to leave for military service (it was during the war). In the meantime the patient was smitten with an incurable disease, leading after a few months to a moribund condition which might bring about the end at any moment. Most of the time she was in a sort of delirious or somnambulistic state, and in this curious mental condition she spontaneously resumed the analytical work. She spoke of her dreams again and acknowledged to herself everything that she had previously denied to me with the greatest vehemence, and a lot more besides. This self-analytic work continued daily for

several hours, for about six weeks. At the end of this period she had calmed herself, just like a patient during normal treatment, and then she died.

810   From this and numerous other experiences of the kind I must conclude that our psyche is at least not indifferent to the dying of the individual. The urge, so often seen in those who are dying, to set to rights whatever is still wrong might point in the same direction.

811   How these experiences are ultimately to be interpreted is a problem that exceeds the competence of an empirical science and goes beyond our intellectual capacities, for in order to reach a final conclusion one must necessarily have had the actual experience of death. This event unfortunately puts the observer in a position that makes it impossible for him to give an objective account of his experiences and of the conclusions resulting therefrom.

812   Consciousness moves within narrow confines, within the brief span of time between its beginning and its end, and shortened by about a third by periods of sleep. The life of the body lasts somewhat longer; it always begins earlier and, very often, it ceases later than consciousness. Beginning and end are unavoidable aspects of all processes. Yet on closer examination it is extremely difficult to see where one process ends and another begins, since events and processes, beginnings and endings, merge into each other and form, strictly speaking, an indivisible continuum. We divide the processes from one another for the sake of discrimination and understanding, knowing full well that at bottom every division is arbitrary and conventional. This procedure in no way infringes the continuum of the world process, for 'beginning' and 'end' are primarily necessities of conscious cognition. We may establish with reasonable certainty that an individual consciousness as it relates to ourselves has come to an end. But whether this means that the continuity of the psychic process is also interrupted remains doubtful, since the psyche's attachment to the brain can be affirmed with far less certitude today than it could fifty years ago. Psychology must first digest certain parapsychological facts, which it has hardly begun to do as yet.

813   The unconscious psyche appears to possess qualities which throw a most peculiar light on its relation to space and time. I am thinking of those spatial and temporal telepathic phenomena which, as we know, are much easier to ignore than to explain. In this regard science, with a few praiseworthy exceptions, has so far taken the easier path of ignoring them. I must confess, however, that the so-called telepathic faculties of the psyche have caused me many a headache, for the catchword 'telepathy' is very far from explaining anything. The limitation of consciousness in space and time is such an overwhelming reality that every occasion when this fundamental truth is broken through must rank as an event of the highest theoretical significance, for it would prove that the space-time barrier can be annulled. The annulling factor would then be the psyche, since space-time would attach to it at most as a relative and conditioned

quality. Under certain conditions it could even break through the barriers of space and time precisely because of a quality essential to it, that is, its relatively trans-spatial and trans-temporal nature. This possible transcendence of space-time, for which it seems to me there is a good deal of evidence, is of such incalculable import that it should spur the spirit of research to the greatest effort. Our present development of consciousness is, however, so backward that in general we still lack the scientific and intellectual equipment for adequately evaluating the facts of telepathy so far as they have bearing on the nature of the psyche. I have referred to this group of phenomena merely in order to point out that the psyche's attachment to the brain, i.e., its space-time limitation, is no longer as self-evident and incontrovertible as we have hitherto been led to believe.

814   Anyone who has the least knowledge of the parapsychological material which already exists and has been thoroughly verified will know that so-called telepathic phenomena are undeniable facts. An objective and critical survey of the available data would establish that perceptions occur as if in part there were no space, in part no time. Naturally, one cannot draw from this the metaphysical conclusion that in the world of things as they are 'in themselves' there is neither space nor time, and that the space-time category is therefore a web into which the human mind has woven itself as into a nebulous illusion. Space and time are not only the most immediate certainties for us, they are also obvious empirically, since everything observable happens as though it occurred in space and time. In the face of this overwhelming certainty it is understandable that reason should have the greatest difficulty in granting validity to the peculiar nature of telepathic phenomena. But anyone who does justice to the facts cannot but admit that their apparent space-timelessness is their most essential quality. In the last analysis, our naïve perception and immediate certainty are, strictly speaking, no more than evidence of a psychological *a priori* form of perception which simply rules out any other form. The fact that we are totally unable to imagine a form of existence without space and time by no means proves that such an existence is in itself impossible. And therefore, just as we cannot draw, from an appearance of space-timelessness, any absolute conclusion about a space-timeless form of existence, so we are not entitled to conclude from the apparent space-time quality of our perception that there is no form of existence *without* space and time. It is not only permissible to doubt the absolute validity of space-time perception; it is, in view of the available facts, even imperative to do so. The hypothetical possibility that the psyche touches on a form of existence outside space and time presents a scientific question-mark that merits serious consideration for a long time to come. The ideas and doubts of theoretical physicists in our own day should prompt a cautious mood in psychologists too; for, philosophically considered, what do we mean by the 'limitedness of space' if not a relativization of the space category? Something similar might easily happen to the category of time (and to that

of causality as well).[1] Doubts about these matters are more warranted today than ever before.

815   The nature of the psyche reaches into obscurities far beyond the scope of our understanding. It contains as many riddles as the universe with its galactic systems, before whose majestic configurations only a mind lacking in imagination can fail to admit its own insufficiency. This extreme uncertainty of human comprehension makes the intellectualistic hubbub not only ridiculous, but also deplorably dull. If, therefore, from the needs of his own heart, or in accordance with the ancient lessons of human wisdom, or out of respect for the psychological fact that 'telepathic' perceptions occur, anyone should draw the conclusion that the psyche, in its deepest reaches, participates in a form of existence beyond space and time, and thus partakes of what is inadequately and symbolically described as 'eternity' – then critical reason could counter with no other argument than the 'non liquet' of science. Furthermore, he would have the inestimable advantage of conforming to a bias of the human psyche which has existed from time immemorial and is universal. Anyone who does not draw this conclusion, whether from scepticism or rebellion against tradition, from lack of courage or inadequate psychological experience or thoughtless ignorance, stands very little chance, statistically, of becoming a pioneer of the mind, but has instead the indubitable certainty of coming into conflict with the truths of his blood. Now whether these are in the last resort absolute truths or not we shall never be able to determine. It suffices that they are present in us as a 'bias', and we know to our cost what it means to come into unthinking conflict with these truths. It means the same thing as the conscious denial of the instincts – uprootedness, disorientation, meaninglessness and whatever else these symptoms of inferiority may be called. One of the most fatal of the sociological and psychological errors in which our time is so fruitful is the supposition that something can become entirely different all in a moment; for instance, that man can radically change his nature, or that some formula or truth might be found which would represent an entirely new beginning. Any essential change, or even a slight improvement, has always been a miracle. Deviation from the truths of the blood begets neurotic restlessness, and we have had about enough of that these days. Restlessness begets meaninglessness, and the lack of meaning in life is a soul-sickness whose full extent and full import our age has not as yet begun to comprehend.

From: *Memories, Dreams, Reflections* (1963), pp. 281–3, 289–92, 297–8

The unconscious helps by communicating things to us, or making figurative allusions. It has other ways, too, of informing us of things which by all logic we could not possibly know. Consider synchronistic phenomena, premonitions, and dreams that come true. I recall one time during the Second World War when I was returning home from Bollingen. I had a book with me, but could not read, for the moment the train started to move I was overpowered by the image of someone drowning. This was a memory of an accident that had happened while I was on military service. During the entire journey I could not rid myself of it. It struck me as uncanny, and I thought, 'What has happened? Can there have been an accident?'

I got out at Erlenbach and walked home, still troubled by this memory. My second daughter's children were in the garden. The family was living with us, having returned to Switzerland from Paris because of the war. The children stood looking rather upset, and when I asked, 'Why, what is the matter?' they told me that Adrian, then the youngest of the boys, had fallen into the water in the boathouse. It is quite deep there, and since he could not really swim he had almost drowned. His older brother had fished him out. This had taken place at exactly the time I had been assailed by that memory in the train. The unconscious had given me a hint. Why should it not be able to inform me of other things also?

I had a somewhat similar experience before a death in my wife's family. I dreamed that my wife's bed was a deep pit with stone walls. It was a grave, and somehow had a suggestion of classical antiquity about it. Then I heard a deep sigh, as if someone were giving up the ghost. A figure that resembled my wife sat up in the pit and floated upwards. It wore a white gown into which curious black symbols were woven. I awoke, roused my wife, and checked the time. It was three o'clock in the morning. The dream was so curious that I thought at once that it might signify a death. At seven o'clock came the news that a cousin of my wife had died at three o'clock in the morning.

Frequently foreknowledge is there, but not recognition. Thus I once had a dream in which I was attending a garden party. I saw my sister there, and that greatly surprised me, for she had died some years before. A deceased friend of mine was also present. The rest were people who were still alive. Presently I saw that my sister was accompanied by a lady I knew well. Even in the dream I had drawn the conclusion that the lady was going to die. 'She is already marked', I thought. In the dream I knew exactly who she was. I knew also that she lived in Basel. But as soon as I woke up I could no longer, with the best will in the world, recall who she was, although the whole dream was still vivid in my mind. I pictured all my acquaintances in Basel to see whether the memory images would ring a bell. Nothing!

A few weeks later I received news that a friend of mine had had a fatal accident. I knew at once that she was the person I had seen in the dream but had been unable to identify. My recollection of her was perfectly clear and richly detailed, since she had been my patient for a considerable time up to a year before her death. In my attempt to recall the person in my dream, however, hers was the one picture which did not appear in my portrait gallery of Basel acquaintances, although by rights it should have been one of the first.

When one has such experiences – and I will tell of others like them – one acquires a certain respect for the potentialities and arts of the unconscious. Only, one must remain critical and be aware that such communications may have a subjective meaning as well. They may be in accord with reality, and then again they may not. I have, however, learned that the views I have been able to form on the basis of such hints from the unconscious have been most rewarding. Naturally, I am not going to write a book of revelations about them, but I will acknowledge that I have a 'myth' which encourages me to look deeper into this whole realm. Myths are the earliest form of science. When I speak of things after death, I am speaking out of inner prompting, and can go no farther than to tell you dreams and myths that relate to this subject.

Naturally, one can contend from the start that myths and dreams concerning continuity of life after death are merely compensating fantasies which are inherent in our natures – all life desires eternity. The only argument I can adduce in answer to this is the myth itself.

However, there are indications that at least a part of the psyche is not subject to the laws of space and time. Scientific proof of that has been provided by the well-known J.B. Rhine experiments.[2] Along with numerous cases of spontaneous foreknowledge, non-spatial perceptions, and so on – of which I have given a number of examples from my own life – these experiments prove that the psyche at times functions outside of the spatio-temporal law of causality. This indicates that our conceptions of space and time, and therefore of causality also, are incomplete. A complete picture of the world would require the addition of still another dimension; only then could the totality of phenomena be given a unified explanation. Hence it is that the rationalists insist to this day that parapsychological experiences do not really exist; for their world-view stands or falls by this question. If such phenomena occur at all, the rationalistic picture of the universe is invalid, because incomplete. Then the possibility of an other-valued reality behind the phenomenal world becomes an inescapable problem, and we must face the fact that our world, with its time, space, and causality, relates to another order of things lying behind or beneath it, in which neither 'here and there' nor 'earlier and later' are of importance. I have been convinced that at least a part of our psychic existence is characterized by a relativity of space and time. This relativity seems to increase, in proportion to the distance from consciousness, to an absolute condition of timelessness and spacelessness.

Although there is no way to marshal valid proof of continuance of the soul after death, there are nevertheless experiences which make us thoughtful. I take them as hints, and do not presume to ascribe to them the significance of insights.

One night I lay awake thinking of the sudden death of a friend whose funeral had taken place the day before. I was deeply concerned. Suddenly I felt that he was in the room. It seemed to me that he stood at the foot of my bed and was asking me to go with him. I did not have the feeling of an apparition; rather, it was an inner visual image of him, which I explained to myself as a fantasy. But in all honesty I had to ask myself, 'Do I have any proof that this is a fantasy? Suppose it is not a fantasy, suppose my friend is really here and I decided he was only a fantasy – would that not be abominable of me?' Yet I had equally little proof that he stood before me as an apparition. Then I said to myself, 'Proof is neither here nor there! Instead of explaining him away as a fantasy, I might just as well give him the benefit of the doubt and for experiment's sake credit him with reality'. The moment I had that thought, he went to the door and beckoned me to follow him. So I was going to have to play along with him! That was something I hadn't bargained for. I had to repeat my argument to myself once more. Only then did I follow him in my imagination.

He led me out of the house, into the garden, out to the road, and finally to his house. (In reality it was several hundred yards away from mine.) I went in, and he conducted me into his study. He climbed on a stool and showed me the second of five books with red bindings which stood on the second shelf from the top. Then the vision broke off. I was not acquainted with his library and did not know what books he owned. Certainly I could never have made out from below the titles of the books he had pointed out to me on the second shelf from the top.

This experience seemed to me so curious that next morning I went to his widow and asked whether I could look up something in my friend's library. Sure enough, there was a stool standing under the bookcase I had seen in my vision, and even before I came closer I could see the five books with red bindings. I stepped up on the stool so as to be able to read the titles. They were translations of the novels of Emile Zola. The title of the second volume read: 'The Legacy of the Dead'. The contents seemed to me of no interest. Only the title was extremely significant in connection with this experience.

Equally important to me were the dream-experiences I had before my mother's death. News of her death came to me while I was staying in the Tessin. I was deeply shaken, for it had come with unexpected suddenness. The night before her death I had a frightening dream. I was in a dense, gloomy forest; fantastic, gigantic boulders lay about among huge jungle-like trees. It was a heroic, primeval landscape. Suddenly I heard a piercing whistle that seemed to resound through the whole universe. My knees shook. Then there were crashings in the underbrush, and a gigantic wolfhound with a fearful, gaping maw burst forth. At the sight of it, the blood froze in my veins. It tore past me, and I suddenly knew: the Wild Huntsman had commanded it to carry away a human soul. I awoke in deadly terror, and the next morning I received the news of my mother's passing.

Seldom has a dream so shaken me, for upon superficial consideration it seemed to say that the devil had fetched her. But to be accurate the dream said that it was the Wild Huntsman, the *'Grünhütl'*, or Wearer of the Green Hat, who hunted with his wolves that night – it was the season of Föhn storms in January. It was Wotan, the god of my Alemannic forefathers, who had gathered my mother to her ancestors – negatively to the 'wild horde', but positively to the '*sälig Lüt*', the blessed folk. It was the Christian missionaries who made Wotan into a devil. In himself he is an important god – a Mercury or Hermes, as the Romans correctly realized, a nature spirit who returned to life again in the Merlin of the Grail legend and became, as the *spiritus Mercurialis*, the sought-after arcanum of the alchemists. Thus the dream says that the soul of my mother was taken into that greater territory of the self which lies beyond the segment of Christian morality, taken into that wholeness of nature and spirit in which conflicts and contradictions are resolved.

I went home immediately, and while I rode in the night train I had a feeling of great grief, but in my heart of hearts I could not be mournful, and this for a strange reason: during the entire journey I continually heard dance music, laughter and jollity, as though a wedding were being celebrated. This contrasted violently with the devastating impression the dream had made on me. Here was gay dance music, cheerful laughter, and it was impossible to yield entirely to my sorrow. Again and again it was on the point of overwhelming me, but the next moment I would find myself once more engulfed by the merry melodies. One side of me had a feeling of warmth and joy, and the other of terror and grief; I was thrown back and forth between these contrasting emotions.

This paradox can be explained if we suppose that at one moment death was being represented from the point of view of the ego, and at the next from that of the psyche. In the first case it appeared as a catastrophe; that is how it so often strikes us, as if wicked and pitiless powers had put an end to a human life.

And so it is – death is indeed a fearful piece of brutality; there is no sense pretending otherwise. It is brutal not only as a physical event, but far more so psychically: a human being is torn away from us, and what remains is the icy stillness of death. There no longer exists any hope of a relationship, for all the bridges have been smashed at one blow. Those who deserve a long life are cut off in the prime of their years, and good-for-nothings live to a ripe old age. This is a cruel reality which we have no right to sidestep. The actual experience of the cruelty and wantonness of death can so embitter us that we conclude there is no merciful God, no justice, and no kindness.

From another point of view, however, death appears as a joyful event. In the light of eternity, it is a wedding, a *mysterium coniunctionis*. The soul attains, as it were, its missing half, it achieves wholeness. On Greek sarcophagi the joyous element was represented by dancing girls, on Etruscan tombs by banquets. When the pious Cabbalist Rabbi Simon ben Jochai came to die, his friends said that he was celebrating his wedding. To this day it is the custom in many regions to hold a picnic on the graves on All Souls' Day. Such customs express the feeling that death is really a festive occasion.

Several months before my mother's death, in September 1922, I had a dream which presaged it. It concerned my father, and made a deep impression upon me. I had not dreamed of my father since his death in 1896. Now he once more appeared in a dream, as if he had returned from a distant journey. He looked rejuvenated, and had shed his appearance of paternal authoritarianism. I went into my library with him, and was greatly pleased at the prospect of finding out what he had been up to. I was also looking forward with particular joy to introducing my wife and children to him, to showing him my house, and to telling him all that had happened to me and what I had become in the meanwhile. I wanted also to tell him about my book on psychological types, which had recently been published. But I quickly saw that all this would be inopportune, for my father looked preoccupied. Apparently he wanted something from me. I felt that plainly, and so I refrained from talking about my own concerns.

He then said to me that since I was after all a psychologist, he would like to consult me about marital psychology. I made ready to give him a lengthy lecture on the complexities of marriage, but at this point I awoke. I could not properly understand the dream, for it never occurred to me that it might refer to my mother's death. I realized that only when she died suddenly in January 1923.

My parents' marriage was not a happy one, but full of trials and difficulties and tests of patience. Both made the mistakes typical of many couples. My dream was a forecast of my mother's death, for here was my father who, after an absence of twenty-six years, wished to ask a psychologist about the newest insights and information on marital problems, since he would soon have to resume this relationship again. Evidently he had acquired no better understanding in his timeless state and therefore had to appeal to someone among the living who, enjoying the benefits of changed times, might have a fresh approach to the whole thing.

Such was the dream's message. Undoubtedly, I could have found out a good deal more by looking into its subjective meaning – but why did I dream it just before the death of my mother, which I did not foresee? It plainly referred to my father, with whom I felt a sympathy that deepened as I grew older.

We lack concrete proof that anything of us is preserved for eternity. At most we can say that there is some probability that something of our psyche continues beyond physical death. Whether what continues to exist is conscious of itself, we do not know either. If we feel the need to form some opinion on this question, we might possibly consider what has been learned from the phenomena of psychic dissociation. In most cases where a split-off complex manifests itself it does so in the form of a personality, as if the complex had a consciousness of itself. Thus the voices heard by the insane are personified. I dealt long ago with this phenomenon of personified complexes in my doctoral dissertation. We might, if we wish, adduce these complexes as evidence for a continuity of consciousness. Likewise in favour of such an assumption are certain astonishing observations in cases of profound syncope after acute injuries to the brain and in severe states of collapse. In both situations, total loss of consciousness can be accompanied by perceptions of the outside world and vivid dream experiences. Since the cerebral cortex, the seat of consciousness, is not functioning at these times, there is as yet no explanation for such phenomena. They may be evidence for at least a subjective persistence of the capacity for consciousness – even in a state of apparent unconsciousness.[3]

Letter to Frau N. (11 July 1944), *Letters*, vol. 1, p. 343

Dear Frau N.,

What happens after death[4] is so unspeakably glorious that our imagination and our feelings do not suffice to form even an approximate conception of it. A few days before my sister died[5] her face wore an expression of such inhuman sublimity that I was profoundly frightened.

A child, too, enters into this sublimity, and there detaches himself from this world and his manifold individuations more quickly than the aged. So easily does he become what *you* also are that he apparently vanishes. Sooner or later all the dead become what we also are. But in this reality we know little or nothing about that mode of being, and what shall we still know of this earth after death? The dissolution of our time-bound form in eternity brings no loss of meaning. Rather does the little finger know itself a member of the hand. With best regards,

Your devoted C.G. JUNG

NOTES

1 [Cf., 'Synchronicity: An Acausal Connecting Principle' (1952), *CW* 8]
2 *Extra-sensory Perception* (1934); *The Reach of the Mind* (1947).
3 Cf., 'Synchronicity: An Acausal Connecting Principle', in *The Structure and Dynamics of the Psyche* (*CW* 8), pp. 506 ff.
4 [This letter is especially significant since Jung himself had been close to death after a severe cardiac infarct at the beginning of 1944. He gives a vivid description of the visions he had during his illness in *Memories*, ch. X [See above, pp. 136–41.–R.M.] The illness accounts for the long gap in the letters between Jan. and July.]
5 [She died in 1935.]

11 UFOs

From: 'Flying Saucers: A Modern Myth of Things Seen in the Skies' (1958) (*CW* 10)

589 It is difficult to form a correct estimate of the significance of contemporary events, and the danger that our judgment will remain caught in subjectivity is great. So I am fully aware of the risk I am taking in proposing to communicate my views concerning certain contemporary events, which seem to me important, to those who are patient enough to hear me. I refer to those reports reaching us from all corners of the earth, rumours of round objects that flash through the troposphere and stratosphere and go by the name of Flying Saucers, *soucoupes*, disks, and 'Ufos' (Unidentified Flying Objects). These rumours, or the possible physical existence of such objects, seem to me so significant that I feel myself compelled, as once before[1] when events of fateful consequence were brewing for Europe, to sound a note of warning. I know that, just as before, my voice is much too weak to reach the ear of the multitude. It is not presumption that drives me, but my conscience as a psychiatrist that bids me fulfil my duty and prepare those few who will hear me for coming events which are in accord with the end of an era. As we know from ancient Egyptian history, they are manifestations of psychic changes which always appear at the end of one Platonic month and at the beginning of another. Apparently they are changes in the constellation of psychic dominants, of the archetypes, or 'gods' as they used to be called, which bring about, or accompany, long-lasting transformations of the collective psyche. This transformation started in the historical era and left its traces first in the passing of the aeon of Taurus into that of Aries, and then of Aries into Pisces, whose beginning coincides with the rise of Christianity. We are now nearing that great change which may be expected when the spring point enters Aquarius.

590 It would be frivolous of me to try to conceal from the reader that such reflections are not only exceedingly unpopular but even come perilously close to those turbid fantasies which becloud the minds of world-reformers and other interpreters of 'signs and portents'. But I must take this risk, even if it means putting my hard-won reputation for truthfulness, reliability, and capacity for scientific judgment in jeopardy. I can assure my readers that I do not do this with a light heart. I am, to be quite frank, concerned for all those who are caught unprepared by the events in

question and disconcerted by their incomprehensible nature. Since, so far as I know, no one has yet felt moved to examine and set forth the possible psychic consequences of this foreseeable astrological change, I deem it my duty to do what I can in this respect. I undertake this thankless task in the expectation that my chisel will make no impression on the hard stone it encounters.

591   Some time ago I published a statement in which I considered the nature of 'Flying Saucers'.[2] I came to the same conclusion as Edward J. Ruppelt, one-time chief of the American Air Force's project for investigating Ufo reports.[3] The conclusion is: *something is seen, but one doesn't know what.* It is difficult, if not impossible, to form any correct idea of these objects, because they behave not like bodies but like weightless thoughts. Up till now there has been no indisputable proof of the physical existence of Ufos except for the cases picked up by radar. I have discussed the reliability of these radar observations with Professor Max Knoll, a specialist in this field. What he has to say is not encouraging. Nevertheless, there do seem to be authenticated cases where the visual observation was confirmed by a simultaneous radar echo. I would like to call the reader's attention to Keyhoe's books, which are based on official material and studiously avoid the wild speculation, naïveté, or prejudice of other publications.[4]

592   For a decade the physical reality of Ufos remained a very problematical matter, which was not decided one way or the other with the necessary clarity despite the mass of observational material that had accumulated in the meantime. The longer the uncertainty lasted, the greater became the probability that this obviously complicated phenomenon had an extremely important psychic component as well as a possible physical basis. This is not surprising, in that we are dealing with an ostensibly physical phenomenon distinguished on the one hand by its frequent appearances, and on the other by its strange, unknown, and indeed, contradictory nature.

593   Such an object provokes, like nothing else, conscious and unconscious fantasies, the former giving rise to speculative conjectures and pure fabrications, and the latter supplying the mythological background inseparable from these provocative observations. Thus there arose a situation in which, with the best will in the world, one often did not know and could not discover whether a primary perception was followed by a phantasm or whether, conversely, a primary fantasy originating in the unconscious invaded the conscious mind with illusions and visions. The material that has become known to me during the past ten years lends support to both hypotheses. In the first case an objectively real, physical process forms the basis for an accompanying myth; in the second case an archetype creates the corresponding vision. To these two causal relationships we must add a third possibility, namely, that of a 'synchronistic', i.e., acausal, meaningful coincidence – a problem that has occupied men's minds ever since the time of Geulincx, Leibniz and Schopenhauer.[5] It is

an hypothesis that has special bearing on phenomena connected with archetypal psychic processes.

594   As a psychologist, I am not qualified to contribute anything useful to the question of the physical reality of Ufos. I can concern myself only with their undoubted psychic aspect, and in what follows shall deal almost exclusively with their psychic concomitants.

780   That there is something beyond the borderline, beyond the frontiers of knowledge, is shown by the archetypes and, most clearly of all, by numbers, which this side of the border are quantities but on the other side are autonomous psychic entities, capable of making qualitative statements which manifest themselves in *a priori* patterns of order. These patterns include not only causally explicable phenomena like dream-symbols and such, but remarkable relativizations of time and space which simply cannot be explained causally. They are the parapsychological phenomena which I have summed up under the term 'synchronicity' and which have been statistically investigated by Rhine. The positive results of his experiments elevate these phenomena to the rank of undeniable facts. This brings us a little nearer to understanding the mystery of psychophysical parallelism, for we now know that a factor exists which mediates between the apparent incommensurability of body and psyche, giving matter a kind of 'psychic' faculty and the psyche a kind of 'materiality', by means of which the one can work on the other. That the body can work on the psyche seems to be a truism, but strictly speaking all we know is that any bodily defect or illness also expresses itself psychically. Naturally this assumption only holds good if, contrary to the popular materialistic view, the psyche is credited with an existence of its own. But materialism in its turn cannot explain how chemical changes can produce a psyche. Both views, the materialistic as well as the spiritualistic, are metaphysical prejudices. It accords better with experience to suppose that living matter has a psychic aspect, and the psyche a physical aspect. If we give due consideration to the facts of parapsychology, then the hypothesis of the psychic aspect must be extended beyond the sphere of biochemical processes to matter in general. In that case all reality would be grounded on an as yet unknown substrate possessing material and at the same time psychic qualities. In view of the trend of modern theoretical physics, this assumption should arouse fewer resistances than before. It would also do away with the awkward hypothesis of psychophysical parallelism, and afford us an opportunity to construct a new world model closer to the idea of the *unus mundus*. The 'acausal' correspondences between mutually independent psychic and physical events, i.e., synchronistic phenomena, and in particular psychokinesis, would then become more understandable, for every physical event would involve a psychic one and vice versa. Such reflections are not idle speculations; they are forced on us in any serious psychological investigation of the Ufo phenomenon.

781 As I said at the beginning, it was the purpose of this essay to treat the Ufos primarily as a psychological phenomenon. There were plenty of reasons for this, as is abundantly clear from the contradictory and 'impossible' assertions made by the rumour. It is quite right that they should meet with criticism, scepticism and open rejection, and if anyone should see behind them nothing more than a phantasm that deranges the minds of men and engenders rationalistic resistances, he would have nothing but our sympathy. Indeed, since conscious and unconscious fantasy and even mendacity, obviously play an important role in building up the rumour, we could be satisfied with the psychological explanation and let it rest at that.

782 Unfortunately, however, there are good reasons why the Ufos cannot be disposed of in this simple manner. So far as I know it remains an established fact, supported by numerous observations, that Ufos have not only been seen visually but have also been picked up on the radar screen and have left traces on the photographic plate. I base myself here not only on the comprehensive reports by Ruppelt and Keyhoe, which leave no room for doubt in this regard, but also on the fact that the astrophysicist, Professor Menzel, has not succeeded, despite all his efforts, in offering a satisfying scientific explanation of even one authentic Ufo report. It boils down to nothing less than this: that either psychic projections throw back a radar echo, or else the appearance of real objects affords an opportunity for mythological projections.

783 Here I must remark that even if the Ufos are physically real, the corresponding psychic projections are not actually caused, but are only occasioned, by them. Mythical statements of this kind have always occurred, whether Ufos exist or not. These statements depend in the first place on the peculiar nature of the psychic background, the collective unconscious, and for this reason have always been projected in some form. At various times all sorts of other projections have appeared in the heavens besides the saucers. This particular projection, together with its psychological context, the rumour, is specific of our age and highly characteristic of it. The dominating idea of a mediator and god who became man, after having thrust the old polytheistic beliefs into the background, is now in its turn on the point of evaporating. Untold millions of so-called Christians have lost their belief in a real and living mediator, while the believers endeavour to make their belief credible to primitive people, when it would be so much more fruitful to bestow these much needed efforts on the white man. But it is always so much easier and more affecting to talk and act *down* to people instead of *up* to them. St Paul spoke to the populace of Athens and Rome, but what is Albert Schweitzer doing in Lambarene? People like him are needed much more urgently in Europe.

784 No Christian will contest the importance of a belief like that of the mediator, nor will he deny the consequences which the loss of it entails. So powerful an idea reflects a profound psychic need which does not simply disappear when the expression of it ceases to be valid. What

happens to the energy that once kept the idea alive and dominant over the psyche? A political, social, philosophical and religious conflict of unprecedented proportions has split the consciousness of our age. When such tremendous opposites split asunder, we may expect with certainty that the need for a saviour will make itself felt. Experience has amply confirmed that, in the psyche as in nature, a tension of opposites creates a potential which may express itself at any time in a manifestation of energy. Between above and below flows the waterfall, and between hot and cold there is a turbulent exchange of molecules. Similarly, between the psychic opposites there is generated a 'uniting symbol', at first unconscious. This process is running its course in the unconscious of modern man. Between the opposites there arises spontaneously a symbol of unity and wholeness, no matter whether it reaches consciousness or not. Should something extraordinary or impressive then occur in the outside world, be it a human personality, a thing, or an idea, the unconscious content can project itself upon it, thereby investing the projection carrier with numinous and mythical powers. Thanks to its numinosity, the projection carrier has a highly suggestive effect and grows into a saviour myth whose basic features have been repeated countless times.

785   The impetus for the manifestation of the latent psychic contents was given by the Ufo. The only thing we know with tolerable certainty about Ufos is that they possess a surface which can be seen by the eye and at the same time throws back a radar echo. Everything else is so uncertain that it must remain for the time being an unproven conjecture, or rumour, until we know more about it. We do not know, either, whether they are manned machines or a species of living creature which has appeared in our atmosphere from an unknown source. It is not likely that they are meteoric phenomena, since their behaviour does not give the impression of a process that could be interpreted in physical terms. Their movements indicate volition and psychic relatedness, e.g., evasion and flight, perhaps even aggression and defence. Their progression in space is not in a straight line and of constant velocity like a meteor, but erratic like the flight of an insect and of varying velocity, from zero to several thousand miles per hour. The observed speeds and angles of turn are such that no earthly being could survive them any more than he could the enormous heat generated by friction.

786   The simultaneous visual and radar sightings would in themselves be a satisfactory proof of their reality. Unfortunately, well-authenticated reports show that there are also cases where the eye sees something that does not appear on the radar screen, or where an object undoubtedly picked up by radar is not seen by the eye. I will not mention other, even more remarkable reports from authoritative sources; they are so bizarre that they tax our understanding and credulity to the limit.

787

If these things are real – and by all human standards it hardly seems possible to doubt this any longer – then we are left with only two hypotheses: that of their *weightlessness* on the one hand and of their *psychic nature* on the other. This is a question I for one cannot decide. In the circumstances, however, it seemed to me advisable at least to investigate the *psychological aspect* of the phenomenon, so as to throw a little light on this complicated situation. I have limited myself to only a few examples. Unfortunately, after more than ten years' study of the problem I have not managed to collect a sufficient number of observations from which more reliable conclusions could be drawn. I must therefore content myself with having sketched out a few lines for future research. Of course, next to nothing has been gained as regards a physical explanation of the phenomenon. But the psychic aspect plays so great a role that it cannot be left out of account. The discussion of it, as I have tried to show, leads to psychological problems which involve just as fantastic possibilities or impossibilities as the approach from the physical side. If military authorities have felt compelled to set up bureaus for collecting and evaluating Ufo reports, then psychology, too, has not only the right but also the duty to do what it can to shed light on this dark problem.

788   The question of anti-gravity is one which I must leave to the physicists, who alone can inform us what chances of success such an hypothesis has. The alternative hypothesis that Ufos are something psychic that is endowed with certain physical properties seems even less probable, for where should such a thing come from? If weightlessness is a hard proposition to swallow, then the notion of a materialized psychism opens a bottomless void under our feet. Parapsychology is, of course, acquainted with the fact of materialization. But this phenomenon depends on the presence of one or more mediums who exude a weighable substance, and it occurs only in their immediate vicinity. The pysche can move the body, but only inside the living organism. That something psychic, possessing material qualities and with a high charge of energy, could appear by itself high in the air at a great distance from any human mediums – this surpasses our comprehension. Here our knowledge leaves us completely in the lurch, and it is therefore pointless to speculate any further in this direction.

789   It seems to me – speaking with all due reserve – that there is a third possibility: that Ufos are real material phenomena of an unknown nature, presumably coming from outer space, which perhaps have long been visible to mankind, but otherwise have no recognizable connection with the earth or its inhabitants. In recent times, however, and just at the moment when the eyes of mankind are turned towards the heavens, partly on account of their fantasies about possible space-ships, and partly in a figurative sense because their earthly existence is threatened, unconscious contents have projected themselves on these inexplicable heavenly phenomena and given them a significance they in no way deserve. Since they seem to have appeared more frequently after the second

World War than before, it may be that they are synchronistic phenomena or 'meaningful coincidences'. The psychic situation of mankind and the Ufo phenomenon as a physical reality bear no recognizable causal relationship to one another, but they seem to coincide in a meaningful manner. The meaningful connection is the product on the one hand of projection and on the other of round and cylindrical forms which embody the projected meaning and have always symbolized the union of opposites.

NOTES

1 'Wotan', first published in the *Neue Schweizer Rundschau*, 1936. [See *CW* 10, pars. 371ff.]
2 In an interview by Georg Gerster, *Weltwoche* (Zurich), XXII:1078 (9 July 1954), p.7.
3 *The Report on Unidentified Flying Objects* (1956).
4 Major Donald E. Keyhoe, *Flying Saucers from Outer Space* (1953), and *The Flying Saucer Conspiracy* (1955). Cf., also Aimé Michel, *The Truth about Flying Saucers* (1956).
5 Cf., my paper 'Synchronicity: An Acausal Connecting Principle', in *The Structure and Dynamics of the Psyche*.

12 Miscellaneous insights and speculations

From: Letter to E.L. Grant Watson (9 February 1956),
Letters, vol. 2, pp. 287–9

You are surely touching upon a most important fact when you begin to question the coincidence of a purely mathematical deduction with physical facts, such as the *sectio aurea* (the Fibonacci series.[1] My source calls him Fibonacci, not -nicci. He lived 1180–1250) and in modern times the equations expressing the turbulence of gases. One has not marvelled enough about these parallelisms. It is quite obvious that there must exist a condition common to the moving body and the psychic 'movement', more than a merely logical *corollarium* or *consectarium*.[2] I should call it an *irrational* (acausal) *corollary* of synchronicity. The Fibonacci series is self-evident and a property of the series of whole numbers, and it exists independently of empirical facts, as on the other hand the periodicity of a biological spiral occurs without application of mathematical reasoning unless one assumes an equal arrangement in living matter as well as in the human mind, *ergo* a property of matter (or of 'energy' or whatever you call the primordial principle) in general and consequently also of moving bodies in general, the psychic 'movement' included.

If this argument stands to reason, the coincidence of physical and mental forms and also of physical and mental events (synchronicity) would needs be a regular occurrence, which, however, particularly with synchronicity, is not the case. This is a serious snag pointing, as it seems to me, to an indeterminate or at least indeterminable, apparently *arbitrary arrangement*. This is a much neglected but characteristic aspect of physical nature: the statistical truth is largely made up of *exceptions*. That is the aspect of reality the poet and artist would insist upon, and that is also the reason why a philosophy exclusively based upon natural science is nearly always flat, superficial, and vastly beside the point, as it misses all the colourful improbable exceptions, the real 'salt of the earth'! It is not realistic, but rather an abstract half-truth, which, when applied to living man, destroys all individual values indispensable to human life.

The coincidence of the Fibonacci numbers[3] (or *sectio aurea*) with plant growth is a sort of analogy with synchronicity inasmuch as the latter consists in the coincidence of a psychic process with an external physical event of the same character or meaning. But whereas the *sectio aurea* is a static condition, synchronicity is a coincidence in time, even of events that, in themselves, are not synchronous (f.i., a case of precognition). In the latter case one could assume that synchronicity is a property of energy, but in so far as energy is equal to matter it is a secondary effect of the primary coincidence of mental and physical events (as in the Fibonacci series). The bridge seems to be formed by the *numbers*.[4] Numbers are just as much *invented* as they are *discovered* as natural facts, like all true archetypes. As far as I know, archetypes are perhaps the most important basis for synchronistic events.

I am afraid this is all rather involved and very difficult. I don't see my way yet out of the jungle. But I feel that the root of the enigma is to be found probably in the peculiar properties of whole numbers. The old Pythagorean postulate![5]

Letter to Gebhard Frei (17 January 1949), *Letters*, vol. 1, pp. 522–3

Dear Professor Frei,

Many thanks for kindly sending me your recent paper on magic.[6] The question of the 'subtle body'[7] interests me too. I try, as my custom is, to approach the problem from the scientific angle. I start with the formula: $E = M$, energy equals mass. Energy is not mere quantity, it is always a quantity of something. If we consider the psychic process as an energic one, we give it mass. This mass must be very small, otherwise it could be demonstrated physically. It becomes demonstrable in parapsychological phenomena, but shows at the same time that though it obeys psychic laws it does not obey physical laws, being in part independent of time and space, which means that psychic energy behaves as though time and space had only relative validity. Thus psychic energy can be grasped only by means of a 4- or multidimensional schema. This can be represented mathematically, but not envisaged. Atomic physics does the same for quantitatively measurable facts. The psychologist, however, sees no possibility as yet of quantitatively measuring his facts. He can only establish them, not explain them. There are, undoubtedly, synchronistic effects with a 'vitalizing' force, i.e., phenomena which are not only synchronistic but also allow the conjecture that psychic energy influences living or inert objects in such a way that, as though 'animated' by a psychic content alien to them, they are compelled to represent it somehow or other. These effects do not come from consciousness but from an unconscious form of existence which appears to be permanently in a merely relative spatio-temporal, i.e., 4- or multidimensional state. Psychic contents in this state act as much *outside* me as *in* me, just as much *outside* time as *in* time.

I think this much can be concluded with sufficient certainty. Of course it isn't an explanation but merely an attempt to formulate conclusions which seem to follow from the empirical premises. The psychic seems to me to be in actual fact partly extraspatial and extratemporal. 'Subtle body' may be a fitting expression for this part of the psyche. With best regards and cordial thanks,

Yours very sincerely, C.G. JUNG

From: Letter to J.R. Smythies (29 February 1952), *Letters*, vol. 2, pp. 44–5

Concerning your own proposition I have already told you how much I welcome your idea of a perceptual, i.e., 'subtle' body. Your view is rather confirmed, as it seems to me, by the peculiar fact that on the one hand consciousness has so exceedingly little direct information of the body from within, and that on the other hand the unconscious (i.e., dreams and other products of the 'unconscious') refers very rarely to the body and, if it does, it is always in the most roundabout way, i.e., through highly 'symbolized' images. For a long time I have considered this fact as negative evidence for the existence of a subtle body or at least for a curious gap between mind and body. Of a psyche dwelling in its own body one should expect at least that it would be immediately and thoroughly informed of any change of conditions therein. Its not being the case demands some explanation.

Now concerning your critique of the space concept:[8] I have given a good deal of thought to it. You know perhaps that the helium atom is characterized by 2×3 space factors and 1 time factor.[9] I don't know whether there is something in this parallel or not. At all events the assumption of a perceptual body postulates a corresponding perceptual space that separates the mind from physical space in the same way as the subtle body causes the gap between the mind and the physical body. Thus you arrive logically at two different spaces, which however cannot be entirely incommensurable, since there exists – in spite of the difference – communication between them. You assume that time is the factor they have in common. Thus time is assumed to be the same physically as well as perceptually. Whereas ψ-phenomena bear out clearly that physical and psychic space differ from each other. I submit that the factor of time proves to be equally 'elastic' as space under ESP conditions. If this is the case, we are confronted with two four-dimensional systems in a contingent contiguity. Please excuse the awfully tortuous ways of putting it. It shows nothing more than my perplexity.

The obviously arbitrary behaviour of time and space under ESP conditions seemingly necessitates such a postulate. On the other hand one might ask the question whether we can as hitherto go on thinking in terms of space and time, while modern physics begins to relinquish these terms in favour of a time-space continuum, in which space is no more space and time no more time. The question is, in short: shouldn't we give up the time-space categories altogether when we are dealing with psychic existence? It might be that psyche should be understood as *unextended intensity* and not as a body moving with time. One might assume the psyche gradually rising from minute extensity to infinite intensity, transcending for instance the velocity of light and thus irrealizing the body. That would account for the 'elasticity' of space under ESP conditions. If there is no body moving in space, there can be no time either and that would account for the 'elasticity' of time.

You will certainly object to the paradox of 'unextended intensity' as being a *contradictio in adiecto*. I quite agree. Energy is mass and mass is extended. At all events, a body with a speed higher than that of light vanishes from sight and one may have all sorts of doubts about what would happen to such a body otherwise. Surely there would be no means to make sure of its whereabouts or of its existence at all. Its time would be unobservable likewise.

All this is certainly highly speculative, in fact unwarrantably adventurous. But ψ-phenomena are equally disconcerting and lay claim to an unusually high jump. Yet any hypothesis is warrantable inasmuch as it explains observable facts and is consistent in itself. In the light of this view the brain might be a transformer station, in which the relatively infinite tension or intensity of the psyche proper is transformed into perceptible frequencies or 'extensions'. Conversely, the fading of introspective perception of the body explains itself as due to a gradual 'psychification', i.e., intensification at the expense of extension. Psyche = highest intensity in the smallest space.

'The Miraculous Fast of Brother Klaus'[10] (1950/1951) (*CW* 18)

1497 The fact that Brother Klaus, on his own admission and according to the reports of reliable witnesses, lived without material sustenance for twenty years is something that cannot be brushed aside however uncomfortable it may be. In the case of Therese of Konnersreuth[11] there are also reports, whose reliability of course I can neither confirm nor contest, that for a long period of time she lived simply and solely on holy wafers. Such things naturally cannot be understood with our present knowledge of physiology. One would be well advised, however, not to dismiss them as utterly impossible on that account. There are very many things that earlier were held to be impossible which nevertheless we know and can prove to be possible today.

1498   Naturally I have no explanation to offer concerning such phenomena as the fast of Brother Klaus, but I am inclined to think it should be sought in the realm of parapsychology. I myself was present at the investigation of a medium who manifested physical phenomena. An electrical engineer measured the degree of ionization of the atmosphere in the immediate vicinity of the medium. The figures were everywhere normal except at one point on the right side of the thorax, where the ionization was about sixty times the normal. At this point, when the (parapsychological) phenomena were in progress, there was an emission of ectoplasm capable of acting at a distance. If such things can occur, then it is also conceivable that persons in the vicinity of the medium might act as a source of ions – in other words, nourishment might be effected by the passage of living molecules of albumen from one body to another. In this connection it should be mentioned that in parapsychological experiments decreases of weight up to several kilogrammes have been observed during the (physical) phenomena, in the case both of the medium and of some of the participants, who were all sitting on scales. This seems to me to offer a possible approach to an explanation. Unfortunately these things have been far too little investigated at present. This is a task for the future.

From: 'Psychological Aspects of the Mother Archetype' (1938/1954) (*CW* 9i)

196 Understood concretely, the Assumption is the absolute opposite of materialism. Taken in this sense, it is a counterstroke that does nothing to diminish the tension between the opposites, but drives it to extremes.

197 Understood symbolically, however, the Assumption of the body is a recognition and acknowledgment of matter, which in the last resort was identified with evil only because of an overwhelmingly 'pneumatic' tendency in man. In themselves, spirit and matter are neutral, or rather, 'utriusque capax' – that is, capable of what man calls good or evil. Although as names they are exceedingly relative, underlying them are very real opposites that are part of the energic structure of the physical and of the psychic world, and without them no existence of any kind could be established. There is no position without its negation. In spite or just because of their extreme opposition, neither can exist without the other. It is exactly as formulated in classical Chinese philosophy: *yang* (the light, warm, dry, masculine principle) contains within it the seed of *yin* (the dark, cold, moist, feminine principle), and vice versa. Matter therefore would contain the seed of spirit and spirit the seed of matter. The long-known 'synchronistic' phenomena that have now been statistically confirmed by Rhine's experiments point, to all appearances, in this direction. The 'psychization' of matter puts the absolute immateriality of spirit in question, since this would then have to be accorded a kind of substantiality. The dogma of the Assumption, proclaimed in an age suffering from the greatest political schism history has ever known, is a compensating symptom that reflects the strivings of science for a uniform world-picture.

From: Letter to Dr. H. (30 August 1951), *Letters*, vol. 2, pp. 21–3

My *modus procedendi* is naturally empirical: how to give a satisfactory description of the phenomenon 'Christ' from the standpoint of psychological experience?

The existing statements about Christ are, in part, about an empirical man, but for the other and greater part about a mythological God-man. Out of these different statements you can reconstruct a personality who, as an empirical man, was identical with the traditional Son of Man type, as presented in the then widely read Book of Enoch.[12] Wherever such identities occur, characteristic archetypal effects appear, that is, *numinosity* and *synchronistic phenomena*, hence tales of miracles are inseparable from the Christ figure. The former explains the irresistible suggestive power of his personality, for only the one who is 'gripped' has a 'gripping' effect on others; the latter occur chiefly in the field of force of an archetype and, because of their aspatial and atemporal character, are acausal, i.e., 'miracles'. (I have just lectured at Eranos on synchronicity.[13] The paper will soon appear in the acts of the Institute.)[14] This remarkable effect points to the 'psychoid'[15] and essentially transcendental nature of the archetype as an 'arranger' of psychic forms inside and outside the psyche. (In theoretical physics the archetype corresponds to the model of a radioactive atom, with the difference that the atom consists of quantitative, the archetype of qualitative, i.e., *meaningful*, relationships, the *quantum*[16] appearing only in the *degree of numinosity*. In physics the *quale* appears in the irreducible quality of the so-called discontinuities,[17] as for instance in the quantum or in the half-life[18] of radioactive substances.)

In consequence of the predominance of the archetype the personality that is 'gripped' is in direct contact with the *mundus archetypus*,[19] and his life or biography is only a brief episode in the eternal course of things or in the eternal revolution of 'divine' images. That which is eternally present appears in the temporal order as a succession. 'When the time was fulfilled' the solitary creator-god transformed himself into a father and begot himself as a son, although from eternity, i.e., in the non-time of the Pleroma or in his transcendental form of being, he is father-son-spirit-mother, i.e., the succession of archetypal manifestations.

Although the psychoid archetype is a mere model or postulate, archetypal effects have just as real an existence as radioactivity. Anyone who is gripped by the archetype of the Anthropos lives the God-man – one can very well say that he *is* a God-man. Archetypes are not mere concepts but are entities, exactly like whole numbers, which are not merely aids to counting but possess irrational qualities that do not result from the concept of counting, as for instance the prime numbers and their behaviour. Hence the mathematician Kronecker[20] could say: Man created mathematics, but God created whole numbers: ὁ θεὸς ἀριθμητίζει.[21]

This description of Christ satisfies me because it permits a non-contradictory presentation of the paradoxical interplay of his human and divine existence, his empirical character and his mythological being.

The wordless or formless 'gripping' is no argument against the presence of the archetype, since the very numinosity of the moment is itself one of its manifestations (and the most frequent), a primordial form of archetypal seizure, cf., *kairos*[22] and Tao or (in Zen) satori. On account of its transcendence, the archetype *per se* is as irrepresentable as the nature of light and hence must be strictly distinguished from the archetypal idea or mythologem (see 'Der Geist der Psychologie'[23] in *Eranos-Jahrbuch 1946*). In this way the transcendence of the theological premise remains intact.

From: *Mysterium Coniunctionis* (1955–56) (CW 14)

661 The mandala symbolizes, by its central point, the ultimate unity of all archetypes as well as of the multiplicity of the phenomenal world, and is therefore the empirical equivalent of the metaphysical concept of a *unus mundus*. The alchemical equivalent is the lapis and its synonyms, in particular the Microcosm.[24]

662 Dorn's explanation is illuminating in that it affords us a deep insight into the alchemical *mysterium coniunctionis*. If this is nothing less than a restoration of the original state of the cosmos and the divine unconsciousness of the world, we can understand the extraordinary fascination emanating from this mystery. It is the Western equivalent of the fundamental principle of classical Chinese philosophy, namely the union of *yang* and *yin* in *tao*, and at the same time a premonition of that 'tertium quid' which, on the basis of psychological experience on the one hand and of Rhine's experiments on the other, I have called 'synchronicity'.[25] If mandala symbolism is the psychological equivalent of the *unus mundus*, then synchronicity is its parapsychological equivalent. Though synchronistic phenomena occur in time and space they manifest a remarkable independence of both these indispensable determinants of physical existence and hence do not conform to the law of causality. The causalism that underlies our scientific view of the world breaks everything down into individual processes which it punctiliously tries to isolate from all other parallel processes. This tendency is absolutely necessary if we are to gain reliable knowledge of the world, but philosophically it has the disadvantage of breaking up, or obscuring, the universal interrelationship of events so that a recognition of the greater relationship, i.e., of the unity of the world, becomes more and more difficult. Everything that happens, however, happens in the same 'one world' and is a part of it. For this reason events must possess an *a priori* aspect of unity, though it is difficult to establish this by the statistical method. So far as we can see at present, Rhine seems to have successfully demonstrated this unity by his

extrasensory-perception experiments (ESP).[26] Independence of time and space brings about a concurrence or meaningful coincidence of events not causally connected with one another – phenomena which till now were summed under the purely descriptive concepts of telepathy, clairvoyance and precognition. These concepts naturally have no explanatory value as each of them represents an *X* which cannot be distinguished from the *X* of the other. The characteristic feature of all these phenomena, including Rhine's psychokinetic effect and other synchronistic occurrences, is *meaningful coincidence*, and as such I have defined the synchronistic principle. This principle suggests that there is an inter-connection or unity of causally unrelated events, and thus postulates a unitary aspect of being which can very well be described as the *unus mundus*.

767   If Dorn, then, saw the consummation of the mysterium coniunctionis in the union of the alchemically produced *caelum* with the *unus mundus*, he expressly meant not a fusion of the individual with his environment, or even his adaptation to it, but a *unio mystica* with the potential world. Such a view indeed seems to us 'mystical', if we misuse this word in its pejorative modern sense. It is not, however, a question of thoughtlessly used words but of a view which can be translated from medieval language into modern concepts. Undoubtedly the idea of the *unus mundus* is founded on the assumption that the multiplicity of the empirical world rests on an underlying unity, and that not two or more fundamentally different worlds exist side by side or are mingled with one another. Rather, everything divided and different belongs to one and the same world, which is not the world of sense but a postulate whose probability is vouched for by the fact that until now no one has been able to discover a world in which the known laws of nature are invalid. That even the psychic world, which is so extraordinarily different from the physical world, does not have its roots outside the one cosmos is evident from the undeniable fact that causal connections exist between the psyche and the body which point to their underlying unitary nature.

768   All that *is* is not encompassed by our knowledge, so that we are not in a position to make any statements about its total nature. Microphysics is feeling its way into the unknown side of matter, just as complex psychology is pushing forward into the unknown side of the psyche. Both lines of investigation have yielded findings which can be conceived only by means of antinomies, and both have developed concepts which display remarkable analogies. If this trend should become more pronounced in the future, the hypothesis of the unity of their subject-matters would gain in probability. Of course there is little or no hope that the unitary Being can ever be conceived, since our powers of thought and language permit only of antinomian statements. But this much we do know beyond all doubt, that empirical reality has a transcendental background – a fact which, as Sir James Jeans has shown, can be expressed by Plato's parable of the

cave. The common background of microphysics and depth-psychology is as much physical as psychic and therefore neither, but rather a third thing, a neutral nature which can at most be grasped in hints since in essence it is transcendental.

769   The background of our empirical world thus appears to be in fact a *unus mundus*. This is at least a probable hypothesis which satisfies the fundamental tenet of scientific theory: 'Explanatory principles are not to be multiplied beyond the necessary.' The transcendental psychophysical background corresponds to a 'potential world' in so far as all those conditions which determine the form of empirical phenomena are inherent in it. This obviously holds good as much for physics as for psychology, or, to be more precise, for macrophysics as much as for the psychology of consciousness.

As an example of 'being in Tao' and its synchronistic accompaniments I will cite the story, told me by the late Richard Wilhelm, of the rain-maker of Kiaochau: There was a great drought where Wilhelm lived; for months there had not been a drop of rain and the situation became catastrophic. The Catholics made processions, the Protestants made prayers, and the Chinese burned joss-sticks and shot off guns to frighten away the demons of the drought, but with no result. Finally the Chinese said, 'We will fetch the rain-maker'. And from another province a dried up old man appeared. The only thing he asked for was a quiet little house somewhere, and there he locked himself in for three days. On the fourth day the clouds gathered and there was a great snow-storm at the time of the year when no snow was expected, an unusual amount, and the town was so full of rumours about the wonderful rain-maker that Wilhelm went to ask the man how he did it. In true European fashion he said: 'They call you the rain-maker, will you tell me how you made the snow?' And the little Chinese said: 'I did not make the snow, I am not responsible.' 'But what have you done these three days?' 'Oh, I can explain that. I come from another country where things are in order. Here they are out of order, they are not as they should be by the ordinance of heaven. Therefore the whole country is not in Tao, and I also am not in the natural order of things because I am in a disordered country. So I had to wait three days until I was back in Tao and then naturally the rain came.'

Letter to Erich Neumann[27] (10 March 1959), *Letters*, vol. 2, pp. 493–6

Dear friend,

Best thanks for your long and discursive letter of 18.II. What Frau Jaffé sent you was a first, as yet unrevised draft,[28] an attempt to pin down my volatile thoughts. Unfortunately the fatigue of old age prevents me from writing a letter as discursive as yours.

I

The question: *an creator sibi consciens est?*[29] is not a 'pet idea' but an exceedingly painful experience with well-nigh incalculable consequences, which it is not easy to argue about. For instance, if somebody projects the self this is an unconscious act, for we know from experience that projection results only from unconsciousness.

Incarnatio means first and foremost God's birth in Christ, hence psychologically the realization of the self as something new, not present before. The man who was created before that is a 'creature', albeit 'made in the likeness' of God, and this implies the idea of the *filiatio* and the *sacrificium divinum*. Incarnation is, as you say, a 'new experience'.

'It has happened almost by accident and casually . . .'[30] This sentence might well characterize the whole process of creation. The archetype is no exception. The initial event was the arrangement of indistinct masses in spherical form. Hence this primordial archetype [mandala] appears as the first form of amorphous gases, for anything amorphous can manifest itself only in some specific form or order.

The concept of 'order' is not identical with the concept of 'meaning'. Even an organic being is, in spite of the meaningful design implicit within it, not necessarily meaningful in the total nexus. For instance, if the world had come to an end at the Oligocene period, it would have had no meaning for man. Without the reflecting consciousness of man the world is a gigantic meaningless machine, for in our experience man is the only creature who is capable of ascertaining any meaning at all.

We still have no idea where the constructive factor in biological development is to be found. But we know that warmbloodedness and a differentiated brain were necessary for the inception of consciousness, and thus also for the revelation of meaning. It staggers the mind even to begin to imagine the accidents and hazards that, over millions of years, transformed a lemurlike tree-dweller into a man. In this chaos of chance, synchronistic phenomena were probably at work, operating both with and against the known laws of nature to produce, in archetypal moments, syntheses which appear to us miraculous. Causality and teleology fail us here, because synchronistic phenomena manifest themselves as pure chance. The essential thing about these phenomena is that an objective event coincides meaningfully with a psychic process; that is to say, a physical event and an endopsychic one have a common meaning. This presupposes not only an all-pervading, latent meaning which can be recognized by consciousness, but, during that preconscious time, a psychoid process with which a physical event meaningfully coincides. Here the meaning cannot be recognized because there is as yet no consciousness. It is through the archetype that we come closest to this early, 'irrepresentable', psychoid stage of conscious development; indeed, the archetype itself gives us direct intimations of it. Unconscious synchronicities are, as we know from experience, altogether possible, since in many cases we are unconscious of their happening, or have to have our attention drawn to the coincidence by an outsider.

II

Since the laws of probability give no ground for assuming that higher syntheses such as the psyche could arise by chance alone, there is nothing for it but to postulate a latent meaning in order to explain not only the synchronistic phenomena but also the higher syntheses. Meaningfulness always appears to be unconscious at first, and can therefore only be discovered *post hoc*; hence there is always the danger that meaning will be read into things where actually there is nothing of the sort. Synchronistic experiences serve our turn here. They point to a latent meaning which is independent of consciousness.

Since a creation without the reflecting consciousness of man has no discernible meaning, the hypothesis of a latent meaning endows man with a cosmogonic significance, a true *raison d'être*. If on the other hand the latent meaning is attributed to the Creator as part of a conscious plan of creation, the question arises: Why should the Creator stage-manage this whole phenomenal world since he already knows what he can reflect himself in, and why should he reflect himself at all since he is already conscious of himself? Why should he create alongside his own omniscience a second, inferior consciousness – millions of dreary little mirrors when he knows in advance just what the image they reflect will look like?

After thinking all this over I have come to the conclusion that being 'made in the likeness' applies not only to man but also to the Creator: he resembles man or is his likeness, which is to say that he is just as unconscious as man or even more unconscious, since according to the myth of the *incarnatio* he actually felt obliged to become man and offer himself to man as a sacrifice.

Here I must close, aware as I am that I have only touched on the main points (so it seems to me) in your letter, which I found very difficult to understand in parts. It is not levity but my *molesta senectus*[31] that forces economy on me. With best greetings,

Sincerely yours, C.G. JUNG

NOTES

1 [G.W. submitted for comment the MS of a chapter on 'Imaginative Fantasy' in a book he was working on: *The Mystery of Physical Life* (1964). Among other things he discusses the phenomenon of phyllotaxis, the arrangement of leaves on the stem of a plant. Their spiral arrangement follows a definite mathematical formula, that of the so-called Fibonacci series, discovered by the Italian mathematician Leonardo of Pisa (or Fibonacci) in the 13th cent.]

2 [*Corollarium* (corollary) denotes the practical consequence of a proposition; *consectarium* (consectary), a logical deduction or conclusion.]

3 [This and the following paragraph are reprinted in W.'s book (p. 48) but with one serious mistake. He has '. . . the coincidence of a *physical* process with an external physical event . . .' thus completely vitiating Jung's argument.]

4 [The function and archetypal role of numbers is discussed at some length in 'Flying Saucers', *CW* 10, pars. 776ff., and 'Synchronicity', *CW* 8, par. 871.]

5 [To the Pythagoreans the whole universe was explicable in terms of the relation of numbers to one another.]

6 ['Magie und Psychologie', *Neue Schweizer Rundschau* (Zurich), No. 48, 1948/49, pp. 680–8.]

7 [In parapsychology, the theory that psychic phenomena in the form of the 'subtle body' can manifest themselves as physical phenomena. Cf., C.A. Meier, 'Psychosomatic Medicine from the Jungian Point of View', *Journal of Analytical Psychology* (London), VIII:2 (July 1963), pp. 111ff.]

8 [Cf., Smythies, *Analysis of Perception* (1956).]

9 [The helium atom has two electrons, each of which has three space co-ordinates, and the whole system has one time co-ordinate.]

10 [Translated from 'Das Fastenwunder des Bruder Klaus', *Neue Wissenschaft* (Baden, Switzerland), 1950/51, no. 7; revised from a letter to Fritz Blanke, 10 Nov. 1948, thanking him for his book *Bruder Klaus von Flüe* (Zurich, 1948). Cf., *Letters*, ed. G. Adler, vol. 1. A prefatory note by the editor of *Neue Wissenschaft* states: 'The period of Brother Klaus's fast lasted from 1467 to 1487. All contemporary witnesses, even those in the immediate neighbourhood of the saint, agree that during this time he took no nourishment'.]

11 [Therese Neumann (1889–1962), generally known as Therese of Konnersreuth, Switzerland, stigmatized since 1926, when she claimed to have re-experienced Christ's Passion.]

12 [The (Ethiopic) Book of Enoch, 2nd-1st cent. BC, the most important of the apocryphal or pseudo-apocryphal Biblical writings. (There is also a Slavonic Book of Enoch and a Book of the Secrets of Enoch.) In Charles, *The Apocrypha and Pseudepigrapha of the Old Testament in English*, II (1913).]

13 ['Über Synchronizität', *Eranos Jahrbuch 1951*; now 'On Synchronicity', *CW* 8, Appendix, pars. 969ff.]

14 [*Studien aus dem C.G. Jung-Institut*, in which Jung's paper on synchronicity, together with Pauli's paper, appeared as vol. IV (1952), *Naturerklärung und Psyche.*]

15 [A term coined by Jung to describe 'quasi-psychic "irrepresentable" basic forms', i.e., the archetypes *per se* in contradistinction to archetypal images (cf., Devatmananda, 9 Feb. 37, n. 1). They belong to the transconscious areas where psychic processes and their physical substrate touch. Cf., 'On the Nature of the Psyche', *CW* 8, pars. 368, 417.]

16 ['A discrete unit quantity of energy proportional to the frequency of radiation' (SOED).]

17 [Discontinuity is a concept stemming from Max Planck's quantum theory, according to which the course of nature does not advance continuously but 'by tiny jumps and jerks' (Jeans, *The Mysterious Universe*, Pelican Books, pp. 31f.; cf., also 'Synchronicity', par. 966).]

18 [The half-life of a given radioactive element is the time required for the disintegration of one half of the initial number of atoms.]

19 [The archetypal, potential world as underlying pattern of the actual world. In the psychological sense, the collective unconscious. Cf., *Mysterium*, *CW* 14, par. 761.]

20 [Leonpold Kronecker (1823–91), German mathematician.]

21 'God arithmetizes', a saying attributed to the German mathematician Karl Friedrich Gauss (1777–1855). Cf., 'Synchronicity', par. 943 and n. 72.

22 The right or proper time, the favourable moment.

23 Cf., 'On the Nature of the Psyche', *CW* 8, par. 417.

24 Cf., *Psychology and Alchemy*, par. 426 and n. 2, fig. 195.

25 Cf., my 'Synchronicity: An Acausal Connecting Principle'.

26 Cf., his *New Frontiers of the Mind* and *The Reach of the Mind*. The relevant phenomena are discussed in 'Synchronicity', pars. 833ff.

27 Parts of this letter were published in Jung and Jaffé, *Erinnerungen, Träume, Gedanken*, pp. 367ff. (not in *Memories*). The whole letter, together with Neumann's of 18 Feb., is in Jaffé, *Der Mythus vom Sinn im Werk von C. G. Jung* (1967), pp. 179ff. (not in tr., *The Myth of Meaning*).

28 The first draft of ch. XII, 'Late Thoughts', in *Memories*.

29 = is the creator conscious of himself?

30 Paraphrase of a passage in *Memories* (which N. had read in MS form): 'Natural history tells us of a haphazard and casual transformation of species over hundreds of millions of years of devouring and being devoured' (p. 339/312). He objected to the 'Darwinistic residue' in 'haphazard and casual transformation' and suggested a different theory 'in which your concept of the archetype and of absolute and extraneous knowledge will play a part'. Concerning N.'s concept of extraneous knowledge – a knowledge steering the life process and in which the division between inner and outer reality, psyche and world, is transcended in a 'unitary reality' – cf., his 'Die Psyche und die Wandlung der Wirklichkeitsebenen', *Eranos Jahrbuch 1952*.

31 = burdensome old age.

Subject index

absolute 147; knowledge 15, 18, 32, 35, 37; unconscious 125

acausal: connecting principle 25, 36, 37, 108, 116, 117; orderedness 33–4; *see also* causality; synchronicity

active imagination 4, 5, 59

affects: *see* emotions

alchemy 8, 14–15, 165

alienation 57

anima/animus 28, 135

anxiety 47

archetypes 3, 6, 9, 14, 19, 20, 28, 29, 61, 75, 77, 88, 107, 109, 115, 125–6, 152–4, 160, 165, 168; activated 18, 38, 106, 109, 110, 117; mother 163; and synchronicity 35–6, 38, 105, 106; *see also* collective unconscious; instinct

astrology 1, 8, 11, 12, 19, 23, 33, 79, 80, 81, 84, 85, 98, 100, 101, 105, 115, 152, 153; experiment 29– 32, 37, 99, 107, 112–21; as a science 98–9; and synchronicity 79–81, 118

baptism, ritual of 134–5

bliss, eternal 139–40

bull-fight, symbolism of 10–11, 73–4

causal relativity 105, 109

causality 10, 12, 13, 16–20, 22–7, 32–4, 74, 85–6, 88, 95–6, 98, 101, 116, 147; magical 14, 19, 108; and synchronicity 118

centre 7, 72, 73

chance 30, 31, 32, 49, 63, 85, 86, 87, 93, 94, 100, 101, 114, 116, 117, 119, 120, 127, 169; *see also* coincidence; statistics

chaos theory 26

Chinese 73–4, 83–6

Christ 38, 164–5, 168; *see also* saviour

clairvoyance 36, 106, 120, 123, 126, 166

coincidence, meaningful 1, 5, 7–10, 12, 14, 28–9, 36, 74, 86, 93–7, 109, 118–20, 124, 127, 153, 158, 166, 169; and astrology 100, 101; and *I Ching* 81, 82; *see also* chance; synchronicity

collective unconscious 6, 8, 56–8, 77, 105, 107, 108, 109, 123, 124, 155, 160, 169; *see also* archetypes

compensation 4, 9, 23, 70, 147, 163

complementarity, principle of 16, 126, 127

complexes 3; integration of 57; psychic 57; soul 55–7; spirit 55, 57; unconscious 6, 56, 57

connection 24, 36, 82; acausal 25, 36, 37, 108, 116–17; synchronicity as principle of 36, 166; *see also* causality; *unus mundus*

conscience 75–6

consciousness: altered states of 54, 126, 133–41, 151; continuity of 150, 151; emptiness of 123; energy of 18; localization of 3; origins of 168, 169; psychology of 167; and synchronicity 2; *see also* psyche; self

content: *see* meaning

correspondence, theory of 14, 19, 24, 37, 88, 101; *see also* synchronicity

countertransference 37

creative imagination: *see* active imagination

death 77, 95, 106, 120, 134, 142–3, 149, 151; *see also* immortality; near-

Name index

Aristotle 26
Aziz, R. 9, 23, 28, 37

Barbault, A. 88–9
Baumann-Jung, G. 3
Baur, B. 11, 80
Beloff, J. 25
Bleuler, E. 122
Bohm, D. 27
Bohr, N. 16

Charet, F.X. 3
Cornell, A.D. 106
Crookes, W. 47
Cysat, R. 70

Dorn, G. 165
Duke University 15
Dunne, J.W. 123
Duprel, K. 47

Einstein, A. 16, 26, 122
Eschenmayer, K.A. von 48

Fibonacci numbers 159
Fierz, M. 17
Flournoy, T. 5
Fordham, M. 29, 30, 35
Franz, M-L. 33, 34
Frei, G. 160
Freud, S. 4, 5, 7, 11, 72, 79
Frey-Rohn, L. 99, 113

Galla Placidia, tomb of 134, 135
Geulincx, A. 107, 120, 153
Giegerich, W. 35
Goddard, V. 97
Goethe, J.W. von 62
Gorres, J.J. vön 48

Grant Watson, E.L. 159

Hu Shih 82
Hyslop, J. 7

James, W. 5
Jeans, J. 16, 166
Jordan, P. 122, 123, 124
Jung, C.G. 1–39, 63, 73; heart attack 7,
  136; Institute 107

Kammerer, P. 124
Kant, I. 35, 47, 61, 86
Keller, A. 122
Kerner, J. 48
Keyhoe, D.E. 153
Klaus, Brother 162
Kling, L. 77
Knoll, M. 98, 153

Leibniz, G.W. von 85, 88, 101, 107,
  120, 153

Meier, C.A. 33, 126
Menzel, D.H. 155
Miller Fantasies 5
Mithras 9, 11
Mount Elgon 62
Mount Pilatus 69, 70

Neumann, E. 167

Passavant, J. 48
Pauli, W. 16, 17, 101,
  122, 124, 126
Penrose, R. 27
Philemon 5, 7, 59, 60
Preiswerk, S. and A. 2
Progoff, I. 29